# TUDOR&STUART
## SEAFARERS

# TUDOR&STUART
## SEAFARERS

The Emergence of a Maritime Nation, 1485–1707

Edited by James Davey

NATIONAL
MARITIME MUSEUM
GREENWICH

ADLARD
COLES

LONDON · OXFORD · NEW YORK · NEW DELHI · SYDNEY

ADLARD COLES
Bloomsbury Publishing Plc
50 Bedford Square, London, WC1B 3DP, UK

BLOOMSBURY, ADLARD COLES and the Adlard Coles
logo are trademarks of Bloomsbury Publishing Plc

First published in Great Britain 2018

In association with Royal Museums Greenwich, the group
name for the National Maritime Museum, the Royal
Observatory, the Queen's House and Cutty Sark.
www.rmg.co.uk

A catalogue record for this book is available from the
British Library

Library of Congress Cataloguing-in-Publication data has
been applied for

ISBN: HB: 978-1-4729-5676-7; ePDF: 978-1-4729-5678-1;
ePub: 978-1-4729-5677-4

2 4 6 8 10 9 7 5 3 1

Designed and typeset in Chaparel Pro by Louise Turpin
Printed and bound in India by Replika Press Pvt. Ltd

Bloomsbury Publishing Plc makes every effort to ensure
that the papers used in the manufacture of our books are
natural, recyclable products made from wood grown
in well managed forests. Our manufacturing processes
conform to the environmental regulations of the country
of origin.

To find out more about our authors and books visit
www.bloomsbury.com and sign up for our newsletters

## ACKNOWLEDGEMENTS

I have accrued many debts of gratitude while editing this book. My first thanks must go to the contributors,
each of whom has provided an outstanding essay that speaks to the broader themes of the publication. It will be
for the reader to decide whether this book is greater than the sum of its parts, but there is no doubting that the
parts themselves are of exceptional quality. My work was made considerably easier by the assistance of Robert
Blyth, whose sound judgment was frequently called upon, and who commented on the book in its entirety.
Pieter van der Merwe also read the book manuscript in full; as ever, I am grateful to him for his keen editorial eye.
At Bloomsbury, Jenny Clark was a dedicated and efficient editor, who helped turn a speculative idea into the
publication you see today. I would also like to thank the numerous external institutions that provided images
or advice. I am particularly grateful to the Plymouth 400 project and its Wampanoag Advisory Committee
for their hospitality and guidance.

This book builds upon the collections of the National Maritime Museum. It follows that numerous individuals
from across the institution have played a role in bringing it to completion. As the two forewords make clear,
Tudor and Stuart Seafarers sits alongside a new permanent gallery of the same name, and I would like to thank all
those who worked on the display team: Lucy Gardner, Laura Humphreys, Dina Ibrahim, Aaron Jaffer, Navjot Mangat,
Kristian Martin, Katherine McAlpine, Clara de la Pena, Clare Richardson, Mary Webb and Ben Weddell.
The quality of the images contained in the book is testament to the expertise of the Museum's conservation
department and the skilled work of its photo studio. Lastly, this book could not have been completed without
the assistance of the NMM's commercial team. Kirsty Schaper offered encouragement from the outset, while
Taragh Godfrey and Poppy Pollitt were unstinting in their support. Most of all, I would like to thank Kate Mason,
whose organisational talents and mastery of detail were invaluable, and who helped steer the book through
to completion with unerring calm and patience.

# CONTENTS

THE CARDE OF the
North coaste of England from
Whitbye vnto Coket Ile

Gifbroghe

Stocktō

Hartlepoole

Efin

Redd cliff

Huntley foote

Skelton

Whitbuy

nhoodes
Bay

# Patron's Foreword

The Tudor period is a source of endless fascination, full of epic moments of drama, such as the Spanish Armada of 1588 as well as the luminescent writing of William Shakespeare. Indeed, it was in the late sixteenth century that England, previously riven with dynastic concerns and religious turmoil, began to look outwards to the sea and the 'New World' as sources of opportunity and adventure. As an American, though one who has lived in the UK, I am aware of the tumultuous and far-reaching consequences of these early encounters on the subsequent history of the European and American continents.

My family is honoured to support the 'Tudor and Stuart Seafarers' gallery at the National Maritime Museum, reflecting the importance of Greenwich in the early modern period. Henry VIII, Mary I and Elizabeth I were born at the Greenwich Palace – a favoured royal residence and a place of pleasure, passion and politics. Henry VIII enjoyed jousting and the thrills of the tournament on the Museum's grounds.

Little remains of Tudor Greenwich following its comprehensive redevelopment by subsequent Stuart monarchs, who created the Queen's House and began work on the Baroque splendour of the Greenwich Hospital complex. However, a new room in the Museum allows visitors to explore the site's many layers of history. Together, this room and the adjacent Gallery bring to life the rich story of Greenwich and its multifaceted connections to this extraordinary historical period, which did so much to shape Britain's relationship with the sea.

Mark Pigott KBE KStJ OBE

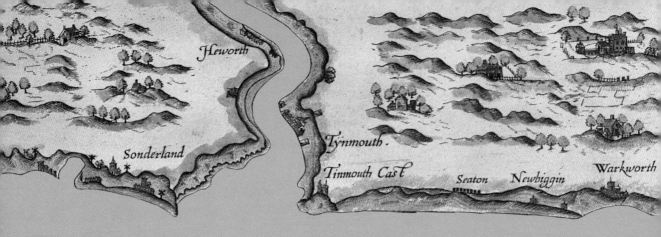

# Director's Foreword

In 1924, Geoffrey Callender, Professor of History at the Royal Naval College in Greenwich, published a textbook entitled *The Naval Side of British History*. The book outlines Britain's rise as a maritime power from the late fifteenth century to victory in the First World War. However, his emphasis is firmly in the age of sail and heavily weighted towards the Tudor and Stuart age. When Callender became the first director the National Maritime Museum in 1934, this narrative of British seafaring endeavour provided the essential intellectual underpinning for the displays.

Our interpretation of the past must, of course, move with the times. Naturally, Callender's outlook now seems hopelessly old-fashioned to modern readers but the Tudor and Stuart period remains an era of popular interest. This book advances the latest scholarship on the sixteenth and seventeenth centuries in an accessible form. It accompanies a new permanent gallery at the Museum – 'Tudor and Stuart Seafarers' – that explores this crucial and foundational period in Britain's maritime history. Whereas Callender focused on great men like Drake, Ralegh and Blake, the gallery examines key themes from a variety of perspectives to give a fuller and more rounded view. By looking anew at events like the defeat of the Spanish Armada and the English settlement of North America, some familiar misconceptions might be overturned and difficult moments in the nation's past be brought into sharper focus.

I hope that readers of this book find it compelling and thought-provoking. Moreover, I expect it will inspire them to visit (and revisit) the Museum to see the many of the objects illustrated here.

The Museum sincerely wishes to thank Mr Mark Pigott and family for their generous support of the 'Tudor and Stuart Seafarers' gallery at the National Maritime Museum and the adjoining Mark Pigott Room which provides visitors with an overview of our site's direct historic links back to Greenwich Palace and the Tudor and Stuart eras.

Dr Kevin Fewster AM
Director, Royal Museums Greenwich

*Chart of the Atlantic Ocean (detail). Nicholas Comberford, 1650. G213:2/.2.*

# Introduction

## James Davey

In September 1620 an old, creaking merchant ship named the *Mayflower* left England, setting out from Plymouth into the Atlantic Ocean. On board were 102 religious separatists, later to become known as the Pilgrims (or Pilgrim Fathers), determined to establish a colony in the 'New World'. There, in the remote, unfamiliar land of North America, the intrepid immigrants hoped they would be free to practise their religion without fear of persecution from James I's government. With their homeland thousands of miles behind them, they established a settlement on the edge of what they believed to be a boundless wilderness. And yet it was here they discovered that England's influence was inescapable. On 16 March 1621, an Indigenous American man named Samoset strode up to the Pilgrims' rudimentary settlement and, to their astonishment, addressed them in their own language. 'Greetings, Englishmen,' he declared, and proceeded to ask if they had any beer. None of the Pilgrims had ever met an Indigenous American before – let alone one who was capable of conversing in their own tongue – and we can only begin to imagine the look of surprise on their faces. There was a further shock in store: the following week Samoset returned, this time with his friend Tisquantum, who spoke English even better.[1]

It seems extraordinary that a group of settlers could sail across the Atlantic to an alien continent and find Indigenous people able to communicate with them in English. However, by the time of the *Mayflower*'s voyage, the people of the British Isles were already devoting considerable attention to the world beyond their own shores. Explorers had sailed to the furthest reaches of the world in a relentless search for wealth and power. In their wake came merchants and settlers determined to exploit these untapped, resource-rich lands. It was these voyages that initiated the spread of the English language around the world. It is likely that Samoset acquired his halting phrases – as well as his taste for beer – from fishermen operating off the coast of Newfoundland. Tisquantum, by contrast, had experienced the darker side of English maritime expansion. In 1614 he had been captured by an English seafarer and taken to London, returning five years later to find his tribe wiped out by diseases transmitted by European explorers. Both had learned enough English to converse with the Pilgrims. That they had done so was testament not only to their gift for language but also to the upswell in English maritime activity at the turn of the seventeenth century.

# Tisquantum

Tisquantum – or Squanto as he was known to the English – was one of the most extraordinary figures of his time. Born to the Patuxet tribe that lived on the western coast of Cape Cod Bay, he was one of 27 Indigenous Americans captured and enslaved by the English adventurer Thomas Hunt in 1614. He was transported to Europe to be sold in Spain, but somehow – the sources are unclear – managed to escape this fate and make his way to England, where he spent the next five years. In 1619 he returned to America as part of an expedition to settle in Newfoundland, and found that his people had been annihilated by an epidemic infection carried by European visitors. He went to live with the Pokanoket tribe and was therefore on hand to greet the *Mayflower* Pilgrims in early 1621.

Perhaps even more surprising than Tisquantum's transatlantic travels was his remarkable generosity. Despite having good reason to distrust and even hate the English, his advice and assistance in the early years of Plymouth Colony was essential to its success. He acted as a translator between English and Indigenous peoples, preventing conflict from breaking out and establishing over ten years of peaceful relations. Tisquantum taught the English how to sow and fertilize native crops, and also helped them economically, introducing them to the lucrative fur trade. Without his many interventions it is barely conceivable that Plymouth Colony would have survived: but for him, the history of English imperialism – and indeed America – would have been very different.

Samoset, Tisquantum and the Pilgrims were all participants in one of the more astonishing developments of the early-modern era: the emergence of England as a major maritime power. In the 1480s, England was an inward-looking, peripheral country, but over the subsequent two centuries the people of the British Isles learned how to use the sea to their advantage, with an expanding mercantile marine, a permanent naval force, and imperial ambitions that were truly global. Indeed, this period saw the English nation come to define itself by its relationship with the maritime world. If many thousands experienced it first-hand, the lives of countless others were shaped by the sea in less direct ways. The explosion of maritime activity saw thousands of people employed in new trades and dockyards, while dinner tables across the land were adorned with exotic commodities brought from the far corners of the world. The exploits of famous sea captains were disseminated in woodcuts and ballads, while paintings, medals and other forms of material culture were produced to celebrate new national heroes. The oceans became a source of inspiration for poets and playwrights, representing a 'sea change' in the way the ocean was understood in the British Isles.[2]

This book tells the story of how England transformed itself into a powerful maritime nation. This development has frequently been reduced to triumphalist and nationalistic histories, in which England would inevitably 'rule the waves'. The defeat of the Spanish Armada looms large in any such discussion, an event that almost single-handedly confirmed England's manifest maritime destiny, and which created a myth of naval superiority that would last for centuries.[3] England's rise, though, was by no means assured, for it was slow to appreciate the opportunities offered by the sea. Indeed, it was not until the 1550s that England began to

The 'Royal Prince' and other Vessels at the Four Days' Battle, 1–4 June 1666. *Abraham Storck, c.1670. NMM, acquired with the assistance of the Art Fund.* BHC0286.

make a concerted effort to exploit the world beyond Europe, and even after this, investment in oceanic endeavour remained limited and unsteady. Authors such as Sir Walter Ralegh and Richard Hakluyt wrote passionate treatises arguing for a larger navy or greater imperial investment, but for much of this period English maritime endeavours were ad hoc, relying on the ambition of private individuals rather than the support of the state. Even when England began to make greater strides into the Atlantic world, failure and disappointment were as common – if not more common – than success. As often as not – and as the Pilgrims could testify – England's expanding position relied as much on good fortune as on any deliberate strategy. Over the sixteenth and seventeenth centuries, though, the English grew more confident and more ambitious. There can be no doubt that by the early 1700s English maritime power was in the ascendancy, poised to dominate the world's oceans.

In recent years a remarkable profusion of new research has opened up fresh perspectives on this story. Scholars from a variety of disciplines have supplemented the traditional focus on strategy, operations and technology with ground-breaking research that has transformed our understanding of the period. We now know far more about the relationship between the sea and the construction of individual and national identities, as well as its impact on art, music and popular culture. Historians have explored the social and cultural realities of life on board ship, the burgeoning communities that supported and depended upon seafaring, and the complex relationships that existed between ship and shore. Ships have been shown to be important places of cross-cultural interaction, while other scholars have shed light on the remarkable diversity of people found on board early-modern vessels. The history of 'discovery' has been replaced with one of 'encounter', focusing on moments of cultural exchange and the numerous incidents of violence and exploitation that came to define European imperialism. Crucially, this research has shown that, in England's case at least, maritime history and national history are intertwined, and that the one cannot be studied without the other.[4]

The chapters that follow build on this wealth of research, bringing together contributions from twelve leading scholars. Individual chapters trace the numerous ways that the English shaped the maritime world of the early-modern era, through exploration, encounter, trade, warfare and piracy. Others focus on key events that were of central importance at the time, and which move the chronology of the book forward. Each chapter has as its spine a selection of objects from the extensive collections of the National Maritime Museum, which offer a rare insight into this history. The Museum holds world-class collections of charts, navigational instruments and ship models that allow us to consider the practicalities of seafaring, the weaponry of warfare and the structure of the sailing ship. Crucially, it houses other artefacts – such as paintings, prints, maps

*Terrestrial table globe.*
*Gerardus Mercator, 1541.*
*NMM, Caird Collection.* GLB0096.

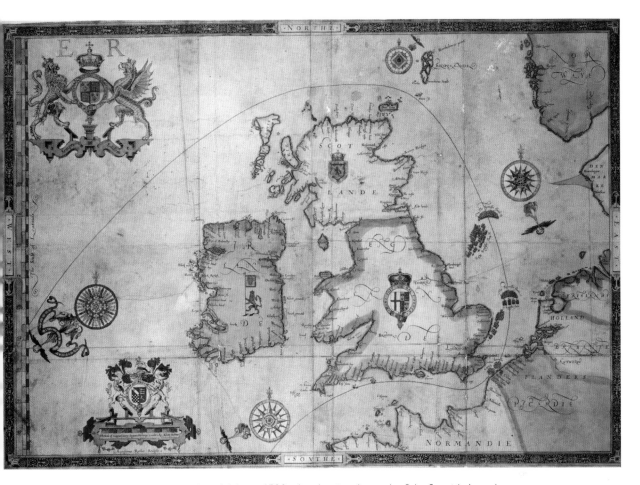

*Print showing the British Isles in 1590, also showing the track of the Spanish Armada.*
*Robert Adams; Augustine Ryther, 1590. PBD8529(2).*

and medals – that demonstrate how the maritime world was represented back in England. In a few places, other international collections have been utilized – for example, those of the Mary Rose Trust – but all of the chapters will use the Museum's collections to demonstrate the impact of maritime endeavours on English society, culture and self-image.

This is, then, fundamentally a book about England. That is not to say that 'Britain' and the people of Ireland, Wales and Scotland are ignored. On the contrary, the early-modern period saw the gradual formation of a federated and composite 'British' state, with the growing adoption of English as a common language across the four nations and the eventual recognition of a single ruler over the British Isles.[5] However, for most of this period, the notion of 'Britain' meant very little. Throughout the sixteenth century, England, Scotland and Ireland were separate nations ruled by different monarchs; Wales had long been subsumed into the English state. The Union of the Crowns in 1603 made James VI of Scotland the new King

Defeat of the Spanish Armada, 8 August 1588.
*Philippe-Jacques de Loutherbourg, 1796.*
*NMM, Greenwich Hospital Collection. BHC0264.*

James I of England, and he subsequently tried his utmost to inculcate a sense of a 'Greater Britain' in a deliberate attempt to shift regional loyalties to his new compound monarchy.[6] It was not until 1707, however, when the Act of Union formally amalgamated Scotland with the English state to form the 'United Kingdom of Great Britain', that 'British' became an accurate descriptor. It follows that this book uses the term 'England' rather than 'Britain', and the countless Irish, Scottish and Welsh protagonists who have a stake in this story will be referred to as such.

Although predominantly about England, this is also a book about England's place in the world. It is not possible, for instance, to understand the voyages of John Cabot without knowing about Columbus's previous expeditions, nor can we grapple with the idea of piracy without some consideration of international law. For much of this period, English eyes remained fixed on European affairs. Indeed, the early-modern era was one of regular and repeated conflict with other Europeans, in no small part *because* of England's rapid maritime expansion. It was Spanish fears about English encroachments at sea that led Philip II of Spain to assemble his vast Armada, while the Anglo-Dutch Wars of the seventeenth century were the direct result of England's seemingly unstoppable commercial and imperial expansion. The rise of an 'English Empire' beyond the British Isles took on global proportions, and explorers and adventurers intervened in and influenced nations and peoples even further afield. Here the English encountered peoples in Africa, America and Asia, establishing diplomatic and trading connections that could have only existed because of maritime communications. As more formalized imperial roots began to be laid down from the 1600s onwards, the impact England had on the world became ever greater.

There is no escaping the fact that in many cases this impact came in the form of violence and exploitation. The early-modern era saw the emergence of the transatlantic slave trade, arguably the greatest stain on English history, which saw millions of Africans forcibly taken from their communities and enslaved to work in European colonies across the Americas. Even where England set up more established trading relationships, these commercial networks frequently relied on indigenous labour and unequal trading agreements. Elsewhere, English settlers disrupted sophisticated societies and communities that had existed for centuries. In North America, English colonization has been accurately – but not uncontroversially – termed an 'invasion', in which settlers displaced peoples who had been living there for millennia. Some groups were forced to re-settle inland as the English intruded further, but others found they had nowhere to turn. The Beothuk people of Newfoundland were forced to huddle in the interior of the island, cut off from their traditional resources and economy by the encroaching English, and by the end of the seventeenth century they were virtually extinct.[7] European settlers also brought with them 'Old World' diseases such as influenza and smallpox, to which Indigenous peoples were extremely susceptible. The consequences were truly devastating: in 1500 there were perhaps 560,000 people living along the east coast of North America; the ravages of disease and conflict halved this population to an estimated 250,000 by 1700, and this decimation continued in the subsequent decades.[8]

This is not an attempt to lambast an entire period of English history. On the contrary, the book grapples with what happened in the past and attempts to understand why people acted as they did. This process necessitates facing uncomfortable truths. Some apologist historians have attempted to explain away the more brutal side of English history, either by pointing out that other European powers had initiated these practices, or suggesting that the deaths of Indigenous Americans were an unhappy but unintended accident. However, these positions do not hold up to even modest scrutiny. Certainly the English were not the first to enslave African

*Print showing male inhabitants of the Gold Coast, West Africa. Johannus Theodor de Bry, 1604.* PAG7537.

people – the Portuguese had long been involved in this trade – but the English quickly eclipsed their Iberian rivals: by the end of the seventeenth century England was the largest transporter of enslaved people in the world. Similarly, while it is true to say that many settlers acted without understanding the impact of their actions, others knew exactly what they were doing: English settlers in Virginia and Maryland conducted deliberate campaigns to raid and destroy local villages, killing thousands of innocent people who stood in the way of English expansion. It is easy to see why some modern scholars have begun to use the word 'genocide' to describe what happened to the indigenous people of North America.[9]

*Portrait depicting a Tudor seafarer. English School, c.1596.*
*NMM, Caird Collection. BHC3152.*

# William Shakespeare

The plays of Shakespeare, one of the most famous writers of his or any age, abound with maritime subjects and imagery. Though he was born in landlocked Stratford-upon-Avon, his work reveals a man who was fascinated by the ocean – so much so that some biographers have wondered if he spent time at sea in his younger years. Even if this is unlikely – the range of explanations for his 'lost years' of 1585–92 is mind-boggling – he was certainly part of a London society that was increasingly aware of the possibilities of maritime endeavour. His plays reveal numerous themes – imperial expansion, ethnicity, trade and warfare – that could only have been written in an age when the sea was beginning to take hold in the public consciousness.

Shakespeare sometimes used the sea as an intimidating, ominous arena, with numerous works highlighting the peril of the ocean. *Twelfth Night* begins with a shipwreck, in which the siblings Viola and Sebastian are separated, with comical consequences. More threateningly, in *The Tempest*, the sorcerer Prospero conjures up a storm to make his rivals to the throne believe they are marooned. However, other works offer a very different picture. In *Antony and Cleopatra*, the Mediterranean Sea is represented as a connecting space, and is the site of numerous political and economic networks. By treating the maritime world as both hostile and full of potential, Shakespeare perfectly encapsulated England's relationship with the sea in the early-modern era.

The story of England's maritime expansion is therefore one that continues to matter today. In the chapters that follow, the book's contributors have not attempted to describe developments as 'good' or 'bad', or individuals as 'heroes' or 'villains'. Such judgements lie beyond the remit of history, and readers will be able to come to their own conclusions about these complex and controversial processes. What follows is a human story that foregrounds the lives and experiences of the many individuals who were participants, and seeks to explain the world in which they lived. These are the 'seafarers' of the book's title, many of whom

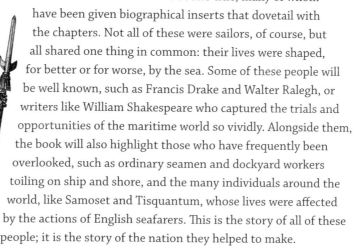

have been given biographical inserts that dovetail with the chapters. Not all of these were sailors, of course, but all shared one thing in common: their lives were shaped, for better or for worse, by the sea. Some of these people will be well known, such as Francis Drake and Walter Ralegh, or writers like William Shakespeare who captured the trials and opportunities of the maritime world so vividly. Alongside them, the book will also highlight those who have frequently been overlooked, such as ordinary seamen and dockyard workers toiling on ship and shore, and the many individuals around the world, like Samoset and Tisquantum, whose lives were affected by the actions of English seafarers. This is the story of all of these people; it is the story of the nation they helped to make.

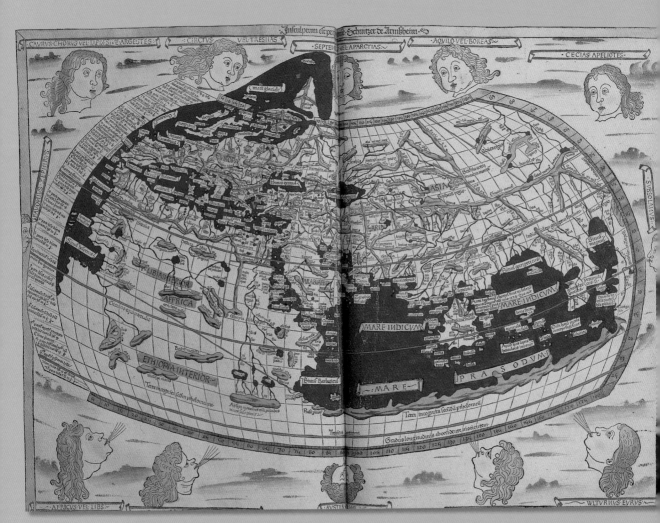

Ptolemy's Cosmographia. *Johann Reger, 1486.* PBD7695.

# 'New Worlds': 1485–1505

## Felipe Fernandez-Armesto

There is plenty of hot air in history, as conventionally told, but not enough wind. For the entire age of sail – that is, for almost the whole of the documented past – winds and currents limited the scope and direction of most long-range contact between cultures. The oceanic highways – the wind corridors, the pattern of currents that link British shores to the rest of the world – form the essential background against which to understand the making of maritime Britain. But the wind system was long enduring and little changing. It raises a further problem: why did English navigators take so long to exploit it? Why did they only begin to overspill their home seas on a large scale in the late fifteenth century? The problem is best approached in the context of all the seagoing communities of western Europe that experienced a similarly long period of hesitation or inertia, followed by a surprisingly sudden breakthrough towards the end of the fifteenth century. That context and that period – from the last couple of years of the 1480s to the first of the sixteenth century – are the subject of this chapter.

British – especially English – mythopoeia smells of tar, tastes of sea salt and resounds with breaking waves and the beat of Drake's Drum. Medieval England, however, was a land power, exhausting its resources in gaining and losing empires across narrow straits in France and Ireland. To some extent, other western European political communities were equally absorbed in landbound conflicts or inward-looking economic endeavours in the same era – France, Sweden, Denmark, Scotland and the Netherlands in internal consolidation and wars with neighbours; Spain in the Reconquista and Mediterranean adventures; north German and Baltic merchant confederacies in eluding other people's wars. Portugal, perhaps by more than coincidence, was the first Atlantic-side state not only to settle its civil wars and, albeit falteringly, its frontiers, but also to reach into the deep and far Atlantic. Yet it would be an error to try to explain the seaward turn of Atlantic-side Europe in terms of state-level politics. The early exploration of the ocean, the establishment of colonies overseas, and the inauguration of long-range, ocean-borne trades owed little to the state beyond the formal legitimation of such enterprises, and almost everything to private initiatives by port communities, merchant-financiers and enterprising adventurers.

Nor can environmental considerations help to explain the timing of the Atlantic take-off. Since the last ice age, the North Atlantic has been regulated by a fairly reliable wind system.[1] Except for occasional interruptions in the normal direction of the wind, usually in spring, and the unpredictable periodic reversal of the North Atlantic currents, a standard pattern prevails. The north-east trades are linked by the Gulf Stream to the northern westerlies that blow into Europe's Atlantic coasts; along the Arctic edge, a series of easterly currents stretches from Scandinavia to Newfoundland, facilitating voyages that can then pick up the westerlies to return home. England was particularly well placed for the winds: except, on a small scale, for Scotland, no other country had a comparable range of harbours to windward, with corresponding defensive advantages, and ready access to the ocean. During cold spells – from the fifth century to the ninth, and again, with some fluctuations, from the fourteenth century through to the seventeenth – glaciation stole south and shifted the system with it, without major disruption (which may help to explain the chronology of Norse navigations to and from Greenland in the Middle Ages). The oceanic outreach of the early-modern period could, as far as the environmental framework was concerned, have happened at any time.

Nor did the breakthrough coincide with any significant technological innovation. Long-range shipping benefited from slow, incremental enhancements in rigging for manoeuvrability in variable weather and from improvements in the construction of water casks – essential for keeping crews alive on long voyages – but the expeditions of the late fifteenth and early sixteenth centuries were made in ship types that had been available for centuries. On land, new direction-finding mechanisms based on astrolabes came into use in the fifteenth century, but no navigator of the critical period is known to have made use of them on board ship (where the motion of the vessel rendered them of little effect); on the contrary, the only evidence we have is of primitive celestial navigation, relying on the naked eye to reckon latitude from observations of the Sun and the Guard and Pole stars;[2] in any case, the much earlier experience of the Norse demonstrates that the Atlantic was traversable without any newfangled techniques. Renaissance scholarship stimulated geographical interest, added knowledge from rediscovered ancient texts and embellished maps and charts, but for the Atlantic, of course, all the additions were speculative.

To make sense of the amazingly accelerated achievements of our period we have to turn from political, environmental and technological history to examine the immediate circumstances. Economic developments, in particular, of the 1470s and 1480s, help to explain why a spectacular breakthrough followed for Atlantic-side European mariners generally and for English adventurers in particular. First, the economic prospects of long-range ventures suddenly improved. Curiosity had never been lacking, and provoked occasional forays from the late thirteenth century onwards, but no initiative made much money – not Genoese efforts to explore an oceanic route to Asia, nor Genoese, French and Iberian efforts to conquer and colonize Atlantic islands; not Portuguese probings of the African Atlantic, nor Flemish investment in trade in the Azores; not fishing and whaling in the northern ocean, nor slaving ventures, nor Norse and Icelandic struggles to keep a trading colony alive in Greenland. In

*The* Bremen Cog,
*a Hanseatic merchant ship,*
*c.1380. 2008.*
ZBA6863.

the 1480s, that changed.[3] In 1481, the Portuguese *Cortes*, or legislature, celebrated the first positive balance sheet from Portugal's Madeira colony. In 1482, the West African fort of São Jorge da Mina began to divert a little of the region's traditional gold trade into Portuguese merchants' hands. Over the next few years, growing Portuguese contact with the kingdom of Kongo enlarged and cheapened the supply of slaves. The costly Castilian enterprise in the Canary Islands began to make money in the same decade as sugar mills entered production. Meanwhile in the North Atlantic, the throughput of whaling products and walrus ivory recovered in Bristol. The fact that an explicitly exploratory Bristolian voyage of 1481 carried salt in enormous quantities suggests that new fisheries may already have been discovered.[4] In consequence of all these successes, the Atlantic became newly attractive to investors. We know little about the backers of the breakthrough voyages of the 1490s, but all those whose activities are traceable had prior experience of investment in Atlantic enterprise.

In the competition for North Atlantic products, activity by Danes, Azoreans and the Hanseatic merchant confederacy attracted interest in England. Bristol was England's second city, with a sense of civic identity reminiscent of a Greek polis or an Italian city republic. Bristolian merchants and shipbuilders endowed huge, sumptuous churches. St Mary Redcliffe is still Britain's biggest parish church, thanks to the munificence of the Canynges family, who

QVI RATE VELIVOLA OCCIDVOS PENETRAVIT AᵖIDOS
PRIMVS ET AMERICAM NOBILITAVIT HVMVM

CHRISTOPHORVS COLVMBVS LIGVR, INDIARV PRIMᵘINVEⁱᵀᴿ AᵒI492

ASTRORVM CONSVLTᵖ ET IPSO NOBILIS AVSV
CHRISTOPHORᵖ TALI FRONTE COLVMBᵖERAT

*Christopher Columbus, 1451–1506. Johannus Theodor de Bry, c.1600.* PAD2286.

rebuilt it after storm damage in 1445. The city's commerce frequented Gascony, Spain and Portugal and touched the Levant across the Mediterranean, but in the 1470s pressure mounted to seek new suppliers and outlets. Rivalry over Icelandic fishing grounds helped to provoke war between England and the Hanse – a league of Baltic and North Sea mercantile states. The Danish king, Christian I, supported the Hanse and tried to ban English merchants from Iceland, where, in the 1480s, his governor exerted a surprising degree of authority over the generally independent-minded islanders. Danish ships, meanwhile, reached Greenland, hoping perhaps to renew the vanished Norse colony, amid Bristolian complaints against Danish 'pirates'.

Expectation was rife that under-exploited riches awaited discovery in the North Atlantic. The new profitability of Atlantic enterprise helped to stimulate it. So did the proliferation of sea charts speckled with speculative isles, and the credence inappropriately bestowed on chivalric romances that credited King Arthur with founding an Atlantic empire and knightly adventurers or peregrinating hermits with unlikely landfalls.[5] A series of voyages from Bristol targeted what their backers called Brasil – a putative island with a long record of featuring in maps and legends. Nothing is known of what, if anything, they found, but in 1497 a Spanish spy reported that 'in the past' Bristolians had 'found Brasil', as well as what we now call Newfoundland.[6] Christopher Columbus added a decisive stimulus by proving on his voyages of 1492 and 1493 that the Atlantic was traversable in both directions. He was not the first navigator to make the attempt but no known predecessor had succeeded, owing to a rarely acknowledged but essential oddity of the history of navigation. Overwhelmingly, except in monsoon seas where sailors can rely on the seasonal turn of the wind and so can be sure of a means of getting home, would-be discoverers have sailed into the wind. It may seem counterintuitive to modern yachtsmen who thrill to the wind at their backs, but there is rarely much point in exploring a route to a new haven unless you can get home to tell people about it. Columbus may not deserve all the praise that adulators have lavished on him, but he had exceptional valour to sail with the wind behind him.

Contemporary opinion was divided about where the wind took him. He had encountered people he optimistically called *indios*; an engraving in one of the earliest printed editions of the first report of his findings showed them trading with oriental merchants. The consensus, however, was that the material culture he observed among Taino and Caribs (whom Columbus identified recklessly with 'people of the Great Khan') was 'savage' and uninfluenced by Asiatic sophisticates. Columbus himself was conflicted about the ethnographic subject matter he had revealed, and saw the *indios* at times as exemplifications of naked human dependence on God, at times as survivors of a classical Golden Age of innocence, and at times as beastly creatures fit only for enslavement.[7] Debate focused on three rival interpretations of the land he found: a forecast but previously uncorroborated antipodean new world; more islands 'like the Canaries'; or, as Columbus claimed, outliers of Asia and the fringe of the world's richest economies at the time.[8] All of these were worth following up, and explorers sailed in his wake, especially from 1499, when the Spanish monarchs admitted interlopers to Columbus's route – which his

*Prints depicting Columbus's voyages. Johannus Theodor de Bry. PAJ3811 (right). PAJ0875 (opposite).*

original royal brief had guaranteed as his personal monopoly. In consequence, much of the coast of Central America and Brazil found its way onto maps by 1502.

Columbus's achievement resonated in England. He had chosen to sail due west from the Canaries because contemporary consensus placed Chinese and perhaps Japanese ports on about the same latitude. As the world is obviously spherical – if anything, savants of the time overestimated its perfect sphericity, and there were probably fewer believers in a flat Earth then than now – the length of the transoceanic journey would be shorter near the North Pole than towards the Equator. From England, if a navigator could find a favourable wind or current during a spring easterly or one of the occasional oscillations of the system, he could, on the basis of Columbus's own claims, beat the record speed to China or its vicinity.

This impeccable reasoning – vitiated only by false premises – was the basis of a plan John Cabot touted in Bristol after Columbus's first return. Like so many fellow explorers, Cabot, as a Venetian citizen, perhaps Genoese-born, exemplified the way Atlantic exploration grew out

of medieval Mediterranean experience.[9] According to the Milanese ambassador in London, Cabot's objective was Cipango, 'where he believes all the spices of the world have their origin, as well as the jewels'. Cipango was an island Marco Polo had vaguely reported (probably on the basis of Chinese accounts of Japan) and Columbus had sought. Cabot importuned merchants in Bristol and the monarch in London for the right and means to make his proposed experiment.[10] In March 1496 Henry VII obliged with a grant of dominion, under the crown, of such lands unknown to Christians and unclaimed by any Christian king as Cabot and his sons discovered. Strictly speaking, the grant was worthless. Spain and Portugal, by papal concession, had exclusive rights of navigation over the seas for which Cabot was bound. In any case, Henry had no right to dispose of land belonging to other people, whether Christian or pagan.

The subsequent story has to be pieced together from stray references in tangentially related documents and from accounts recorded at second hand in largely unverifiable commentaries. If an account presented to Columbus can be trusted, Cabot's first attempt at an Atlantic

# John Cabot

The navigator and explorer John Cabot has been overlooked by historians obsessed with Christopher Columbus's momentous voyages. Cabot, though, is deserving of more attention. His expedition of 1497, commissioned by Henry VII of England, was the first European exploration of North America since the Vikings. Cabot was fêted on his return to England, and preparations were made for a second voyage the following year. It remains unclear what became of him: some sources suggest that he was lost at sea, but recent research suggests that some members of his crew returned safely to England.[12]

crossing in 1496 was unsuccessful, apparently because of short supplies, bad weather and a recalcitrant crew.[11] Presumably, adverse winds contributed. On a second attempt in 1497, in what all the sources confirm was a single small vessel, Cabot benefited from a sustained spell of springtime wind from the east on the outward journey, setting out in May and returning in August with the prevailing westerlies that had borne the Norse and Columbus. According to the most circumspect narrative of the voyage at the time, Cabot explored a length of coast on the far side of the ocean between the latitudes of Dorsey Head in Ireland and the mouth of the Garonne – roughly from 46 to 51 degrees north. Readings of latitude at sea are often said to have been unreliable at the time, but navigators practised in primitive celestial navigation, or using a simple gnomon, could check their estimates by consulting tables of latitude, printed or in manuscript, for selected places in Europe. If the readings ascribed to Cabot were accurate, he had hardly exceeded the limits of the coast of Newfoundland; the current becomes adverse at about the southernmost tip of that island. Cabot reported just such a rich cod fishery as Newfoundland possessed. Up to that point, therefore, his report was plausible.

If contemporary reportage is reliable, he went on to claim that he had 'discovered mainland 700 leagues away, which is the country of the Great Khan'. The ruler of China had borne no such title since 1368, but communications across Eurasia had dwindled in the intervening period so that European information on the celestial kingdom had become seriously out of date. Columbus, on his way to what he hoped would be China, had carried letters from the Spanish monarchs addressed to the same potentate. Cabot's speculations on the availability of silk in the vicinity of his supposed discoveries presumably also arose from his expectation that he would come close to China. Like Columbus, and indeed like most explorers of the time who were usually inspired by romantic fictions, he affected the role of a hero of chivalric romance, promising to bestow the governorships of islands on his crew, down to his Genoese barber. But however much thoughts of undiscovered islands filled the adventurers' minds, the hard-headed commercial objective remained access to China: the world's most prosperous economy and biggest market.

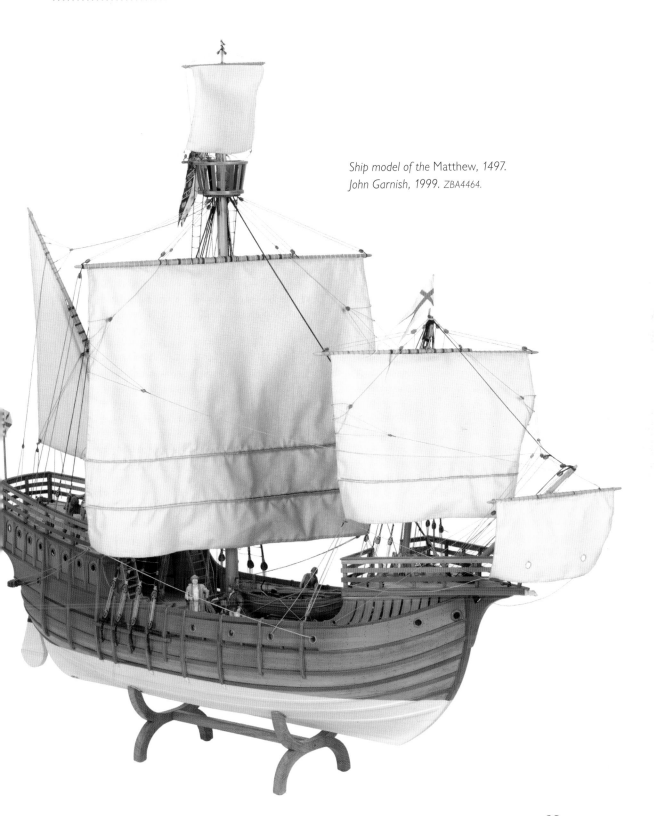

*Ship model of the Matthew, 1497.*
*John Garnish, 1999.* ZBA4464.

Henry VII was sufficiently impressed by Cabot's claims to invest in further enterprises. Cabot's immediate reward was a bounty of £10, which he spent, according to his fellow Venetian Pasquale Pasqualigo, on swaggering apparel; after his next crossing, an annual pension of £20 was added, to be paid from the Bristol customs. On a scale enhanced by expectations of success and inflated by ready money, a further voyage was planned in an impressive flotilla of six ships. The king contributed at least £221 and 16 shillings and a ship, apparently hired from two London merchants and provisioned for a year. Foreign ambassadors reported that the king proposed to enlist convicts as colonists, but if so, the intention came to nought. London chroniclers reported that London merchants provided modest trading goods. Most of the finance probably came from Bristol merchants, including William Weston, who was mentioned in the king's commendation to Cabot the following year. In the next generation, the head of one of the city's leading merchant dynasties claimed to have inherited an exploring urge from 'the discoverers of Newfoundland', Robert Thorne and fellow merchant, Hugh Elyot.[13]

The voyage was a disaster. Polydore Vergil, the king's Italian chronicler, said Cabot was 'believed to have found the new lands nowhere but on the bottom of the ocean'. The leader disappeared, never to be seen again. Of the five ships that set out, one got back to Ireland, badly storm-damaged. Yet faith in the transatlantic enterprise was not extinguished, thanks mainly to the efforts of Azorean explorers. At least 16 attempts to cross the Atlantic from the Azores are mentioned in Portuguese records as having sailed, or in some cases having at least been planned, from 1452 to 1486. The prevailing westerlies frustrated them, but in 1499 João Fernandes received a commission for a further attempt to be launched from Terceira. His route is unknown, though the historical consensus locates him in Labrador. The following year, Gaspar Corte-Real, son of the governor of Terceira in the Azores, set out northwards and made landfall on Greenland, at or near Cape Farewell. Follow-up voyages by Gaspar and his brother Miguel, starting in Lisbon in 1501 and 1502 respectively, ended in catastrophe, with the loss of both leaders and their ships, but surviving vessels brought home native slaves from Newfoundland – 'fit,' according to Gaspar, as reported by Pasqualigo, 'for every kind of labour'. Reports arrived of the potential fertility of Labrador, which the explorers named 'land of the farmer', and of Newfoundland, which Gaspar Corte-Real called the 'Green Country'. Contemporaries described the explored lands as populous, endowed with wooden constructions, rich in salmon and well forested.[14]

Meanwhile, João Fernandes and two other Terceirans, João Gonsalves and Francisco Fernandes, transferred to Bristol in the hope of finding sponsors for the resumption of Cabot's voyages. Such transfers of allegiance were common. Columbus had been a supplicant in Portugal before switching to Spain. Vespucci made the same shift, as did Magellan in the next generation. For Azorean entrepreneurs, England was, perhaps, a more likely source of patronage than their own kingdom, especially when intelligence-gathering missions of the early 1490s suggested that the Indian Ocean was accessible by sea and deflected Portuguese rulers and investors from the Atlantic. The profits yielded by voyages to India in 1497 and

# Amerigo Vespucci

Amerigo Vespucci, who had worked for one of Columbus's bankers, took to sea in 1499 as an assessor of pearls on a voyage to fisheries Columbus had reported, off what is now Venezuela. Setting himself up as a purported authority on navigation and cartography, he transferred his allegiance to Portugal and took part in a further expedition, of disputed extent, along the coast of South America and into the South Atlantic in 1501–02. Returning to Spain, he obtained an official position training pilots and checking charts of the route across the Atlantic. There is no evidence that he discharged either responsibility, though he drew the corresponding salary until his death in 1510. Meanwhile, in 1507, geographers in St Dié in Lorraine, impressed with false claims that Vespucci had discovered the western hemisphere, hailed him as the new Ptolemy and proposed naming the New World after him. The name 'America' stuck.

*Amerigo Vespucci's first voyage, 1497–99. PAG7429.*

1500 concentrated Portuguese attention on the riches of maritime Asia. Anyone marginalized on the western extremities of the Portuguese monarchy or fixated on Columbus's chimerical theories of a western route to China had cause to look elsewhere for backing.

The Portuguese arrivals reignited Atlantic exploration in Bristol. The terms of their letters patent from Henry VII recall Cabot's, and the presumption that they were bound for Cabot's discoveries seems irresistible.[15] João Fernandes died on the first expedition the newcomers mounted from Bristol, but survivors continued the work in partnership with some of Cabot's former backers, including Hugh Elyot and the brothers Thorne. Traces of their voyages litter the archives. In January 1501 the exchequer paid 100 shillings to 'the men of Bristol that found the isle'. Further bounty followed in 1502 'to the merchants of Bristol that have been in the new found land'. Francisco Fernandes and João Gonsalves received 10 pounds each in September 1502 'as captains into the new found land'. Hugh Elyot was among investors for a voyage that year. Meanwhile, three 'savages' who wore hides, ate raw meat and jabbered unintelligibly were presented at court.[16] It is not clear where any of the voyages went – the allegedly newfound land may have been no farther away than Greenland. By 1502, however, to judge from insecure but suggestive cartographic evidence, a substantial stretch of coast had been revealed, probably from Hudson Strait to the southern tip of Nova Scotia.

Though the achievement looks substantial in retrospect, disappointment prevailed at the time. As more coastline appeared, inhabited by 'savages' and unproductive of spices, silks, precious metals or fancy manufactures, the less likely it seemed that Cabot's trajectory would lead to China or anywhere near it. The heavy losses – ships sunk, commanders vanished – were uncompensated by the sort of pecuniary profits that consoled Portugal, say, for the high cost in shipping of the voyage to India. The gamble on a western route to Asia had always seemed reckless to geographically informed observers. The true size of the globe – known since antiquity – precluded fantasies about a narrow Atlantic. Spanish intelligence reports revealed anxiety about the potential the Bristolians displayed, but the winds blew Englishmen back and forth along northerly routes that led only to what seemed a profitless obstacle. Eventually, English navigators resigned themselves to the need to follow Columbus's route to and from America. It was a long way out to the colonies England had established, sailing with the north-east trades – typically six weeks or so, compared with about four to the Spanish Caribbean – but it was at least viable and reliable. Cabot's northern route had led only to a cul-de-sac.

Nor did mariners from England follow up on the decoding of the South Atlantic wind system (more or less a mirror image of that of the North Atlantic), or on the discovery via the South Atlantic winds of a route to the Indian Ocean. These achievements occurred in consequence of laborious Portuguese exploration of the west coast of Africa during the 1480s in adverse sailing conditions, along lee shores and against contrary currents. Probably as a result of a foray into the high ocean by Bartolomeu Dias in 1488, it became apparent that the best route around the Cape of Good Hope – as the Portuguese called that dangerous promontory in a conscious application of promotional rhetoric – was via the southeast trades and the unremitting westerlies of the far south. In 1497–98, Vasco da Gama demonstrated the value

# Vasco da Gama

Vasco da Gama was born in Portugal probably in 1460 and became a major figure in the history of exploration. He commanded a fleet of four ships seeking a sea route to India, which left Lisbon on 8 July 1497 with a crew of about 170 men. Sailing south, they passed the Cape of Good Hope and entered the India Ocean. At Malindi (in present-day Kenya) da Gama employed a pilot, who navigated the course for Calicut in south-west India. But he took no such advice on the way back. His ships struggled against the opposing monsoon, taking three months to reach Malindi at the cost of half the crew. Two ships and only 55 men finally returned to Lisbon after more than two years at sea. Nevertheless, the voyage was a success, bringing back lucrative spices and the promise of further voyages. For the next century Portugal dominated European trade with India until England's successful challenge in the 1600s.

Vasco da Gama, c.1460–1524. *António Manuel da Fonseca, after an earlier miniature, 1838. NMM. Greenwich Hospital Collection. BHC2702.*

of using the South Atlantic system: he justified apparently disastrous losses in ships and men by opening direct trade with India. In 1500 Pedro Álvares Cabral deviated so far in pursuit of the westerlies that he hit Brazil. Spanish navigators from 1499 onwards explored the route of the southeast trades in probing South American coasts. In England, Scotland and Ireland, however, such opportunities aroused little interest and inspired almost no efforts. Britain's home seas were a long way from the relevant winds. The available shipping was fully occupied on existing routes. The Iberian powers seemed to have pre-empted competition.

Henry VII's grandiloquent letters patent disclose imperial ambitions that were doomed to frustration. There were to be ceremonies of possession. Indeed, Cabot celebrated such a ceremony on his second voyage, hoisting, according to various reports, English, Venetian and papal banners. Governors – so the king hoped – would follow, with colonists, missionaries and every kind of economic exploitation. None of it came to pass. For the rest of the sixteenth century, England managed only sporadic forays. None achieved the professed objectives – neither a route to China nor a colony in America. English ships were largely confined to piratical exploits, flitting and stinging on the edge of the Spanish Main (the coastal waters of the Spanish American mainland), like insects irritating the hide of some great beast, while Elizabethan projectors raged at England's inability to challenge Spanish dominance. Not until 1607 would a lasting English presence in the New World begin to take shape, when a fragile colony settled at Jamestown in Virginia.

*Map depicting emerging European knowledge of the Indian and Atlantic Oceans. Claudius Ptolemy; published by Martin Waldseemüller, 1513. G201:1/63.*

Until then the new worlds for which English seamen reached may have contributed less overall to the making of a maritime 'nation' than to the increasing volume and range of commerce with well-known oceanic destinations in Iceland, the Azores, the western coasts of France, Portugal and Spain, and the mainland ports and islands of the African Atlantic. A further problem abides. 'One Englishman, an idiot,' quipped George Santayana; 'two Englishmen, a sporting event; three Englishmen: the British Empire.' The notion that empire comes easily to the British – in a feat of *sprezzatura* or a fit of absence of mind – is a beloved part of a tenacious myth. Instead, however, of celebrating a supposed golden age of national greatness under the Tudors, we should, perhaps, ask why, by Spanish and Portuguese standards, English effort overseas was feeble and England's imperial maritime vocation weak and unsustained.

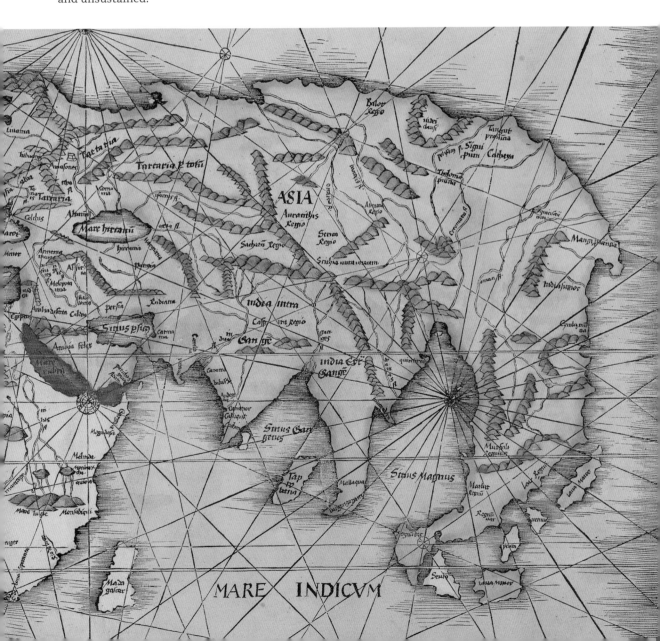

CORVS

CIRCIVS

Terra de ca[n]metta

GERMANIA

GALLI

HISPA

TANIA

ASIA

MINOR

H[...]MANE

INSVLE

FORTVNA[...]

MAVRI

TANIA

ARM

IA[...]

ILLA CANCRI

C. dee caballos

[...]

ETHI

OPIA

SVB

REGIS

[...]O

CRVC[...]

EQVINOCTIALIS

TERRA S CRVCIS SIVE
MVDVS NOVVS

C CAPRICORNI

cefa

ANTARTIC[...]

FR

AVIS[...]

LIBO AVSTER

AVSTER

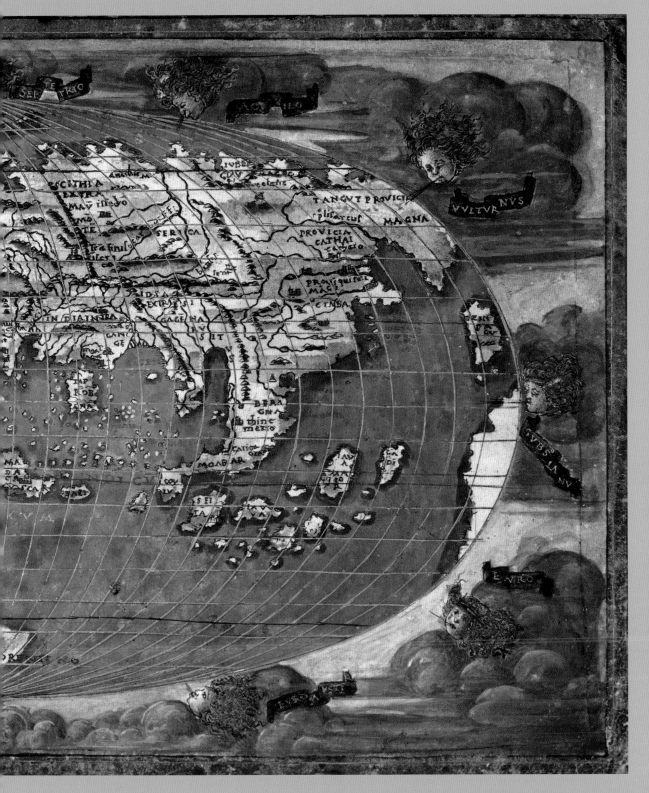

*Venetian map depicting the known world after the voyages of Columbus, Vespucci, Cabot and da Gama. Francesco Rosselli, 1508. NMM. Caird Collection. G201:1/53.*

*Triple portrait depicting Thomas Cavendish, Sir Francis Drake and Sir John Hawkins.*
*British School, seventeenth century. NMM, Greenwich Hospital Collection. BHC2603.*

CHAPTER

2

# Adventurers: England Turns to the Sea, 1550–80

## James Davey

Were we able, through some quirk of time and space, to wander through England in the early 1500s, we would hear little talk of the sea. For the first half of the sixteenth century, the English ignored the possibilities presented by the remarkable voyages of Columbus, Cabot and da Gama, their attention firmly fixed on the British Isles and its immediate environs. And yet, from the 1550s onwards, the English nation 'turned to the sea' with an insatiable fervour, fuelled by the prospect of boundless wealth and power. This transformation was not the result of state investment or any grand strategic plan. Instead, it was a policy born out of greed and ambition, as individuals from a variety of backgrounds sought to make their name and fortune on the oceans. Whether through legitimate trade, aggressive piracy, ferocious warfare or the brutal exploitation of indigenous peoples, these seafarers contributed to the emergence of a new kingdom defined by its maritime prowess. Where before England had been withdrawn and peripheral, a second-rate power, by the 1580s it was a nation with global reach and the confidence to assert its burgeoning power.

If the English were slow to appreciate the opportunities provided by the 'shock of the new', their Iberian rivals demonstrated no such restraint. No sooner had Columbus set foot in the Caribbean than the Spanish put down imperial roots, following this up with a series of assertive colonizing ventures. Portugal quickly monopolized trade with Africa and South America, and also extended its influence into the Indian Ocean. Not everyone in England was blind to these movements. One unnamed Royal Councillor noted in 1511 that 'England alone is a just empire', and argued for English resources to be directed 'that way we can, and to which it seems the eternal providence hath destined us, which is by sea'.[1] However, such statements were decidedly unpopular with the newly enthroned Henry VIII. He faced numerous European enemies and their threat only increased following his schism with the Roman Catholic Church in 1527, which sparked the English Reformation. For the entirety of his reign (1509–47) Henry VIII pursued ambitions that were inherently parochial, squandering what resources he had on expensive and ultimately futile attempts to reclaim English lands in France.

When it came, England's decision to exploit opportunities away from the European continent had little to do with providence, and everything to do with circumstance and raw opportunism. The 1550s ushered in a great recession in England, prompted by a catastrophic decline in the price of woollen cloth – the nation's most important export commodity. English merchants searched frantically for new markets and also for other products that could be traded. In 1553, a group of London merchants, assisted by the aged explorer Sebastian Cabot, established the 'Mystery and Company of Merchant Adventurers for the Discovery of Regions, Dominions, Islands and Places Unknown' (or the 'Merchant Adventurers' for short). With Spain and Portugal dominant in the Atlantic World and the Ottoman Empire commanding the overland route to Asia, they were forced to look north in their attempt to locate untapped sources of wealth. They fell upon the prospect of the 'north-east passage', a seaward

*Map of Africa. Abraham Ortelius, 1570. G290:1/10.*

route to the riches of the Indies that would pass along the northern coast of Russia. For these desperate merchants, it appeared to be the only viable way of securing access to the riches of the East.

The first attempt was made in May 1553, when Sir Hugh Willoughby headed north with three ships. They were soon beset by storms. Beaten by freezing winds, the vessels became separated off the northern tip of Norway. Two of Willoughby's ships sought relief in a sheltered bay, but the crews of both vessels were appallingly unprepared for the brutal cold of an Arctic winter; their bodies were discovered by Russian fishermen the following spring. The third ship, led by Willoughby's second-in-command, Richard Chancellor, did manage to escape the icy tempest, and struggled into the White Sea. There, Chancellor was summoned to the court of the Russian tsar, Ivan IV Vasilyevich. More popularly known as 'Ivan the Terrible', he was a fearsome man famous for outbreaks of mental instability and hardly renowned for his hospitality. Nonetheless, through adept diplomacy Chancellor left Russia months later with a commercial treaty establishing a trade route that stretched from England to Persia, over sea and land. A disastrous voyage was transformed into a significant trading success; Chancellor returned to London in triumph. On 26 February 1555, the charter of the 'Merchants of Russia, granted upon the discovery of the said country', known more popularly as the Muscovy Company, was established. The expansion of England's global trading position had begun.[2]

There would be further attempts to find a north-east passage to the Indies, but it was beyond the capabilities of early-modern seafarers to navigate the icy northern barrier. English attention turned instead to the Atlantic Ocean and particularly to West Africa, where the English were more conspicuous interlopers. The Portuguese had established an extensive trading network along the West African coast over the preceding decades, and saw no reason to relinquish their influence over the region. English merchants cared little for diplomatic niceties and stubbornly attempted to break into the lucrative trade in gold, ivory and pepper. The first English trading ship arrived at Benin in the Niger delta in 1553, commanded by Thomas Windham, and was welcomed by West African communities pleased to have another, rival European power to trade with. Windham was able to exchange cloth, metals and other hardware for 2,400 ounces of gold, and also negotiated to take 80 tons of pepper on credit. His obvious commercial success prompted many repeat voyages, and although violence between those European nations with an interest in West Africa was common, the Portuguese could do little to prevent English merchants from returning on an almost annual basis. Indeed, between 1553 and 1567 there were 12 voyages by English merchants to Africa. English interest in the Atlantic, dormant since the voyages of Cabot in the 1490s, had been revived.[3]

None of this interchange would have been possible without the cooperation of Africans on the 'Gold Coast'. The English dealt with professional African merchants well versed in commodity exchange and skilled in commercial transactions; in 1554, the English merchant

John Lok admiringly noted one African's skill in weighing gold. With their own transportation and currency systems, African people had developed commercial networks that had been in place for hundreds of years and extended across the continent. Most commercial transactions were conducted on a reciprocal, egalitarian basis. Certainly there were instances of European deception – for example, when poor-quality materials were traded – but in the main, the trade offered economic opportunities to both English and African people. Many Africans were eager to participate in the Atlantic economy and some grew rich through the trade with English seafarers. These commercial encounters were also moments of cultural exchange and inquisitiveness. In 1555 Lok brought five African men back to England with him so that they might learn English and serve as interpreters; at least three of them later returned and became brokers and intermediaries in the Anglo-African trade.[4]

If these early English voyages were marked by a significant degree of mutual reliance and gain, the 1560s ushered in a far more brutal and exploitative practice: the slave trade. Portugal had been trading African people for decades, but the English had had little opportunity to follow suit. This changed in 1562 when Sir John Hawkins commanded an expedition to the coast of Africa, where he captured a Portuguese slave ship. Understanding the price they would fetch in the Caribbean, he transported 301 enslaved people across the Atlantic to be sold in the Spanish colonies. For Hawkins it was a risky venture, with many in England regarding the practice as immoral. Initially Queen Elizabeth I called the slave trade 'detestable' and prophesied that Hawkins's voyage 'would call down the vengeance of heaven'. She soon changed her mind when she realized the enormous profits on offer, quietly authorizing him to continue trading. He led three subsequent voyages between 1564 and 1569, supported by courtiers, financiers and the queen herself, all attracted by the vast revenues that could be made from supplying Spanish America with African slave labour. Hawkins's methods were initially aggressive, sometimes using violence to kidnap and imprison Africans, but this proved too dangerous and costly a tactic. He subsequently employed Portuguese merchants to supply enslaved people, or even supported African tribal leaders against their enemies in exchange for a share of the prisoners taken. Across his four voyages, Hawkins enslaved an estimated 1,000 African people.[5]

This was the beginning of English involvement in the transatlantic slave trade, a practice that over the coming centuries saw millions of African people uprooted from their communities and forcibly transported across the Atlantic Ocean to be sold as slaves in the Americas. In its early days, it was a limited and uncertain venture

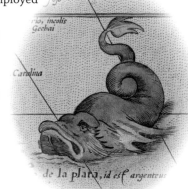

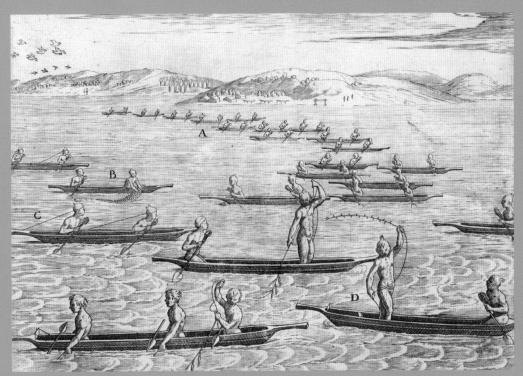

*Print depicting African people fishing by day. Voyage of the Dutch to the Gold Coast of Guinea, 1600; natives fishing by day. Johannus Theodor de Bry, 1604. PAG7540.*

*Print depicting African people fishing by night. Johannus Theodor de Bry, 1604. PAG754.1.*

# Sir John Hawkins

John Hawkins dominated the maritime world of Tudor England. Born in 1532, he followed in his father's footprints by seeking a career at sea, organizing a series of semi-piratical voyages to Africa and the Caribbean. The first, in 1562, saw the establishment of the English slave trade, and made him and his sponsors very rich. His second voyage in 1564–65 – in which he was joined by his second cousin, Francis Drake – secured the financial support of Elizabeth I, and saw his profits reach new levels. Though his next venture in 1568 ended in disaster, he continued to win favour in court, becoming MP for Plymouth and subsequently Treasurer of the Royal Navy. In this role he played a crucial part in the restructure of the English navy, advocating for faster and more manoeuvrable ships: it was these nimble yet powerful vessels that helped see off the Spanish Armada. Along with Drake, he continued to fight the Spanish after 1588; the following year they made an unsuccessful attempt to capture the Spanish treasure fleet. In 1595 both died of disease during a privateering voyage to the West Indies.

*Portrait of Sir John Hawkins.*
*English School, 1581.*
*NMM, Caird Fund.* BHC2755.

for those traders prepared to pursue it. Hawkins himself met with financial disaster on his final voyage to Africa in 1568 after a clash with the Spanish at San Juan de Ulúa in Central America. In the 50 years that followed there were very few English slave voyages, and it was not until the seventeenth century that England's own colonizing efforts would see the demand for slaves increase. Compared with that of the Portuguese and, increasingly, the Dutch, who dominated slave shipments to Brazil, the scale of English slave trading in the sixteenth century was limited, but the foundations of a horrendous system had been laid. By the end of the seventeenth century English traders had become the largest carriers of enslaved people on the Atlantic (see Chapter 7).[6]

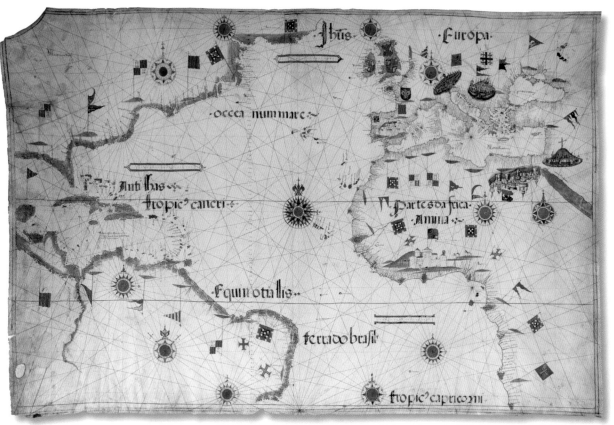

*Portolan chart of the Atlantic Ocean, depicting the
spread of European empires, c.1535. G213:2/4.*

Elizabeth's tacit approval of Hawkins's expeditions suggested that for the first time, England had a monarch who was prepared – indeed determined – to enforce a more aggressive maritime strategy. Certainly, she and her ministers understood that many of the problems she had inherited on her accession to the throne in 1558 – including a national debt of £300,000 and a hostile opposition abroad – could be tempered by the further expansion of overseas trade. The imperative to pursue new markets, particularly those of the Ottoman Empire and the states of northern Africa, not only brought her wealth, but also established closer relations with major military powers that were also hostile to Catholic Spain. Tudor fascination with the Islamic world went back at least as far as Henry VIII, after which English merchants had begun importing exotic commodities from Islamic lands, including cotton, sweet wines and Moroccan sugar (which Elizabeth consumed in such large quantities that her teeth turned black). It was clear that such trade warranted further official support, and Elizabeth's first parliament enacted reforms to encourage overseas commerce. Within a decade England was importing 250 tons of Moroccan sugar each year, valued at £18,000. Total imports from Morocco were worth £28,000 – nearly 25 per cent more than the entire revenue from trade with Portugal.[7]

*Sir Martin Frobisher, c.1535–94. Early seventeenth century. PAD4572.*

As England became more and more isolated from Catholic Europe, its determination to forge closer ties with the Islamic world – and particularly the Ottoman Empire – grew ever stronger. Throughout the 1570s, Asian spices, pepper and silks arrived in ever-larger quantities via the overland route, culminating on 11 September 1581 with the establishment of the 'Turkey Company', a joint-stock company capable of laying out the remarkable sum of £45,000 in start-up costs. By 1586, the Turkey Company (renamed the Levant Company in 1592) was thriving, exporting cloth and metal in return for silk, spices, cotton, currants, carpets, indigo and drugs of various kinds. At its height, it was despatching an average of five voyages a year to trade with Ottoman-controlled ports. The commercial benefit was obvious: on some voyages profits were estimated at over £70,000, producing returns of 300 per cent. More than this economic vitality, though, the burgeoning trade with Turkey ushered in a remarkable period of cross-cultural exchange between England and the Islamic World. By the late 1580s, hundreds, perhaps thousands, of Elizabeth's subjects were plying their trade in the waters between England and North Africa.[8]

While England's emerging trading network was a tangible boon to Elizabeth (and particularly her coffers), she and her ministers were only too aware of Spain's expanding global position, and were extremely jealous of the vast wealth pouring out of its American possessions. Spanish rule extended across the Caribbean, Central America, and the northern and western coasts of South America, the whole imperial system designed to transport gold and silver back to the mother country. The English knew that an all-out war would be suicidal, for Spain was the economic and military superpower of the day. Still, those in power believed that something needed to be done to check Spain's power and secure a slice of the fabulous wealth emanating from across the Atlantic. In 1563, Elizabeth ordered a decree permitting 'reprisals by general proclamation' that opened up the prospect of state-sanctioned raiding

Sir Francis Drake, 1540–96. *Marcus Gheeraerts the Younger, 1591.*
*NMM, Caird Collection.* BHC2662.

on a grand scale. A law existed whereby 'letters of reprisals' could be given to shipowners who had been robbed by the subjects of a foreign prince in a time of peace, and they were thus authorized by an Admiralty court to recoup their losses up to a specified sum. This system was far more limited than the later 'letters of marque' that allowed sailors in the seventeenth and eighteenth centuries to attack enemy shipping. However, these were laws that could be easily twisted by an unscrupulous queen.[9]

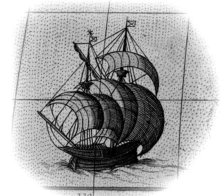

The next 20 years were marked by a series of unofficial actions at sea, a 'cold war' in all but name, as the activities of English pirates and adventurers steadily tested international relations. Few in Spain were fooled by English proclamations of innocence; for them, the actions of English adventurers were nothing short of piracy, and the Spanish king, Philip II, became increasingly irate as reports of English depredations fed back to Madrid in ever-greater numbers. English seafarers took to privateering with relish: freed from any real legal restraint, men such as John Hawkins, Martin Frobisher and Thomas Cavendish were able to use whatever means they could countenance to seize goods and plunder, while Elizabeth, who frequently gave financial support to the missions, quietly pocketed much of the winnings. The bolder captains won fame, capturing the public imagination and inspiring others to follow their lead. Chief among these 'Sea Dogs' was Francis Drake, a man who failed even to pretend to be interested in trade and yearned only for plunder and celebrity. The sea, he wrote, was 'the path to fame, the proof of zeal, and the way to purchase gold'.[10]

Born in 1540, in Devon, Drake served his seafaring apprenticeship with his kinsman John Hawkins, and had been present on two of his slaving voyages. He quickly developed ambitions of his own, though his early efforts met with mixed success. He was present on Hawkins's disastrous voyage of 1567–69, but was able to escape with a quarter of his men and substantial booty – enough, at least, to pay for two more voyages in 1570 and 1571. It was at this time that Drake began to make a name for himself, waging a war against the Spanish in the Caribbean that exposed their vulnerability to opportunistic raids conducted by small, nimble opponents. The prize he sought above all others was the town of Nombre de Dios, in present-day Panama, from which the annual Spanish treasure shipment left. In 1572 Drake made his attempt but was defeated in a night attack. However, he had the patience and tenacity to hide for months, appearing out of nowhere to capture a mule train in February 1573. Though the treasure seized represented only 5 per cent of Spain's silver shipments that year, for Drake and England it was a significant windfall. He returned to England having made his name and fortune; in the Spanish-speaking world, he became known rather more pejoratively as 'El Draque', the dragon.[11]

Drake was the ideal candidate to lead a new expedition, devised by the Secretary of State, Sir Francis Walsingham, and sponsored in part by the queen. Ostensibly his task was to explore

# Diego

The sailor and interpreter Diego was a crucial member of the *Golden Hind*'s crew. Likely to have been born in Senegambia, West Africa, he was enslaved by the Spanish and transported to Nombre de Dios in Central America, where he was on hand to witness Francis Drake's abortive attack in 1572. He subsequently came to work for Drake, though accounts differ as to whether he was captured or whether he joined him of his own volition. Either way, he became a crucial member of Drake's following. Diego helped negotiate an alliance with the Cimarron people (former enslaved Africans who had run away from their Spanish masters to found settlements in the hinterland of Central America), and with their assistance captured a Spanish treasure train in 1573. Diego's knowledge of Central America, along with his language skills (he spoke Spanish), made him highly useful, and he returned to Plymouth with Drake, spending the next four years living as a free man in England. In 1577 he once again set sail with Drake, voyaging across the Atlantic and Pacific oceans. He did not complete the circumnavigation, however, and died near the Moluccas in 1579.[12]

*Map depicting North and South America shortly before Drake's circumnavigation. Abraham Ortelius, 1573. PBD7640(2).*

the Pacific coast of the Americas, but secretly he was instructed to target Spanish ships and possessions in the region. In November 1577 Drake set sail from Plymouth in the *Pelican* (later renamed the *Golden Hind*) along with four other vessels and headed to the tip of South America. Drake was a ruthless commander who required total obedience from his crew, and in the turbulent southern seas his obsession with order soon turned to paranoia. He came to believe his deputy was plotting mutiny and had him removed from command, then imprisoned and finally executed after a trial of dubious legitimacy. In the subsequent weeks, two other subordinates were removed from their roles. The voyage was hard, and many sailors died in dark, stormy, unhealthy conditions as they negotiated the Strait of Magellan. One ship, the *Marigold*, was wrecked, swallowed by a wave, while the crew of the *Elizabeth* simply could not face further hardships and turned for home. By 1578 the *Golden Hind* was alone, with only 60 of its original 160 crew still alive.[13]

For those who persevered and survived, the pay-off was close at hand. After entering the Pacific Ocean, Drake turned north towards the Spanish settlements on the western coast of South America and found them completely unprotected. His crew raided and robbed towns up the coast, using every means possible to maximize their winnings, threatening hangings

*Terrestrial and celestial pocket globe, with the tracks of Drake's voyage of circumnavigation marked. Charles Price and John Senex, 1710. GLB0013.*

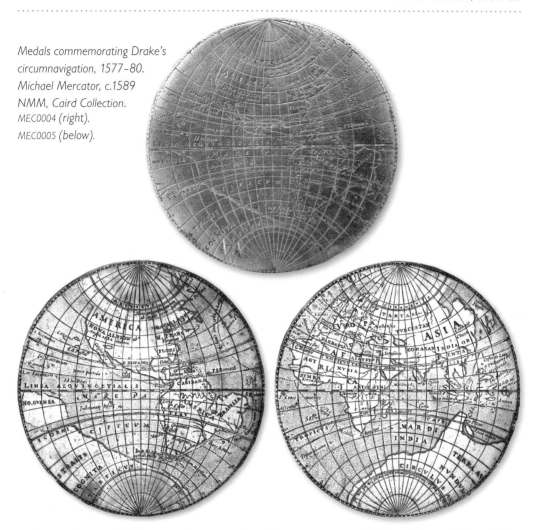

*Medals commemorating Drake's circumnavigation, 1577–80. Michael Mercator, c.1589 NMM, Caird Collection. MEC0004 (right), MEC0005 (below).*

and executions to frighten men into revealing where treasure was hidden. At sea, he boarded and captured ship after ship, stripping them of their valuable cargoes. His greatest prize was the *Nuestra Señora de la Concepción*, known to its crew by the wonderful nickname 'Cacafuego', or 'fire-shitter'. The vessel failed to show any fiery resolve, and it surrendered with little resistance; Drake found it so laden with treasure that he used captured silver and gold for ballast. Remembering that his mission was supposed – publicly at least – to be one of exploration, he voyaged as far as present-day Seattle, claiming the province for England as 'Nova Albion' in the process. Having ventured so far, and unwilling to navigate through the treacherous Strait of Magellan again (especially given that the Spanish were now alerted to his presence), Drake decided it would be easier to return to England by continuing westwards, across the Pacific and Indian oceans. It was an incredible feat of navigation and seamanship, sailing for thousands of miles through uncharted waters; during one stretch, his men saw nothing but saltwater for 68 days. In September 1580, he finally returned home, with just one of the original five ships he set out with.[14]

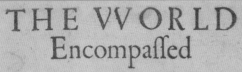

# THE WORLD
## Encompaſſed
### By
### Sir FRANCIS DRAKE,

Being his next voyage to that to *Nombre de Dios* formerly imprinted;

Carefully collected out of the notes of Maſter FRANCIS FLETCHER *Preacher in this imployment, and divers others his followers in the ſame* :

Offered now at laſt to publique view, both for the honour of the actor, but eſpecially for the ſtirring vp of *heroick ſpirits, to benefit their Countrie, and eternize their names by like noble attempts.*

LONDON,
Printed for NICHOLAS BOVRNE
and are to be ſold at his ſhop at the
Royall Exchange. 1628.

*AVXILIO·DI·VINO*

*SIC PARVIS MAGNA*

*Drake pervgti novit quem terminus orbis,*
*Et quem bis mundi vidit vterq Polus;*
*Si taceant homines, facient te Sidera notum,*
*Sol neſcit comitis non memor eſſe ſui.*

THIS PAGE AND OPPOSITE The World Encompassed by Sir Francis Drake, *1628.* PBB1876.

Drake's achievements on his voyage were remarkable. He had, almost accidentally, circumnavigated the world, and was the first to do so since Magellan's crew 50 years earlier. However, as he approached England for the first time in three years, he did so with some trepidation; he was, after all, returning with a shipload of stolen treasure, taken from a nation with which England was not at war. He need not have worried, though, for Elizabeth had no intention of punishing him. The treasure in his ship was valued at £307,000, an enormous sum, with investors enjoying a 4,700 per cent return; the queen's share alone paid off her entire foreign debt, with some left over to invest in the Levant Company. Elizabeth's gratitude knew no bounds: she knighted Drake, and did so wearing plundered Spanish jewellery in full view of Philip II's ambassador. Once the excitement had died down, Elizabeth became slightly more circumspect about her role in the operation, and suppressed the circulation of information about the expedition: the map and voyage journal Drake presented to her were never seen again and Richard Hakluyt was instructed to omit any mention of Drake's voyages in his *Principal Navigations*. It was not until 1628 that Drake's nephew was allowed to publish an account of the circumnavigation, *The World Encompassed by Sir Francis Drake*.[15]

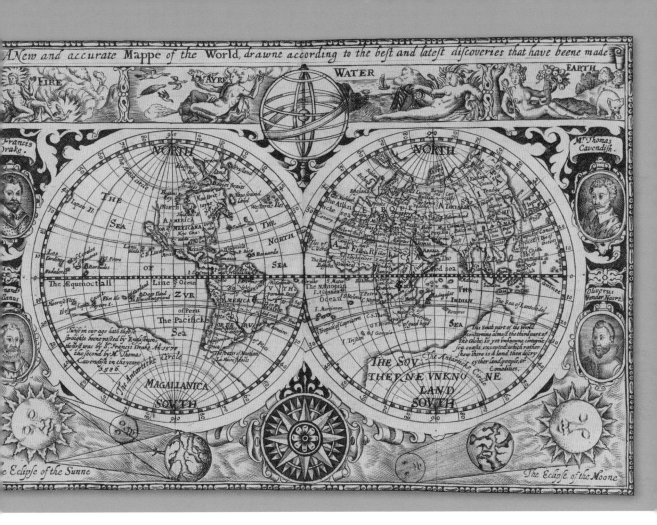

The reputation of English seafarers had risen to new heights. Writing in the 1590s, the Italian political philosopher Giovanni Botero described the English as 'marvellous expert in maritime actions, then whom at sea there is not a valianter and bolder nation under heaven'.[16] This period saw a growing identification between committed Protestantism, piracy, naval service and experimental trade, and this was only cemented further as English seafarers became ever more adventurous.[17] Britannia was not yet ruling the waves but it is clear that, both domestically and internationally, England was becoming closely associated with maritime expansion and naval prowess. England was a nation transformed, and this development was all the more remarkable because it happened so quickly. English mariners rarely ventured out of home waters before the 1550s, and in those days the idea that an Englishman could circumnavigate the world would have been laughed at across Europe. Nevertheless, by 1580 English maritime enterprise had taken on a truly global and threatening character. There was, however, a downside to this, for, like all upstarts who assert their position so violently, the English and their seafaring activity grabbed the attention of a major rival. The actions of adventurers like Drake placed England and the mighty Spanish empire on a collision course – one that would lead directly to the greatest naval invasion attempt of the early-modern era.

English Ships and the Spanish Armada, August 1588 (detail). English School, sixteenth century. NMM, Caird Fund. BHC0262.

CHAPTER

3

# The Spanish Armada and England's Conflict with Spain, 1585–1604

## David Scott

The Spanish Armada's descent on England in the summer of 1588 was a critical period in European and world history. Upon its outcome rested the fate of not just the Tudor monarchy and its subjects, but also of Protestantism in Britain and throughout western Europe. That the Armada would end not in Counter-Reformation glory but in England's greatest military victory since Agincourt could not have been predicted with confidence at the time – a victory, moreover, that would turn more upon strategic errors by the Spanish than the superiority in seamanship and naval technology enjoyed by the English. Four decades earlier, Henry VIII had similarly courted disaster by waging war against the might of France without a continental ally worthy of the name – and the Elizabethan state that defied the still mightier Spanish empire in the 1580s was, if anything, even weaker than its Henrician predecessor had been. For all the bluster of its Protestant propagandists, Tudor England was a second-rate power. Its resources and its population of roughly four million were dwarfed by those of the Spanish king, Philip II, whose possessions included (besides Spain itself) large swathes of the Italian peninsula, the Low Countries, and vast colonial territories in the Americas. His annual income from New World silver and domestic taxation was at least ten times that of Elizabeth, and sustained battle fleets in the Atlantic and Mediterranean as well as the *tercios* (massed infantry formations) that were the Roman legions of their day. To provoke invasion by such an enemy was in itself a calamity for Elizabeth and her people, redeemed only by the fact that the 1588 Armada and the two that would follow in the 1590s all failed to find their target.

The legacy of the 'Black Legend' – the myth of the Spanish as uniquely cruel and domineering Catholic zealots – has lent a sense of naturalness, almost inevitability, to the idea of war between England and Spain that the conflict itself never possessed. In fact, for several centuries before the 1560s the two nations had enjoyed close trading links and been allies against their common enemy, France. Moreover, viewed in the long term, the duration of their quarrel would prove remarkably transient. Within less than three generations on from the Armada their respective national interests would realign in the face of renewed French aggression against their neighbours. Admittedly, Spain's claim to exclusive access to the riches of the New World north of the Equator – granted by papal decree in 1493 – had strained the 'ancient amity' with England. As the previous chapter has shown, a few of the more intrepid English seafarers had been encroaching upon Spain's colonial waters since the 1540s, while Tudor experiments with 'reprisals by general proclamation' – that is, peacetime privateering – in 1544, 1557 and 1563 had revitalized the centuries-old pirate trade in the Channel, taking a heavy toll on Spanish merchant shipping.[1] Yet although these violations were winked at,

Philip II of Spain. *Netherlandish School, seventeenth century. NMM. Caird Collection.* BHC2951.

Elizabeth I, *c.1590. British School, sixteenth century. NMM. Caird Collection.* BHC2680.

sometimes even covertly sanctioned, by the English authorities, the damage they did to Anglo-Spanish relations might have been containable. It was England's slow and fitful emergence as a Protestant nation – a development that defeating the Armada did much to consolidate – that would put the two nations on collision course.

The death of Mary I and the succession of her half-sister, the 'heretic' Elizabeth I, in 1558 threatened no immediate breach with Spain and its 'most Catholic king', Philip II. The new queen's piety was closer to the Bible-centred anti-papalism of the first generation of English reformers than to the strident anti-Catholicism of Europe's second-generation Protestants and their spiritual figurehead, the Genevan theologian John Calvin. Elizabeth had no appetite for joining Europe's Calvinists in their struggle against 'popery'. Indeed, she disliked fanatical Protestants almost as much as she did rigid papists. Philip, for his part, was initially more worried about French designs upon England than about Elizabeth reversing Mary's Catholic revival and leading her subjects back into heresy. Despite his devout Catholicism, he was prepared to support Elizabeth, even offering her his hand in marriage in 1559. His motive in proposing was as logical as it was unromantic – to preserve the Anglo-Spanish alliance against France.

But then suddenly, in the early 1560s, this strategic imperative was undermined by the outbreak of a civil war between French Calvinists (the Huguenots) and Catholics that would divide and weaken their kingdom for decades to come. Fear of the French crown's territorial ambitions had been the main force pushing England and Spain together since the Middle Ages: without it, they had only their commercial ties to fall back on (and these were vulnerable to English piracy and retaliatory Spanish trade embargoes).[2] The two countries were still digesting this new and destabilizing twist in their relations when Philip's subjects in the Low Countries – including a sizeable community of Dutch Calvinists – revolted against Spanish rule. Having lost his patience and exhausted his political options, Philip sent a Spanish grandee, the Duke of Alva, into the Netherlands in 1567 at the head of 10,000 troops, to restore obedience and Catholicism by force. This presented Elizabeth with a serious dilemma. She recoiled at the idea of assisting rebels against their rightful sovereign; yet it was hardly in the national interest to have a Catholic army stamp out Dutch Protestantism or operating within such easy striking distance of the English coastline. If the Netherlands fell under Spanish military occupation, argued some of Elizabeth's councillors, then England would surely be next.

Philip's resort to armed force in the Low Countries succeeded in quelling the rebellion there, at least temporarily, but at the cost of entrenching the rebels' friends at the heart of the Elizabethan state. In 1540, Henry VIII had sacrificed his chief minister Thomas Cromwell, the architect of the English Reformation, to satisfy the conservative faction at court and the Catholic powers on the Continent. In the late 1560s, Elizabeth did the exact opposite. With a Spanish army encamped across the North Sea and some of her own noblemen plotting with Spain to replace her on the throne with her Catholic cousin, Mary, Queen of Scots, Elizabeth stuck by her ardently Protestant administrator-in-chief, William Cecil, and so antagonized his lordly rivals that they rebelled against her and were executed. In thus undermining the pro-Spanish interest, Elizabeth's actions tilted the balance of power at court in favour of the 'forward' Protestant faction – a group led by

Cecil, the Earl of Leicester and Sir Francis Walsingham, and defined by its unshakeable conviction that Philip, the papacy and France's Catholics had joined forces 'for recovery of the Tiranny to the Pope'.[3]

What made this reading of European politics – as a cosmic struggle between 'true religion' and the 'popish Antichrist' – so compelling to England's 'hotter sort' of Protestants was their sense of themselves as an embattled minority even in their own country. Nevertheless, it greatly exaggerated both the unity and the purposefulness of their enemies. As his relations with Elizabeth deteriorated in the late 1560s, Philip certainly began to give serious consideration to regime change in England, and the result was a series of Spanish-backed plots against her throne and life. But as master of a global empire, he generally had more pressing demands on his time and money than dealing with what he regarded as a divided and unstable country. Equally, his relationship with the papacy was often far from harmonious, and he would not conclude a formal alliance with France's Catholics until the 1580s. Yet few of these facts registered with Cecil, Leicester and their followers. Alva's reign of terror in the Low Countries seemed to confirm their apocalyptic view of the international scene – and the Elizabethan government reacted accordingly. Spanish ships and their cargoes of money for Alva's troops were seized, 30,000 Dutch rebels were given asylum in England, and Dutch and Huguenot privateers were allowed to operate out of ports along the south coast, joining their English confederates in attacking ships of all nations, but especially those of Spain. For the English crews involved, piety and piracy ran in happy accord: 'we cold not do God better service than to spoyl the Spaniard both of lyfe and goodes'.[4] By 1570, a state of cold war could be said to exist between England and Spain.

Elizabeth was determined to resist pressure for full-scale confrontation, however. A pragmatist in an age of ideologues, as well as being penny-pinching to a fault, she was unmoved by arguments that defeating Spain was the only guarantee of Protestantism's survival or that it would pay for itself in the spoils of victory. It was only after much arm-twisting by her councillors that she agreed to provide refuge and money for the Dutch rebels and the Huguenots. Her preferred method of trying to keep Spanish power in check, while stopping short of provoking war, was to invest in the buccaneering-cum-business ventures of a growing band of English privateers eager to gain fame and fortune by seizing Spanish treasure-ships and raiding Spain's colonies in the New World. Their 'trading' expeditions cost Elizabeth

English Ships and the Spanish Armada, August 1588. *English School, sixteenth century.*
*NMM, Caird Fund. BHC0262.*

very little in terms of money upfront, and yet could prove hugely profitable. Even better, as ostensibly private initiatives they allowed her to 'dysavowe', as she put it, her subjects' piratical proceedings – what today would be termed 'plausible deniability'.[5] Except, of course, that Philip found such denials highly implausible, while Elizabeth failed to grasp that he put a somewhat different construction on these attacks than the one she intended. To her they were warning shots; to him they were the prelude to all-out war upon his dominions – an understandable mistake, as this was precisely how Leicester and Walsingham wished to see them too.

The exploits of Elizabethan 'Sea Dogs' – adventurers like Drake, Hawkins and Cavendish who took to the oceans and earned the favour of the queen – would convince future generations of English people that it was their God-given right to rule the waves, and not just around England, but globally.[6] Yet until the 1560s, English mariners had rarely ventured beyond European waters, and knew little about deep-sea navigation. Meanwhile, the Spanish had been establishing colonies around the world, their ships plying back and forth across the Atlantic, crammed on the homeward journey with bullion from the silver mines of Peru. It was the arrival of Huguenot privateers, driven to England during the 1560s by Catholic victories in France, that turned English seamen into deep-water warriors for the Protestant cause. Not content with plundering Spanish shipping in the English Channel, Huguenot fleets had

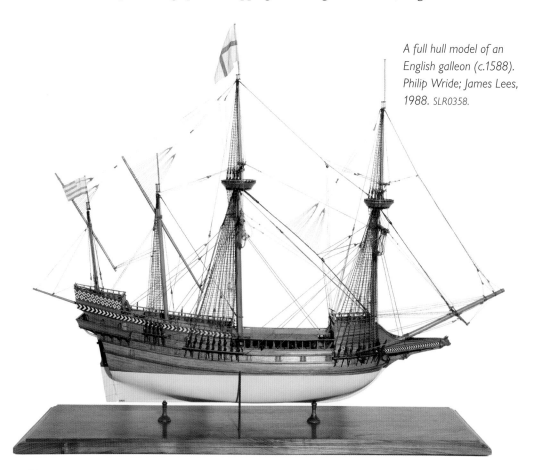

*A full hull model of an English galleon (c.1588). Philip Wride; James Lees, 1988. SLR0358.*

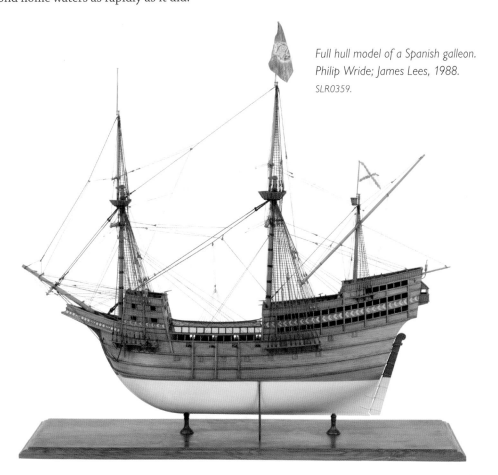

*Iron smoothbore muzzle-loading gun, 4in calibre, used by the Spanish during the Armada expedition, c.1588. On loan from a private lender. KTP0019.*

crossed the Atlantic in the 1550s and 1560s to attack Spanish settlements in the Caribbean. With assistance and encouragement from the Huguenots, the English followed in their wake. The daring escapades of Sir John Hawkins and his protégé Sir Francis Drake inspired more and more gentlemen and merchants to follow their example, so that by the 1580s the English themselves were forced to admit that they were infamous throughout Europe for 'outeragious, common, and daily piracies'.[7] But it was Huguenot navigators who helped steer Drake and his like to their targets across the Atlantic; and it was Huguenot – as well as Iberian, Flemish and Scottish – mapmakers who taught the English to become expert cartographers themselves. Without this French connection it is unlikely that English sea power would have spread beyond home waters as rapidly as it did.

*Full hull model of a Spanish galleon. Philip Wride; James Lees, 1988. SLR0359.*

61

England was already a formidable naval power by the time the Huguenots reached its shores. One of Henry VIII's more sensible reactions to the isolated position he found himself in after breaking with Rome was to build up the royal fleet from seven warships to almost 50, while English shipwrights, borrowing from the Portuguese and other naval innovators, developed the 'sailing-galley', or galleon, carrying heavy cannon firing through gunports. The need for military economies in the 1550s led to some streamlining, but Elizabeth was still left with what for the time was an exceptionally well-equipped and well-maintained fleet of about 30 sailing ships. Most of these warships had been specially built, or adapted by the 1580s, along sleek, 'race-built' lines – a term derived from the 'razing' (lowering) of a ship's forecastle, stern castle and other upper works. Lowering, lightening and elongating ships in this way not only improved speed and handling, it also meant that they could fight effectively as gun platforms in addition to using the traditional tactics of grappling and boarding.[8] The technological requirements for hunting and overpowering Spanish and other prizes endowed the queen's fleet and the English privateering sector with the most state-of-the-art warships in the world, and although smaller than the high-castled galleons of Spain and Portugal, they carried considerably heavier guns. Tudor England's emergence as a maritime power owed much to its status as one of Europe's leading manufacturers of high-quality ordnance. English cannon were more durable and powerful than those of any other nation, and English gun crews better trained. The relative ease and cheapness of acquiring heavy ordnance in England helps to explain the unusual willingness of English ships, however small, to give battle, and the English propensity to steal colonial goods from others rather than go to the trouble of founding colonies themselves.

English attacks upon Spanish shipping and colonies, and the resurgence of Dutch resistance to Philip from 1572, had brought England and Spain to the precipice by 1580, but it was the vagaries of continental geopolitics that would push them over it. Philip's brilliant new general in the Low Countries, Alessandro Farnese (created Duke of Parma in 1586), began to reassert royal authority in Flanders from the late 1570s, heightening concern in England that Spanish forces would soon overrun the entire Netherlands. Even more menacing was Philip's conquest of Portugal in 1580 following the extinction of the Portuguese royal line. At a stroke, Spain acquired Portugal's powerful Atlantic fleet, another global empire and the port of Lisbon, which possessed Europe's finest and most strongly defended harbour. The slide towards war became virtually unstoppable in 1584. With town after town falling to Farnese's troops, the assassination of the Dutch leader William of Orange in July 1584 threw the rebels into even greater disarray. In England, a majority of the queen's councillors now pushed for open military intervention to help the Dutch before it was too late.

Philip, too, was preparing to widen the conflict. Having cooperated informally since the mid-1570s, he and the French Catholics signed a military alliance late in 1584 that threatened

*OPPOSITE Prints depicting a voyage in 1585 made by 23 English ships that raided the towns of St. Iago: Sto. Domingo, Cartagena and St Augustines. Giovanni Baptista Boazio, 1588. PBC4053(1) (top), PBC4053 (bottom).*

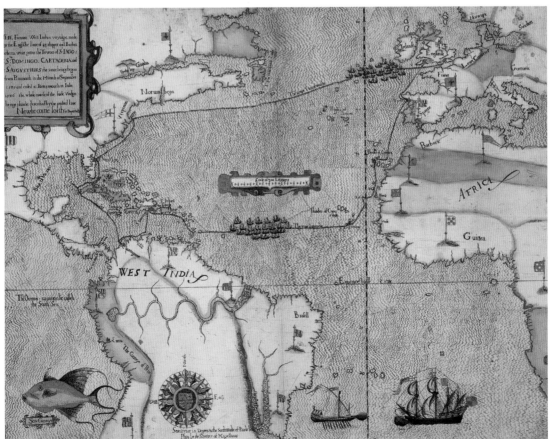

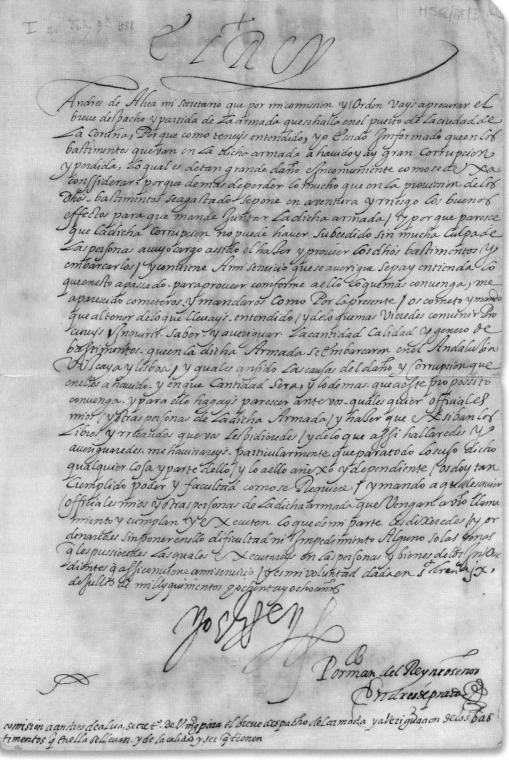

*Instructions from Philip II of Spain to Andres de Alva about the provisions for the Armada, 9 July 1588. HSR/HF/4.*

France, as well as the Netherlands, with Spanish domination. The Protestant nightmare of an international Catholic league 'for the ruyne and overthrow of the professours of the Ghospell' had finally become a reality.[9] Reluctantly, in August 1585, Elizabeth agreed to support the Dutch rebels with 7,500 English troops under the command of the Earl of Leicester. The long-suffering Philip had been weighing up whether to invade England since the early 1570s: Elizabeth's treaty with the Dutch rebels and raids by Drake late in 1585 on the Spanish coast and Indies made up his mind. Preparations for the 'enterprise of England' began in earnest, and went into high gear early in 1587 following the execution of Mary, Queen of Scots, who had been in English custody since fleeing Scotland in 1568. Her demise left her Calvinist son, James VI of Scotland, heir apparent to the English throne. When Philip learnt of Mary's death he wept for the new Catholic martyr, and then issued a flood of orders for assembling the Armada. In the words of his secretary, it was time to put England 'to the torch'.[10]

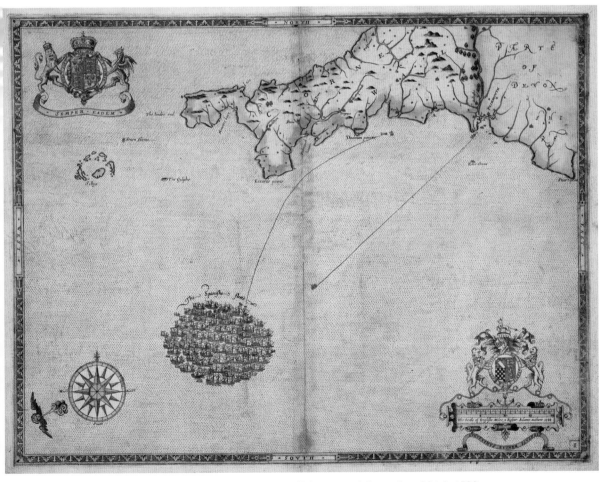

*Print depicting the Spanish fleet off the coast of Cornwall on 29 July 1588.*
*Robert Adams; Augustine Ryther, 1590.* PBD8529(3).

The Armada sailed from Lisbon in May 1588, and although it would be nearly two months before it encountered the English in battle, the Spanish were already relying on divine intervention to secure their victory. For despite the Armada's immense size and firepower, they were under no illusions as to the challenge they faced:

> *the English, who have faster and handier ships than ours and many more long-range guns, and who know their advantage just as well as we do, will never close with us at all but stand aloof and knock us to pieces with their culverins [heavy cannon] without our being able to do them any serious hurt.*[11]

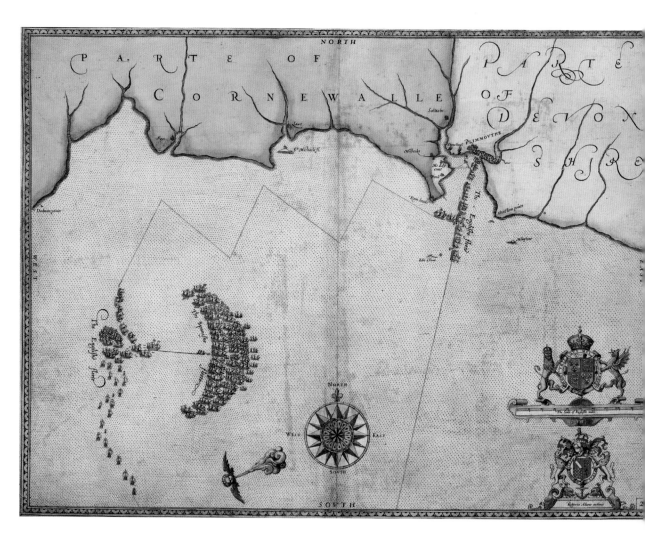

*Print showing the Spanish and English fleets near Plymouth on 30–31 July 1588. Robert Adams; Augustine Ryther, 1590. PBD8529(4).*

What the Spanish had not reckoned with, although it posed a far greater danger than the English culverins, was their own king's strategy for the Armada's deployment. The safest and most practical option would have been to make directly for England or Wales with an invasion force already on board – as Henry VII had done in 1485 and as William III would do in 1688. Philip, however, the age's premier armchair strategist, set his mind inflexibly on something more ambitious. The Armada was to sail up the Channel, anchor in the Strait of Dover, and then transport over to Kent an army that Parma had been ordered to assemble in the Netherlands. The advantage of this plan – that it would bring Europe's finest troops to bear on England's ramshackle and ill-prepared land defences – was nullified by the near impossibility

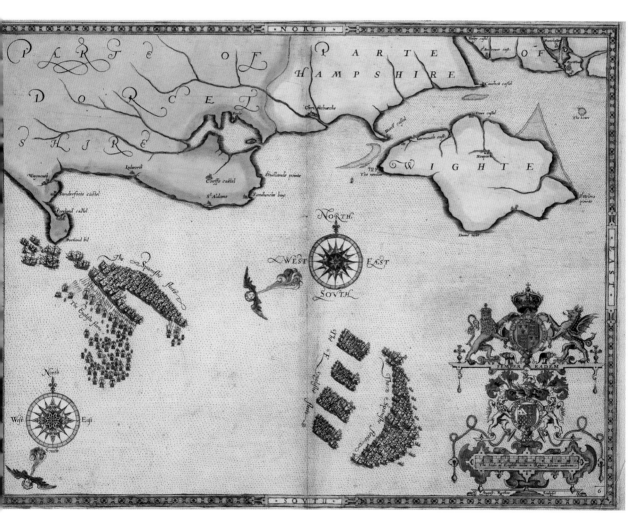

*Print showing the English and Spanish fleets between Portland Bill and the Isle of Wight on 2–3 August 1588. Robert Adams; Augustine Ryther, 1590. PBD8529(8).*

# Charles Howard, Lord Effingham

Born into the English aristocracy – he was a cousin of Elizabeth I – Charles Howard was a prominent Tudor statesman. Named Lord High Admiral in 1585, he was designated 'lieutenant-general and commander-in-chief of the navy prepared to the seas against Spain'. In this role he commanded the English force that was assembled to repulse the Spanish Armada in 1588. He proved a highly effective commander, whose organizational talents meshed perfectly with those of his more audacious second-in-command, Sir Francis Drake. He subsequently led an expedition to Cádiz in 1596, and was again appointed to command English naval forces when another Spanish Armada threatened in 1597. Following Elizabeth's death in 1603 he continued to serve under James I, but it is for his steady hand during the turbulent events of 1588 that he is best known.

*Miniature of Charles Howard, 2nd Baron Howard of Effingham and 1st Earl of Nottingham. Attributed to Rowland Lockey, 1605. NMM, Caird Fund.* MNT0136.

of the Armada and Parma's army combining successfully in the first place. Philip's strategy, which he insisted should be rigidly adhered to, simply invited disaster. Its slim chances of success were also not improved by his choice of the Duke of Medina Sidonia to command the fleet. A more experienced and resolute commander would have set Philip's instructions aside where circumstances dictated, and pursued victory by the best course available. The Armada's progress up the Channel presented opportunities for it to destroy the English fleet in port or to establish a bridgehead on the south coast. Skilfully deployed, it might also have landed an army that the under-powered Elizabethan state would have found very hard to dislodge. But Medina Sidonia lacked the initiative and confidence to depart significantly from his master's plan. In the end, England's Sea Dogs, with help from the weather, merely applied the *coup de grâce*.

Nevertheless, for the English sailors who first sighted the Armada off the Lizard in mid-July 1588, it must have presented a daunting spectacle – about 130 warships and support vessels spread across the horizon in a crescent formation, carrying 18,000 troops (mostly new recruits), and mounting 150 heavy guns. The English fleet that left Plymouth on 20 July to confront it, under the command of Lord Howard of Effingham, would swell in size to some 80 ships that between them carried about 250 heavy cannon.[12] Fewer than half of these vessels

# Duke of Medina Sidonia

The Duke of Medina Sidonia was an important Spanish nobleman. Philip II chose him to command the Spanish Armada, presumably because he was considered a competent and safe pair of hands. But Medina Sidonia was far from convinced of his own suitability and wrote to the king indicating that he lacked any knowledge of military command and was prone to seasickness. It is likely Philip II never saw the letter, however, and the duke had to begin preparing the Armada. Despite his doubts, Medina Sidonia proved an effective administrator, and ensured the Spanish ships were well equipped. At sea, though, his inexperience resulted in overcautiousness when engaging the English fleet, and as a result, he failed to give Spain the necessary advantage. While the duke cannot be singled out for the failure of the Spanish Armada – the complexity of Philip II's plan and the weather were major factors – his reputation was badly damaged.

*Miniature believed to depict Sir Francis Drake. Nicholas Hilliard, 1581. NMM, Caird Collection.* MNT0023.

belonged to the queen; the rest were provided by port towns, the London merchant companies, and privateer shipowners such as Drake and Hawkins. The English galleons were faster and more manoeuvrable than the floating fortresses of the Spanish, with crews better practised in standing-off and out-gunning opponents. The one obvious weakness on the English side was that Howard's captains had no experience of fighting in a large, disciplined formation – in other words, as a fleet – which was the only way to attack the Armada effectively.[13] Drake, for example, abandoned his station after the first day's action to seize a rich Spanish galleon that had become detached from the Armada, instead of leading his division as he had been ordered; but the English were so accustomed to fighting as privateers that he was not even reprimanded. Howard and his captains made another unwelcome discovery in the heat of battle, which was that even their heaviest guns could hardly penetrate the thick oak planking of the Spanish warships, let alone do serious damage, unless fired at such close range – less than 100 yards – that the attacker risked being boarded.[14] As long as the Spanish maintained good order, which they did, the English ships had little chance of making their superior firepower tell. By the time the Armada dropped anchor off Calais on 27 July it had endured several prolonged gun battles with Howard's fleet, and yet not one Spanish ship had been put out of action by English gunfire, much less sunk.

Medina Sidonia had done what Philip had required of him: he had brought the Armada intact to its rendezvous point with Parma's army. But that still left the problem of how the two

ARMÉE NAVALE DES
SVRNOMMÉE INVINCIB.
PAR LES ANGLOIS LE·22·

forces were actually to combine. Even if the duke had felt secure enough to ignore the English fleet (which was lurking just to windward) to detach ships from the Armada to clear a way through the hostile Dutch craft patrolling the inshore waters, Parma's troop barges needed calm conditions to cross the Channel safely; and by late July, the weather was worsening. While Medina Sidonia waited for something little short of a miracle to occur, his ships, anchored against a lee shore, were sitting ducks. At midnight on 28 July, the English launched fireships towards the Armada, and at the sight of these most feared naval weapons, many Spanish captains panicked and broke formation. At last the English were able to get in among

The Armada in the Strait of Dover. *Flemish School, c.1600–10.* PAJ3949.

the enemy and assail them at close quarters, sometimes surrounding Spanish warships and pounding them from all sides. Several took such a battering that they sank or lost steerage; all were holed and leaking, their masts and rigging shot through, their decks littered with dead. Hundreds of Spaniards were killed and as many as 6,000 more wounded. And although all but half a dozen ships survived the English bombardment, the prevailing winds then forced the Armada out into the North Sea and beyond all hope of a conjunction with Parma's army.

71

Painting representing the launch of fireships against the Spanish Armada, 7 August 1588. Netherlandish School, c.1590. NMM, Caird Collection. BHC0263.

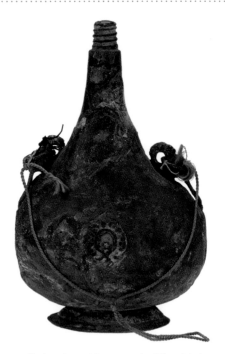

Pewter flask salvaged from wrecked Spanish Armada
galleon San Juan de Sicilia, c.1588. *REL0252.*

Mortar salvaged from wrecked Spanish Armada
galleon San Juan de Sicilia, c.1588. *REL0228.*

The Armada's long journey home round Scotland and down the west coast of Ireland, battered by gales and low on food and water, took a far greater toll on men and materiel than the English had. By the time Medina Sidonia's fleet had limped its way back to Spain, at least half of its ships had foundered or been wrecked, or were damaged beyond repair, and perhaps as many as two-thirds of its original complement of 30,000 had perished.[15] Yet the victorious English seamen fared little better. Whereas Philip felt honour-bound to pay and care for the Armada's wretched survivors, Elizabeth begrudged even the minimum expenditure on those who had risked their lives to save her throne. Having kept his combat losses to below 60, Howard watched in anguish during August as his exhausted and malnourished sailors succumbed to disease by their thousands in the ports of southern England. If he and other captains had not used their own money to succour their men, the death toll would have been even higher.

The fight against the Armada would be no more than the opening broadside in the war at sea. In 1589, the English mounted a major seaborne offensive of their own against northern Spanish naval ports and Lisbon, this time with Drake acting in his more familiar role of aggressor. But the 'English Armada', as it became known, was no more successful than its Spanish predecessor: Drake's force lost 40 ships, some in actions off the coast of Spain, but the vast majority to storms on its retreat home. Elizabeth's attempt to capitalize on the advantage gained in 1588 came to nothing, allowing Philip time to rebuild and strengthen his navy. Drake and Hawkins returned to attacking Spanish ports and ships, until fatigue and disease

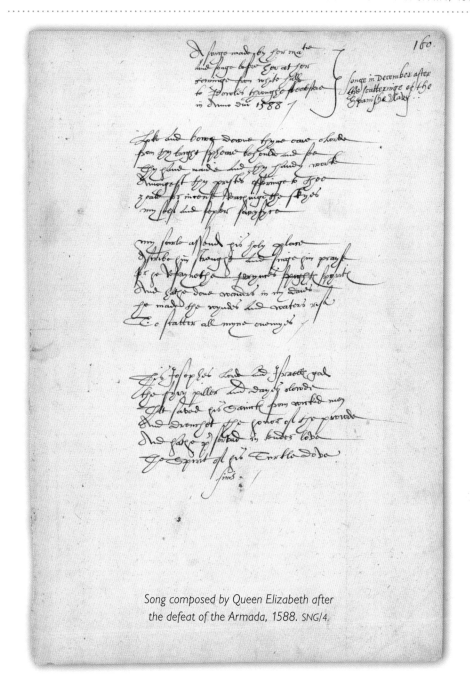

*Song composed by Queen Elizabeth after the defeat of the Armada, 1588.* SNG/4.

claimed them both during a joint raiding expedition in the Caribbean in 1595–96. Spain, its Atlantic fleet refitted with English-style warships, launched two further armadas in 1596 and 1597 – the second even larger than that of 1588 – only for the 'Protestant wind' to rise up, as it had off Flanders in 1588, and again repulse its enemies. If nothing else, the failure of the various armadas launched in the 1580s and 1590s demonstrated the difficulty in organizing

*Playing cards celebrating the English defeat of the Spanish Armada.*
*PAD0181, PAD 0183.*

and executing long-range naval operations in the early-modern period. The anti-Spanish privateering offensive that both preceded the first Armada and continued afterwards proved far more decisive. Decades of attrition by Protestant privateers would ruin Spain's merchant marine for centuries to come, while expanding the range and scale of England's overseas commerce beyond all recognition.[16] Yet the principal long-term beneficiaries of the Anglo-Spanish War of 1585–1604 were not the English but the Dutch. England's troops in the Low Countries and its victories at sea contributed significantly to the birth of a new state, the Dutch Republic, that in the seventeenth century would eclipse both friend and foe as Europe's greatest maritime power. It was the Dutch who would mount the last successful invasion of England exactly a century after the Armada's defeat.

This chapter is based upon D. Scott, *Leviathan: the Rise of Britain as a World Power* (London: William Collins, 2013), ch. 2.

*Medal commemorating the defeat of the Spanish Armada, 1588. Gerard van Bylaer. 1588.* MEC0012.

*Counter commemorating the defeat of the Spanish Armada, 1588.* MEC0047.

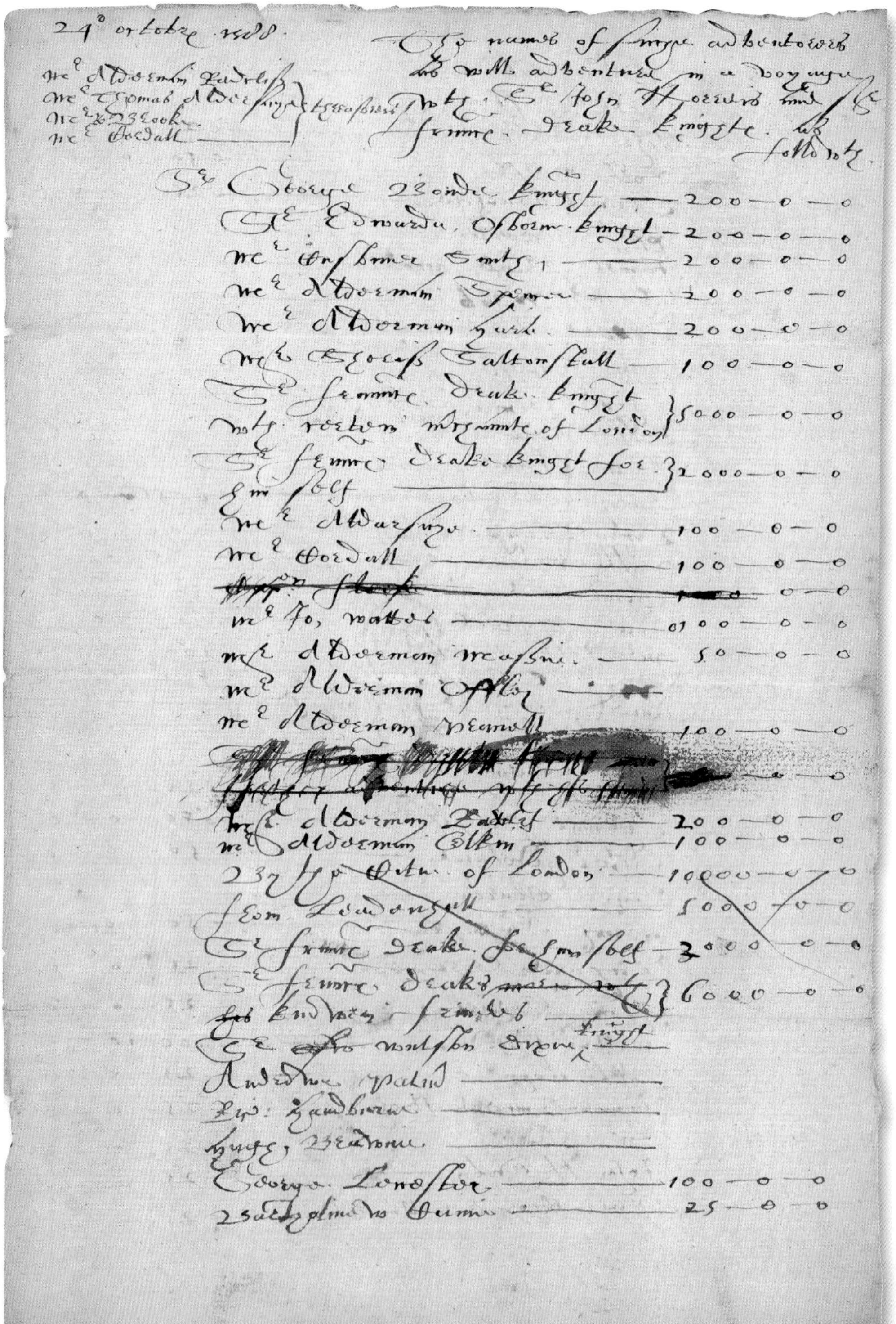

24° October 1588.

The names of suche adventurers
as will adventure in a voyage
with Sir John Norris and
Sir Frauncis Drake knighte

Mr Alderman Radclyff
Mr Thomas Woesing treasurers
Mr Rooke
Mr Goddall

folio 10

| | |
|---|---|
| Sr George Bonde knyght | 200 — 0 — 0 |
| Sr Edwarde Osborn knyght | 200 — 0 — 0 |
| Mr Custmer Smyth | 200 — 0 — 0 |
| Mr Alderman Spencer | 200 — 0 — 0 |
| Mr Alderman Harde | 200 — 0 — 0 |
| Mr Thomas Saltonstall | 100 — 0 — 0 |
| Sr Frauncis Drake knyght | 5000 — 0 — 0 |
| the reste of the merchaunts of London | |
| Sr Frauncis Drake knyght for him self | 2000 — 0 — 0 |
| Mr Aldworthe | 100 — 0 — 0 |
| Mr Goddall | 100 — 0 — 0 |
| ~~Mr Staper~~ | ~~100 — 0 — 0~~ |
| Mr Jo. Watsel | 0100 — 0 — 0 |
| Mr Alderman Mashne | 50 — 0 — 0 |
| Mr Alderman Flex | |
| Mr Alderman Beamell | 100 — 0 — 0 |
| ~~...~~ | ~~...~~ |
| Mr Alderman Radclyf | 200 — 0 — 0 |
| Mr Alderman Ellem | 100 — 0 — 0 |
| 237 the Cittie of London | 10000 — 0 — 0 |
| from Leadenhall | 5000 — 0 — 0 |
| Sr Frauncis Drake for him self | 3000 — 0 — 0 |
| Sr Frauncis Drake more | 6000 — 0 — 0 |
| the Kendray symble | |
| Sr the welshe knyght | |
| Andrew palm | |
| Edw. Leadman | |
| Hugh Bradone | |
| George Lanoster | 100 — 0 — 0 |
| Bartholmewe Bonne | 25 — 0 — 0 |

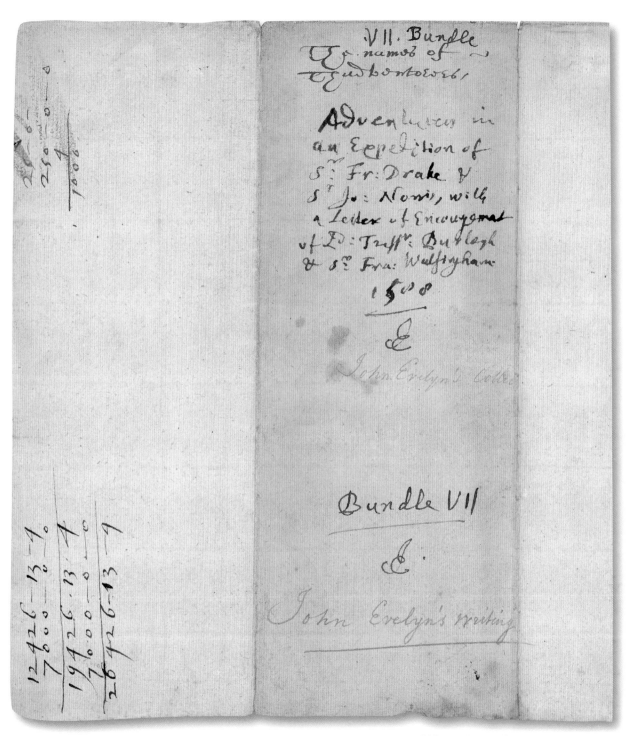

*OPPOSITE AND ABOVE* Phillipps-Upcott. *List of adventurers who joined the 1589 expedition to Spain, 24 October 1588.* UPC/5/2.

Charles II (1630–85). *Sir Peter Lely*, c.1670.
*NMM, Caird Fund.* BHC2609.

# Building a Navy

## J. D. Davies

The sixteenth and seventeenth centuries are invariably known as the age of the Tudors and the Stuarts, but this 'definition by surname', with its implicit focus on personalities, is misleading in all kinds of ways. For example, the 'Tudor' monarchs did not actually call themselves by that name at all, and hardly any of their subjects would have known them, or described them, by the now-iconic dynastic moniker.[1] This is also true of naval history. Only one 'Tudor' monarch, Henry VIII, had a genuine interest in the navy, and even that was intermittent. The Stuarts did rather better: Charles I, and especially his sons Charles II and James II, loved ships, were directly involved in naval administration, and oversaw substantial expansions and reforms of the service. Indeed, the younger Charles had an enthusiasm for the sea that went far beyond the merely formal. He introduced yachting to England and developed a scientific interest in the art of shipbuilding which was said by informed individuals in private, not just by sycophants in public, to rival that of a master shipwright.[2] Two 'non-royal' regimes were also responsible for significant improvements to the navy. The Duke of Buckingham, Lord High Admiral from 1619 to 1628, might have owed his initial rise to his sexual appeal to James I, but he proved a dynamic and effective reformer. The Rump Parliament of 1649–53, the first parliament of the republican regimes that governed the Commonwealth established after the execution of Charles I, drove through an unprecedented expansion of the navy, doubling its size by building 20 new ships in just over two years.[3] Although this was essentially a security measure born of the insecure republican regime's desperate vulnerability to domestic rebellion and foreign invasion, it established the principle of a large, powerful, permanent navy, consisting primarily of warships owned and operated by the state. This replaced the more ad hoc system of supplementing a core of royal warships with those owned by other institutions or individuals.

The expansion of the navy and its increasing permanence were by no means inevitable, and were by no means a continuous, uninterrupted progression. Henry VII inherited six royal warships when he took the throne at Bosworth in August 1485, but by the following March, only one was left. Although new building, in the shape of the impressive four-masted carracks *Sovereign* and *Regent*, commenced soon afterwards, Henry's navy was never as impressive

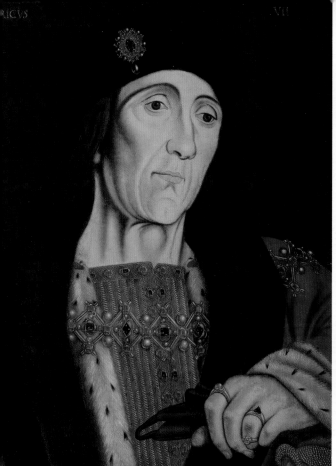

Henry VII, 1457–1509. *British School,
sixteenth century, after Hans Holbein, c.1505.*
NMM, Caird Collection. BHC2762.

Henry VIII, 1491–1547. *British School,
sixteenth century, after Hans Holbein, c.1505.*
NMM, Caird Collection. BHC2763.

even as that commanded by his son-in-law James IV, King of Scots, who by 1513 possessed the
*Michael*, one of the largest warships in the world. The powerful fleet was unable to influence
the outcome of the catastrophic Flodden campaign in that year, during which James and
10,000 other Scots were killed. The Scottish navy never again compared seriously with that
of England. By 1520, though, Henry VIII had 30 royal warships, a number that doubled by
the end of the reign, thanks partly to an unprecedented shipbuilding programme in 1544–45
that added 18 new ships to the fleet.[4] This force was splendidly recorded for posterity in the
pictorial survey of 1546 known as the 'Anthony Roll', which demonstrated the extraordinary
diversity of the king's vessels, ranging from large ships such as the *Mary Rose* – which had
sunk in the previous year – to galleys and rowbarges.[5] But this great 'Navy Royal' declined
during the two succeeding reigns: at her accession in 1558, Elizabeth I inherited just 31
warships of her own, ten of which were said to be too worn out for further service. As always,
though, the monarch could call upon the entire maritime strength of the kingdom during

# Jacques Francis

Jacques Francis (or 'Jaques Frauncys') was an enslaved African diver who salvaged equipment from the wreck of the *Mary Rose* during the reign of Edward VI. He came from Arguin Island, off the coast of present-day Mauretania, and was in his twenties when he worked on the wreck of Henry VIII's ill-fated ship. The authorities were particularly anxious to bring up the vessel's valuable guns, hoping that some of England's lost prestige might be recovered with them. Francis's Venetian master, Piero Paolo Corsi, employed him as lead diver on the operation in 1547.

Corsi subsequently became involved in a legal dispute with another recovery team, who accused him of stealing reclaimed metal and salvage equipment. Francis gave an articulate and ultimately successful defence of his master in court, refuting these allegations. The plaintiffs tried to prevent him from giving evidence, declaring that an enslaved 'infidel' was unfit to stand, but the High Court of Admiralty accepted his testimony. Francis thus became one of the earliest seafaring Africans to leave his mark on English state records.[7]

emergencies. In 1577 it was estimated that this comprised 136 ships of over 100 tons and another 656 of 40–100 tons.[6] It was this kind of composite fleet, partly a state and partly a private enterprise, that fought against the Spanish Armada.

During the seventeenth century, the nature of the navy changed. By the 1650s and 1660s in particular, merchantmen no longer had the strength or armament to withstand the impact of new tactics, with their emphasis on a huge weight of fire on the broadside (as deployed in the so-called line of battle). Thus the navy became more and more a fighting force exclusively owned, operated and paid for by the state. Inevitably, it became ever more expensive. In 1557, Queen Mary's Lord High Treasurer estimated that it would be possible to run the peacetime navy on £10,000 a year; a little over a hundred years later, it proved nigh-on impossible to run the equivalent force on £400,000 a year, even allowing for the fact that the great majority of ships were mothballed – or laid up 'in ordinary' – in the dockyards.[8] In wartime, when the entire fleet was mobilized, the costs were phenomenal. During the 1650s, a period of virtually continuous mobilization, the average annual expenditure on the navy was £663,000: during the 1690s, it was £1,763,000.[9] These mind-boggling sums nearly bankrupted the state more than once: the fact that Charles II had no money to set out a fleet for a third year of the second Anglo-Dutch war (1664–67) contributed directly to one of Britain's greatest national humiliations, the Dutch attack on the Medway in 1667.

Despite the erratic pace and nature of their expansion, the slowly changing character of the state's naval forces demanded concomitant changes to the administration and infrastructure. The position of Lord High Admiral was invariably occupied by a prominent nobleman, and the incumbents' interest in the administrative and military aspects of the role, as opposed to the substantial income they could garner from wrecks and prizes, varied considerably.

# Samuel Pepys

Samuel Pepys, perhaps England's most famous diarist, was also one of the Royal Navy's most important administrators. While his diary outlines his thoughts on theatre, music and wine – as well as detailing his numerous sexual escapades – it also shows him as a conscientious naval employee. Pepys entered the administration of the Royal Navy in 1660, and through a combination of intelligence, application and contacts rose quickly through the ranks. In 1673 he became Secretary to the Admiralty, the most influential person in the navy, answerable only to the king. He was also a Member of Parliament, first for Castle Rising and then for Harwich, where he became a leading advocate for naval expansion. Generally credited with introducing lieutenants' exams into the navy, he played an integral role in the professionalization of the Royal Navy in the seventeenth century.

*Samuel Pepys, 1633–1703. Sir Godfrey Kneller, 1689. NMM, Caird Collection. BHC2947.*

At the end of Henry VIII's reign, John Dudley, later Duke of Northumberland, was a dynamic and proactive Lord High Admiral, as was the Duke of Buckingham 80 years later and the Duke of York 40 years after that, but many other holders of the office were little more than ornamental. In 1628, following the assassination of Buckingham, Charles I put the Admiralty into commission for the first time, with a committee of senior courtiers and office-holders exercising the functions of the office. This pattern was essentially resumed under the various republican regimes from 1649 to 1660, when a number of Admiralty and navy committees presided over the service. It was nominally under Charles II from 1673 to 1679, although in practice much of the authority of the Admiralty during those years was directly exercised by the king, assisted by a remarkably able Londoner of relatively humble origins, Samuel Pepys. In 1679, a political crisis forced Charles to grant the authority of the Admiralty to a commission composed of opposition Parliamentarians. This system was abandoned in 1684, when the king resumed control of the navy himself, albeit with Pepys restored in an entirely new office, essentially a Secretary of State for the Navy; but it returned in 1689, and with a few brief interruptions, formed the pattern for all Admiralty administrations until the department was finally abolished in 1964 with the creation of the Ministry of Defence.[10]

In 1546, a major change was made to the day-to-day running of the navy. A 'Council of Marine Causes' was established, presided over by a Lieutenant Admiral (an office which later evolved into the honorific post of Vice-Admiral of England). Sitting on the council were the holders of the two existing subordinate naval offices of Controller and Clerk of the Ships, together with three new ones: the Treasurer, the Surveyor and the Master of Naval Ordnance. From 1557 onwards, this body worked with a more certain and steady supply of money, following the establishment of an 'ordinary' for the navy (a sum which covered its day-to-day expenses, as opposed to any 'extraordinary' charges incurred from time to time – for

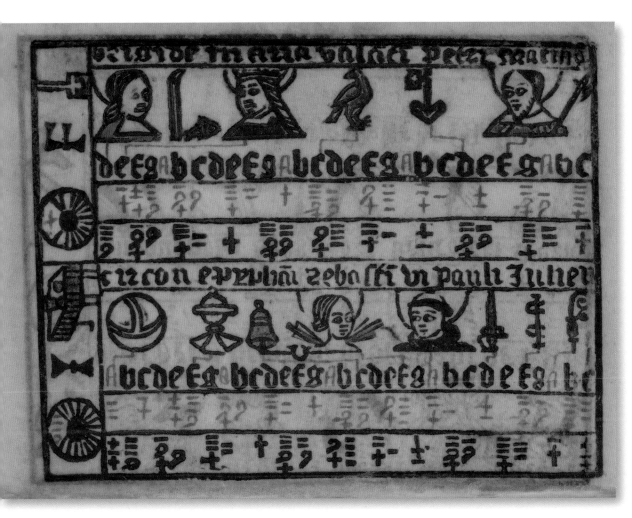

*Pepys's Nautical Almanac, c.1546. NVT/40.*

instance, during war).[11] The name of this body changed over the years, with the Navy Board eventually becoming its usual shorthand title; from 1656, this met in a substantial building in Seething Lane, close to the Tower of London. The Commonwealth abolished the system of 'principal officers' (the Master of Naval Ordnance had long ceased to exist) and replaced them with commissioners until the Restoration in 1660, when the Stuart brothers restored the old system, albeit adding three commissioners to the four principal officers. Nominally the most junior of the latter was the official now known as the Clerk of the Acts, essentially the secretary to the board; but from 1660 to 1673 the office was held by Samuel Pepys, whose insatiable curiosity and appetite for hard work soon made him the most indispensable cog in the naval administration. As Clerk, and then during two periods as Secretary to the Admiralty (1673–79 and 1684–89), Pepys was directly responsible for, or helped to implement, a number of hugely important reforms, ranging from the working methods of pursers to a new system of appointing naval chaplains and the introduction of a qualifying examination for lieutenants.[12]

At the heart of the navy's administrative system were the dockyards. The 'royal dockyards' per se were first established under the Tudors when, in 1495, a dry dock was formed at Portsmouth, complementing the large natural harbour that had long been a traditional assembly point for fleets sailing for France. Henry VIII subsequently established facilities nearer to London. A storehouse was built at Erith, although the dockyard there survived no more than 30 years. The facilities established at Woolwich (1512) and Deptford (1513) proved much more durable, and continued to serve the navy until 1869. Deptford's unique feature, a large basin (or 'wet dock'), was built in 1517, and it also seems to have been the first dockyard to have dock gates, installed in the late 1570s or early 1580s, which enabled a much faster turnaround of ships than the old system of building and then demolishing mud walls at the mouth of the dock.[13] During the 1540s and 1550s, royal ships also began to use the River Medway. Although the navigation was tortuous, the long, deep-water straight between Chatham and Gillingham was ideal for laying up vessels when not in commission, despite being 11 miles from the open sea, and shore facilities to support the ships were gradually established at Chatham during the first decades of Elizabeth's reign. Little further development of the facilities of the dockyards took place until the Duke of Buckingham became Lord High Admiral in 1619. Between then and the death of James I in 1625, major expansion took place at Deptford, Woolwich and Chatham: the number of dry docks in those yards increased fourfold between 1603 and 1626. Hardly any development took place at Portsmouth during the sixteenth and early seventeenth centuries, but the yard was substantially expanded under the Commonwealth and Protectorate, and it became a major building and laying-up facility under the later Stuarts.

The dockyards were far and away the largest workplaces in the country. Even by the late seventeenth century, the largest mill contained no more than perhaps a few dozen workers. As early as 1562–63, though, Deptford dockyard alone had 62 shipwrights, 24 carpenters, 31 labourers, 15 watermen and several dozen other workers and officials of

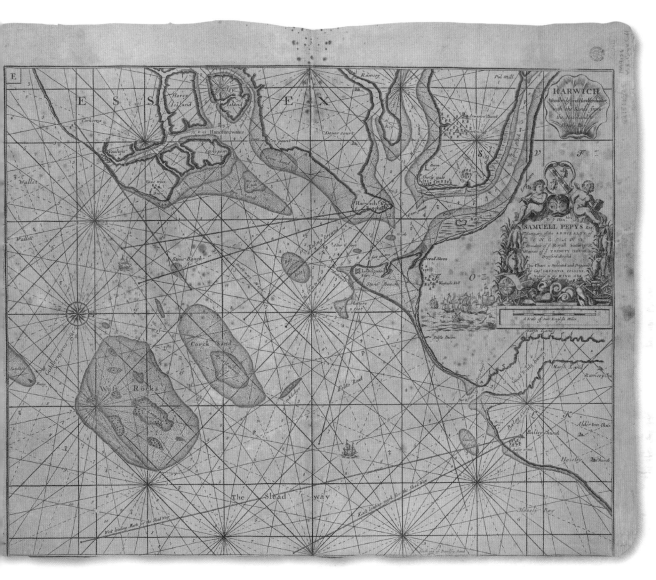

*Chart of Harwich, Woodbridge and Handfordwater dedicated to*
*Samuel Pepys Esq. Captain Greenvile Collins, 1686. G218:11/25.*

different kinds. These were the 'ordinary', the permanent establishment of the yard, but as it was a period when several new ships were under construction, additional workers were employed on an 'extraordinary' basis – thus forming a welcome boost to the incomes of the local widows and goodwives who ran the lodging houses that accommodated them.[14] As the fleet increased in size during the seventeenth century, so did the manpower of the yards. In 1675, a quiet peacetime year when the establishments were being kept to a bare minimum, the five dockyards contained a combined total of 986 workers; but in 1694, five years into a great war against France, Chatham alone had about 1,400.[15] Like the fleet, they were truly national institutions. In peacetime, the yards could draw their manpower exclusively from the immediately adjacent communities and, unsurprisingly, dockyard 'dynasties' grew up: generation after generation was employed in the same place, with famous shipbuilding families like the Petts and the Shishes being just the tip of the iceberg. In wartime, however, the yards had to draw in shipwrights from wherever they could obtain them, and men from East Anglia, Bristol and Newcastle all worked in the Stuart royal dockyards.[16] The dockyards also employed, or did business with, significant numbers of women: during the latter part of the seventeenth century, Martha Bradford and 'Widow Evans' were the keeper and water-carrier of the payhouse at Chatham; 'Widow Braman' was the lockmaker at Deptford and – some years earlier – Margaret Browne was the chief supplier of lead to the same yard.[17]

Such huge and diverse workforces required sophisticated systems of governance, including exact timekeeping: the dockyards were perhaps the first major institutions to have clocks mounted in towers, visible to every worker and dictating their hours of work. Firmer control from the centre was also established. From the 1650s onwards, both Chatham and Portsmouth were under resident commissioners, who were nominally members of the Navy Board. Although contemporaries as well as some historians have condemned the dockyards as 'corrupt' or 'inefficient', such judgements are inevitably subjective and often loaded with hindsight. In fact, the dockyards were capable of quite astonishing feats, perhaps none more so than that of the summer of 1666: many ships of the fleet were badly damaged during the Four Days' Battle against the Dutch at the beginning of June, but the dockyards were able to refit them so that the fleet was at sea again, and able to defeat the Dutch in the Saint James's Day fight, just seven weeks later.[18]

*Model of the Royal Dockyard at Woolwich.*
*Richard Pickthorne; John Haley, 1772–74.*
*SLR2905.*

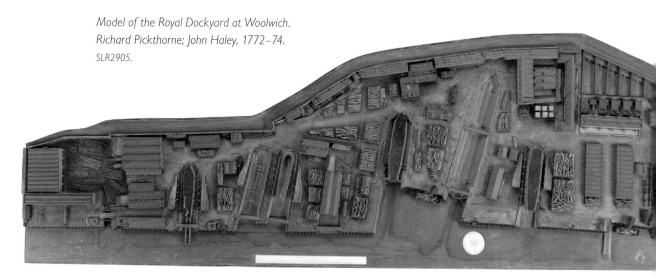

*Royal coat of arms of King William III, formerly displayed over the gate at Deptford Dockyard, 1689–1702. HRA0014.*

The chief occupation of the dockyards was to build and repair ships. The origins of almost all the major advances in ship design during the period have generated considerable debate. The older clinker-built pattern of hull construction gave way to the much stronger carvel-built method early in the sixteenth century, a development that occurred at much the same time as the introduction of gunports. These seem to have been in use from at least the 1470s and were certainly present in the *Mary Rose*, launched in 1511, and in the *Henry Grâce à Dieu* of 1514, which carried 19 heavy guns.[19] The innovation permitted the deployment of much larger weapons than those that had appeared on earlier warships: Henry VII's *Regent* of 1486 carried no fewer than 225 guns, but those were largely small 'serpentines'. The guns themselves also grew in size and power as gun-founding technologies improved. However, the

*Ship model of the* Mary Rose *(1509).
Bassett-Lowke Ltd, 1986–91.
SLR3012.*

greater emphasis on artillery was not accompanied by any significant change in tactics: warships continued to rely above all on boarding, using their heavier guns to 'soften up' the enemy first.[20] During the third quarter of the sixteenth century, the relatively cumbersome 'great ships', with their high castles fore and aft, were partly supplanted in English service by the 'race-built galleon', a narrower, faster hull form with a much lower forecastle, which carried a greater proportion of its guns on the broadside. These ships seem to have been a response to the tactical advantages enjoyed by galleys, but fine lines came at the expense of capacity, making them unable to sustain the sort of lengthy ocean voyages that Spanish and Portuguese galleons regularly undertook. It was once believed that the race-built galleon was the brainchild of one man, John Hawkins of Plymouth, based on the lessons that he and his kinsman Francis Drake learned during their semi-piratical Caribbean raiding in the 1560s, but it is more likely that the design evolved across several decades, with innovations taking place in several countries.[21] Indeed, towards the end of his reign, Henry VIII's personal inclinations moved away from 'great ships' towards vessels with lower profiles, which were essentially intermediate between the huge carracks and the race-built galleons.[22]

As designs changed, so did the nature of the shipwright's traditionally carefully guarded mysteries. Although they still worked primarily to 'rules of thumb' handed down from one generation to the next, there was an increasing knowledge of mathematical principles, and greater use of scientific method in designing ships. In 1608, for example, Thomas Harriot, essentially a layman who had made just one major sea voyage, used Apollonian geometry to devise a new rule for calculating the ideal height of a mast, and passed this on to Matthew

*Portrait of Fisher Harding,*
*Master Shipwright*
*1664–1706, depicted*
*with the* Royal Sovereign.
*Jonathan Richardson, c.1701.*
*NMM, Caird Collection.*
*BHC2743.*

Baker, one of the most eminent shipwrights of the day, who may have been the first member of his profession to produce designs on paper.[23] Pepys subsequently held up his friend Sir Anthony Deane as an exemplar of a new breed of shipwright. Deane produced a detailed 'Doctrine of Naval Architecture' in 1670, probably at Pepys's behest, to demonstrate how a ship could be built using mathematical and scientific principles.[24] But for all Pepys's special pleading, Deane was clearly not unique among his contemporaries. Edward Bushnell had already published a book entitled *The Complete Shipwright* in 1652, and others, too, were clearly working in a similarly systematic way. John Shish, master shipwright at Deptford, was an illiterate alcoholic according to Pepys, who systematically denigrated all of Deane's rivals in his constant efforts to advance his friend; but Shish certainly produced detailed paper draughts, as Pepys well knew since he received copies of them.[25] Moreover, the ships that Deane built were little superior to those of any of his contemporaries.

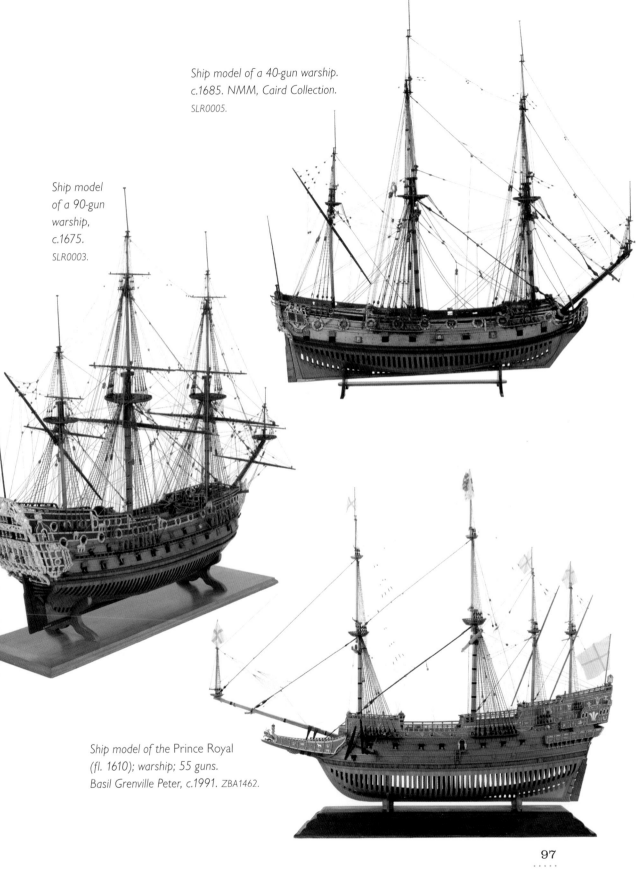

*Ship model of a 40-gun warship.*
*c.1685. NMM, Caird Collection.*
*SLR0005.*

*Ship model*
*of a 90-gun*
*warship,*
*c.1675.*
*SLR0003.*

*Ship model of the* Prince Royal
*(fl. 1610); warship; 55 guns.*
*Basil Grenville Peter, c.1991.* ZBA1462.

97
. . . . .

Painting showing the
Britannia in two positions.
Isaac Sailmaker, 1689–1702.
NMM, Caird Collection. BHC3743.

French and Venetian designs. The attempt to separate the rowing sweeps and rowers from the gun battery, which could then be made continuous on one deck, was not entirely successful in the prototypes, but the principle of the single gundeck was taken forward by the frigates of the eighteenth century and into the early years of the nineteenth.[30]

In conclusion, then, at the beginning of the Tudor period, the 'Navy Royal' was a moveable feast: impermanent, useful principally for transporting armies, and small enough to be in the effective charge of one man. Its ships were indistinguishable from those of merchants and were, indeed, often hired out for trading voyages. By the end of the seventeenth century, though, it was a great department of state, the country's largest industry and the principal defence of the realm: or, as the preamble to the 1661 naval Articles of War put it, 'wherein under the good Providence and protection of God, the Wealth, Safety, and Strength of this Kingdom is so much concerned'.

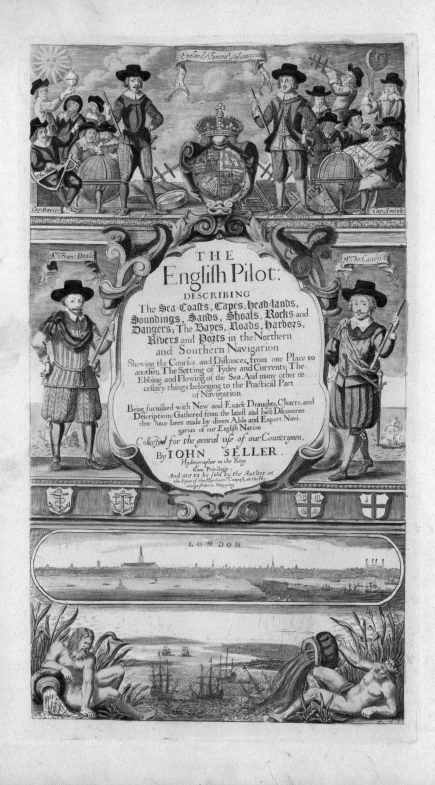

*Frontispiece to John Seller's* The English Pilot, *c.1671.* PBE6857.

# Using the Seas and Skies: Navigation in Early-Modern England

## Megan Barford and Louise Devoy

John Seller's *The English Pilot*, first published in 1671, was fêted as the first English sea atlas. The book's title page is an explicit celebration of England's growing navigational expertise, with well-known explorers from the previous century such as Walter Ralegh, Hugh Willoughby, Francis Drake and Thomas Cavendish placed in a scene of conversation alongside some of the iconic navigational instruments of the day. One man looks skywards with a cross-staff; another measures with dividers. A third, resting a backstaff on his knee, points towards a banner over the whole scene: 'Englands Famous Discoverers'. The atlas was presented as a triumph of England's maritime activity, 'furnished with New and Exact Draughts, Charts, and Descriptions ... from the latest and best Discoveries ... of our *English* Nation'. Despite its patriotic overtones, Seller's publication was largely made from old plates already used to print Dutch atlases, and its celebration of England as a maritime nation depended on skills and knowledge that came from elsewhere. The famed English navigators of Seller's picture relied on the assistance of Portuguese pilots and the charts taken from them, while the impressive array of instruments on the top half of the page gives little indication of the English navigators' debt to centuries of mathematical development and the shared practical expertise of Arab, Chinese, Greek and European scholars and seafarers. Indeed, this process of assimilation had begun over a century before Seller's *English Pilot*, as Tudor explorers sought to reach further into the Atlantic World, and in so doing enshrined navigation as a subject of state and scholarly interest.

For generations, mariners had relied on their local knowledge for navigation, hugging the coastline and looking for landmarks to guide their way between ports. Gaining practical experience at sea was essential as these skills were transmitted orally from one generation to the next, with no formal training. Mariners relied on their ability to gauge the strength of the wind, tides and currents, combined with a directional bearing gained from a magnetic compass, to assess their position. How much rope it took for a sounding lead – normally a long lead weight – to reach the bottom of the sea was used to measure depth, and a piece of tallow on the lead would allow detection of changes in the nature of the seabed, which would correspond to written descriptions of particular routes. For example, one fifteenth-century guide, covering the route from the west coast of France to English ports, informed mariners that near the mouth of the Loire they would find 'striped stones and white shells'.[1] Similarly, the log-line gave mariners the means to measure their speed: a small plate of wood known as a log attached to a coiled rope full of equally spaced knots was thrown over the side of the vessel alongside the boat and the number of knots issued into the water was measured in 28-second intervals using a sandglass (hence the nautical speed of knots, still used today). Mariners kept track of this information, along with a record of their direction (their 'bearing'), by inserting pegs into a compass-shaped traverse board. This technique of assessing one's position by direction and speed became known as 'dead reckoning', a deductive process that formed the mainstay of navigation for centuries. By using this combination of environmental factors and local knowledge, mariners could negotiate the waters safely as they plied their trade between coastal ports.

During the fifteenth century, however, additional techniques were devised, in part because of the opening up of new trade routes between Europe, Africa, Asia and the Americas. Sailors were now leaving the safety of familiar coastlines to explore uncharted shores across featureless oceans. A new range of navigational instruments was required to help them make the most of these lucrative trade routes, and navigators began to think more globally about their position on the Earth. Ideas from Ancient Greek astronomical manuscripts became more widely available during the medieval period, thanks to a centuries-long process of translation and assimilation across Byzantine, Islamic and European centres of learning. From this collaborative effort emerged a new breed of navigational instruments that relied on the Earth's magnetic field, the apparent motion of the Sun and stars, and the interplay between the tides and the changing phase of the Moon. One of the most useful and widespread navigational instruments at this time was the magnetic compass, an instrument believed to have originated in China several centuries earlier and first recorded in Europe during the twelfth century.

*Mariner's compass. This is the earliest compass in the National Maritime Museum collection and dates from the second half of the sixteenth century. The case, lid and compass bowl are made of turned ivory. The compass is mounted in a brass gimbal ring, which reduces the effects of the ship's motion at sea, c.1570. NMM, Caird Collection. NAV0276.*

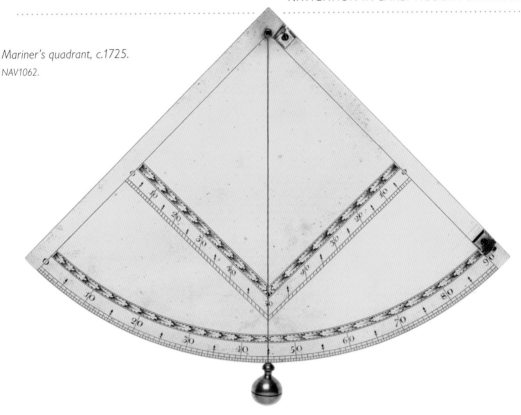

*Mariner's quadrant, c.1725.*
*NAV1062.*

The compass was mainly used for direction-finding, since a ship's course could be established with reference to the instrument's north-pointing needle. By the sixteenth century, mariners had realized that they could also use the compass to help estimate the time of high tide by measuring the position of the Moon as observed from specific ports.

While the magnetic compass offered mariners a valuable means of direction-finding when the skies were cloudy, it still only provided a general sense of direction, and they soon discovered discrepancies between magnetic and true north. Mariners turned their attention to the North Star, Polaris, the height of which above the horizon could also be used as a measure of latitude (north–south position relative to the Equator). During the fifteenth century, European mariners began to use angle-measuring instruments to determine the height of Polaris and other celestial bodies, something that Chinese and Arab mariners had been doing for centuries. One of the instruments used by European navigators was the mariner's quadrant, a quarter-circle wedge-shaped plate with a degree scale along the curved limb, sighting vanes along the straight-edged top and a plumb bob attached to the apex. It could be used to measure the altitude of Polaris at night and the Sun during the day, especially at local noon, when the Sun reaches the highest point of its apparent daily journey across the sky. Astronomers knew that the Sun's altitude at noon varied according to the observer's latitude, hence mariners could use data tables to compare their readings hence determine their latitude. Using the Sun to measure latitude became essential when sailing south of the Equator, since

*Mariner's astrolabe. This example was found in 1845 under a rock on Valentia Island, close to the point off southern Ireland where three ships of the Spanish Armada were wrecked in 1588. NAV0022.*

the northern navigators' most important star, Polaris, was no longer visible above the horizon.

While the mariner's quadrant provided seafarers with a measure of their latitude, the instrument was difficult to use at sea on a pitching vessel in windy conditions. An alternative instrument was the mariner's astrolabe, an adaptation of a complex astronomical device that was developed centuries earlier by Greek and Islamic scholars. For elite astronomers, the astrolabe was an expensive but useful didactic tool. However, it remained physically and intellectually out of reach for mariners. Instead, they relied on a simplified version with a weighted lower part to give stability and a plate with cut-out sections to allow the wind to pass through. Used in a similar fashion to the quadrant, sighting vanes on the reverse of the instrument allowed the user to measure the height of the Sun and stars above the horizon.

The instrument of choice for most mariners, however, was the cross-staff. Cheaper and easier to use than the mariner's astrolabe, it was invented during the fourteenth century by the Jewish scholar Levi ben Gershon. The instrument was composed of a central rod (staff)

*Use of a cross-staff BELOW, and use of a backstaff ('quadrant') RIGHT, as depicted in John Davis's The Seaman's Secrets (1595). PBE5163.*

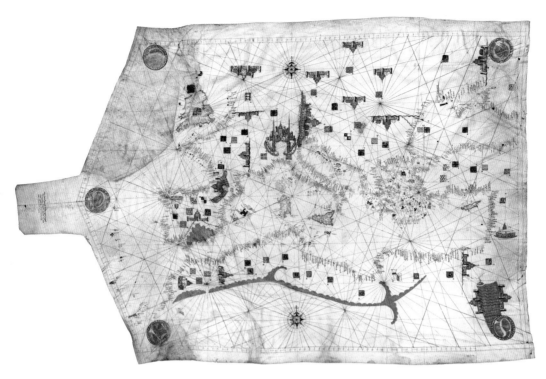

*Chart of the Mediterranean Sea and the North-East Atlantic. The oldest portolan chart in the Museum's collection. Bertran Jacopo and Berenguer Ripol, 1456. G230:1/7.*

with a set of movable vanes that could be interchanged and adjusted to enable the observer to measure the apparent angular distance between two celestial bodies. Like the astrolabe, the cross-staff was initially designed for astronomical purposes rather than navigation, but once again, a simplified version for seamen enabled them to measure the altitude of Polaris with relative ease. Mariners risked their eyesight by observing the Sun directly, so a modified instrument that relied on measuring the Sun's shadow, known as a backstaff, was described by the English explorer John Davis in his navigation manual, *The Seaman's Secrets* (1595).

Navigational instruments made of wood and metal helped mariners to make specific observations in relation to direction and position. Such observations were used in conjunction with charts and written directions, which recorded and described particular routes. Some of the earliest marine charts – known as 'portolan' charts after the coastal sailing directions on which they were based – were developed in the Mediterranean in the thirteenth century. They typically included pronounced depictions of the coastline, indications of rocks and shallow water, and networks of criss-crossing rhumb lines, which indicated compass bearings. These charts tended to be centred on the Mediterranean, whereas the cartography of the British Isles is typically much less developed, indicating how peripheral this region was to the rich trading networks of the Italian city states, the Ottoman Empire, Spain and Portugal. These early charts were made by drawing and painting on specially prepared sheep or goat skins, known as vellum. As techniques of printing onto paper from engraved copper plates developed through the fifteenth and sixteenth centuries, such methods also began to be used to produce maps and charts more readily in multiple copies.

In the later sixteenth century, maps and charts bound into volumes became an important format for presenting navigational information. This development was particularly significant in Amsterdam, where expansion of the Dutch maritime empire and a burgeoning book trade meant that there was both demand and capacity for the production of sea atlases. The most important of these volumes in the sixteenth century was the work of Lucas Janszoon Waghenaer, a Dutch cartographer whose *Spieghel der Zeevaert* (1584) was the first printed volume to combine detailed charts, instructions and tables of data for navigating between the ports of Europe. Translated into English as *The Mariners Mirrour* (1588), the volume was so important among English-speaking mariners that similar volumes including both written descriptions and charts came to be known as 'wagoners', a corruption of Waghenaer's name.

In spite of the growing range of instruments and charts, mariners were still dependent upon pilots, who were employed specifically for their local knowledge. Walter Ralegh's voyages to North America, for example, relied heavily on the navigational expertise of Portuguese pilot Simao Fernandes. Francis Drake gave much credit to the assistance provided by Nuno de Silva,

*Detail from Lucas Janszoon Waghenaer's* The Mariners Mirrour, *1588.* PBD8264(26).

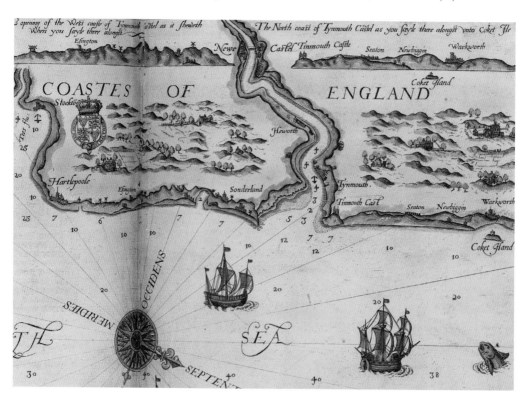

a Portuguese pilot he captured in the Atlantic in 1578. This was particularly important because of the way the Spanish and Portuguese guarded navigational information, only permitting navigational charts to be produced in manuscript, and closely managing who had access to them. At the same time, mariners could be sceptical about the use of charts and instruments, aware of the effectiveness and continuing importance of local knowledge and rule-of-thumb methods. One commentator in the early seventeenth century noted that 'I have knowne within these 20 yeres, that they that were auncient Masters of Ships have derided and mocked them that have occupied their Cardes and Plattes ... saying: that they care not for their sheepes skinnes', referring to the sheets of vellum on which sea charts were made.[2]

Despite their functional appearance, maps, charts and instruments were not just used for practical purposes. They were, in general, objects of high value and status. Particularly in a period when European understandings of geography were undergoing significant change, representations of distant territories served to show off their owners' commercial and cosmopolitan outlook. Many of the maps and charts that survive are not examples of practical documents taken on ships and used for navigation, but are finely coloured and sometimes illuminated objects, intended for the libraries of the wealthy. For most of the sixteenth century, English mariners had to rely on purchasing their charts and instruments from established centres of scholarship and craftsmanship on mainland Europe, such as Amsterdam and Nuremberg. Although a relatively sophisticated range of astronomical instruments designed for navigation was available, there was little interest in or need for such items among English mariners, who rarely ventured beyond known coastlines. As the century progressed, however, the combination of involvement in long-distance voyages of exploration and intensifying trade networks stoked interest in different navigational techniques. Within a few decades, a new community of instrument and chart-makers in London began to emerge, along with a scholarly interest in navigational theory.

An early influence on the uptake of navigational techniques in England was the Venetian Sebastian Cabot. His life as a mariner, cosmographer and Pilot Major at the *Casa de Contratación*, the institution which managed Spanish exploration and colonization, provided him with a wealth of experience, which he brought to England in 1548. Unable to slot into an equivalent institutional structure on his arrival, since none existed in England, Cabot was nonetheless involved in organizing some major mid-century mercantile voyages, and was one of the founders of the Muscovy Company in 1555. He was heavily involved in drawing up instructions for mariners on English ships, as well as highlighting to prominent figures what were seen as the navigational inadequacies of English seamen. A more scholarly advocate of astronomical navigation in England was John Dee, a sixteenth-century mathematician from

*OVERLEAF Atlas sheet from an edition of* Theatrum Orbis Terrarum, *depicting the world on an oval projection, surrounded by sky, 1573. PBD7640(1).*

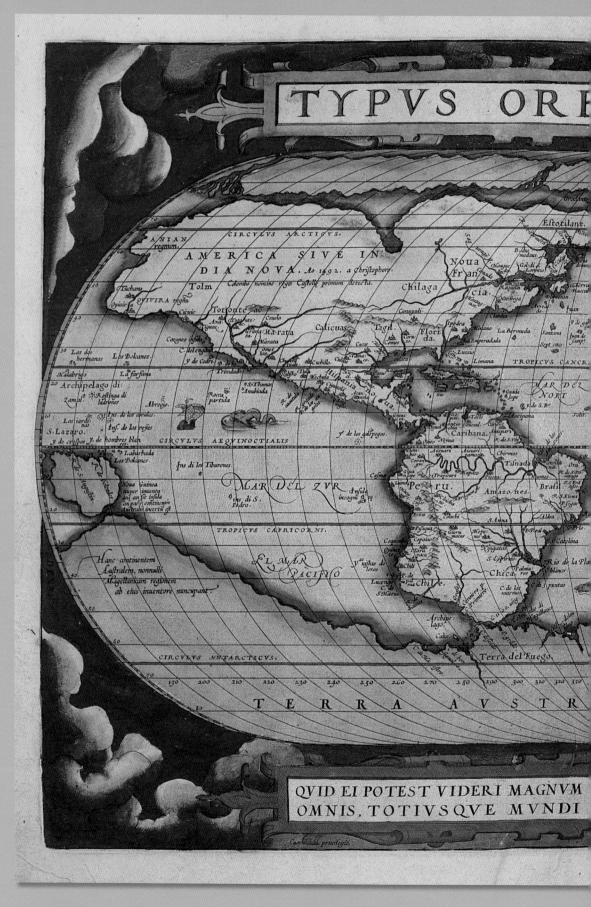

# TERRARVM.

Norvegia
Nova Zembla
Tartata
Tangut
Mongol
Suedia
S. Nicolas
Ohin
Naiman
Mongul
Cattigara
Weling
Wilki
Calami
Cosim
Turfon
Canghi
EVROPA
Russia
Grustina
Kinai
Cotam
Cathaio
Moscou
Bulgar
Cogia
Marmo
rea
Paquisu
Kituar
Tenduc
Singui
Zangut
Brema
Germa
nia
Tartaria
Tainsu
Prustent
Congu
Camba
Quinzu
Miaco
Gallia
Bon
Cuizar
A S I A
Sedah
Curauan
Iaci
Mar de Bachu
Turcheftan
Samarchand
Voci
am
China
Natolia
Armn
nia
Coral an
Danno
Perfia
Rey
Candabar
Saura
Sirar
Turbet
Hochestan
Aegyptus
Guzarate
India orien
talis
Delli
Orixa
Brema
AFRICA
Nubia
Arabia
Goa
Narf
Licht
Decan
Agi
Zibit
Farradg
Calecut
Palcban
Nubia
Aden
Abiffi
ni
Melinda
Gilam
Vasco de Aema
S. Francesco
Due Compagne
Manicon
go
Mel
inde
Don Garçia
Poueada
Jona
Lantchidol
mare
ANVS AE
PICVS.
Adarno
Barxos de Nazaret
Macareñas
Lycach
S. Apollonia
MAR DI INDI
MALETVR
Iuan de
Lisboa
Tomeri
Vastissimas hic esse
regiones ex M. Pauli Ven. et
Lud. Vartomanni scriptis pe
regrinationibus constat.
Los Romeros

Psitacorum regio,
sic à Lusitanis appellata ob in
credibile earum auium ibidem
magnitudinem.

S   N O N D V M   C O G N I T A.

1573.

Cambridge University who travelled to Louvain during the summer of 1548. Dee visited the renowned workshop established by cartographers Gerardus Mercator and Gemma Frisius, immersing himself in his hosts' research into new theories and practical applications of astronomy, cartography and astrology.

Upon his return to England, Dee faced two problems in convincing his fellow countrymen of the opportunities of astronomical navigation: the lowly status of mathematics in universities, and a lack of available instruments. When Dee w as asked in 1570 to provide a preface to a new translation of the Ancient Greek mathematical textbook *The Elements* by Euclid, he used the opportunity to promote the subject and advocate its use in numerous applications, including navigation:

> *It is obvious that the Master Pilot requires knowledge of the Arts of Hydrography, Astronomy, Astrology, and Horometry, as well as the common Base and foundation of all Arts, Arithmetic and Geometry. Thus he will be able to read the necessary Instruments, whether he has constructed them himself or they have been skilfully crafted by experts.*[3]

At this time, the only significant instrument-maker available in London was the engraver and map-seller Thomas Gemini, a former pupil of Mercator and Frisius who brought expertise from Louvain to England. Based on the similarity between Gemini's instruments and those produced later by the goldsmith Humfrey Cole, England's first native instrument-maker, we can infer that Cole gained at least some of his knowledge from his European predecessor.

By the 1570s, there was a growing awareness of the political and economic benefits of applied mathematics and Cole was able to exploit this new demand for precision instruments. While mainly working as a die-sinker at the Royal Mint, he found time to produce surveying instruments in response to the demand generated by the new landowners who had benefited from the dissolution of the monasteries under Henry VIII and the subsequent reallocation of estates. Meanwhile, merchants and

*Astronomical compendium dial for latitudes 0°–90° North. Humfrey Cole, 1569. This oval-shaped instrument has five leaves held together by small brass pegs. NMM, Greenwich Hospital Collection. AST0172.*

# Sebastian Cabot

In 1548, the Venetian Sebastian Cabot, esteemed by navigators across Europe, arrived in Bristol. Permitted a short absence from his position as Pilot Major at the *Casa de Contratación* in Seville, he in fact took up residence in England, much to the chagrin of Charles V, then ruler of the Spanish Empire. As Pilot Major, Cabot had been responsible for the training and examination of Spanish pilots in the use of navigational instruments and charts, and for inspecting all such navigational equipment. Such a role meant that when Cabot moved to England, he took with him a sophisticated understanding of cartography and celestial navigation which he had developed in over 30 years' service in Spain.

His move in 1548 was in fact a return, as he had lived and worked in Bristol in the first decade of the sixteenth century, and gained recognition as a merchant and cartographer. Back in England, he was received with enthusiasm and became one of the founders of the Muscovy Company, in which role he was deeply involved with the English attempts to find a northern passage to Asia. He insisted that pilots working for the Muscovy Company develop skills in celestial navigation and that the company provide them with the necessary instruments and charts. At the same time, he stressed the importance of practical experience, ridiculing cosmographers who insisted on the truth of their geographical speculations without the experience of travel.

The long-distance trading networks which certain English merchants so desired would not develop until long after Cabot's death. But the impulse which he gave to navigation in England, based on his long maritime experience in the service of the Spanish Empire, and his emphasis on the importance of theoretical training and practical experience were undeniably influential.

*Print of a painting by Hans Holbein of Sebastian Cabot, 1824. PAD2347.*

politicians in London watched the Iberian states profiting from overseas empires with some envy. One response to this sense of competition was a series of three voyages organized by Martin Frobisher and Michael Lok, who sought to find the north-west passage to Asia, known as 'Cathay'. Acting on the English belief that the success enjoyed by the Spanish was in part rooted in their navigational expertise, Frobisher and Lok hired Dee as a navigation instructor for the crews' training sessions, while the accounts reveal that over £50 (approximately £10,000 today) was spent on instruments supplied by 'Humfrye Cole and others'. The shopping list was impressive: armillary spheres, maps, globes, compasses, charts and a cross-staff, although it is unlikely that the instruments were used fully, given the adventurers' admission upon their return that they had struggled to follow Dee's instructions.

While Cole's instruments were designed for wealthy noblemen and merchant adventurers who were prepared to invest in high-quality products for risky voyages, the average navigator continued to depend on the simple instruments described earlier. When Cole died in 1591, his work was continued by a new generation of London-based instrument-makers. Within a few decades, the city had a burgeoning community of such artisans based in workshops clustered around the Tower of London and St Paul's Cathedral. Like Cole, many

of these craftsmen combined their expertise in engraving, printing, metalwork and mechanics so that the trades of chart-making and instrument-making often overlapped. This was most often the case for charts printed from copper plates, as techniques of engraving were relevant to both. Many of these skills were introduced by immigrant craftsmen, often religious refugees from the European continent. One example of this is the engraver Jodocus Hondius, who fled his native Ghent during the wars of the Counter-Reformation. Already a skilled engraver, he established himself in London in 1584 and worked on several very prestigious projects. These included engraving some of the charts for the English translation of Waghenaer's sea atlas, and gores (printed paper segments) for globes made by Emery Molyneux, which were the first to be produced in England.

Chart- and instrument-makers were based principally along the north banks of the Thames

RIGHT *The earliest extant printed English globe. Emery Molyneux, 1592. Courtesy of Middle Temple Library.*

OPPOSITE *Map of the East Indies. Nicholas Comberford, 1665. G256:1/1.*

QVINCII
XANTVM
NANQVIN
CHEQVIAM
CANTAN

CORAY

IAPAN

Checoco

TRO       PI       CVS   CAN      CRI

TONQVIN    QVANCII

SIAM

CAMBOIA

MALAYA

SVMATRA

LAPHILIPINIA

MINDANO

BORNEO

CELLE
BI

Æ QVI      NOC      TI   AL

NOVAGVIN
EA

IAVA MALOR

113

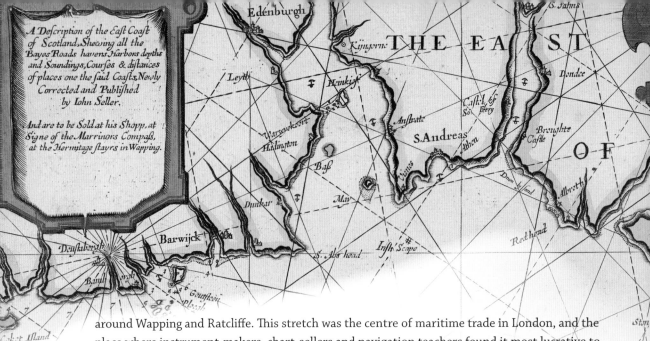

around Wapping and Ratcliffe. This stretch was the centre of maritime trade in London, and the place where instrument-makers, chart-sellers and navigation teachers found it most lucrative to work. It was here that the so-called Thames School of mapmakers developed. The artisans were connected as masters and apprentices over several generations, and developed a particular style of manuscript chart, generally made on vellum and pasted onto hinged wooden boards, called 'platt[e]s', which could be closed to protect the surface of the chart. They were in some ways similar to the portolan charts, including extensive networks of rhumb lines with ornate 'roses' at their centre. Typically these were small-scale oceanic charts, rather than larger-scale examples showing a specific area in great detail, and those that survive tend to be highly decorative. Little is known about this group of chart-makers, perhaps because, despite the striking appearance and contemporary renown of the objects they produced, their occupation was not judged to be particularly prestigious.[4]

The riverside area of Wapping was also home to John Seller, who produced *The English Pilot*, and with whom this chapter began. In a period when England was recurrently at war with the Dutch Republic over profitable trade routes, any potential reduction in dependence on enemy charts mattered a great deal to those involved. Appointed as Hydrographer to the King by Charles II in March 1671, Seller was also granted protection for his cartography. There was a 30-year ban on reproducing the charts from the atlas, as well as on importing atlases from the continent. Seller himself had not been so restrained in his use of others' work. In the 1660s, it is thought that Seller made a trip to the Low Countries, where he acquired some 63 old engraved copper plates. These were then re-used to make *The English Pilot*. In several of the sheets of this atlas, there are visible traces of Dutch text having been removed from the plates, and some Dutch names remain among those changed to English (see map above). Samuel Pepys was blunt in his commentary, reporting the accusation that Seller 'bought the old worn Dutch copper plates for old copper, and has used them in his pretended new book'.[5]

This was not so unusual. The transfer of plates between publishers

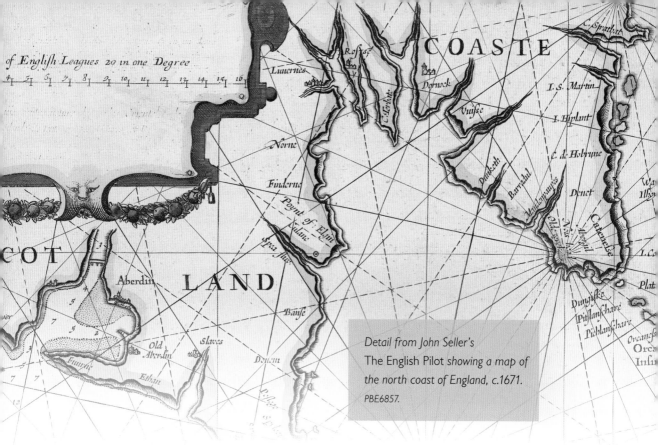

Of English Leagues 20 in one Degree

*Detail from John Seller's*
The English Pilot *showing a map of*
*the north coast of England, c.1671.*
PBE6857.

was common, and cartographic copying even more so.[6] The Dutch plates that went into the making of *The English Pilot*, for example, had already passed through the hands of two Dutch cartographers and had initially been made to produce an atlas that was a counterfeit of a volume by a third.[7] This is only one example of the way in which cartographic information might be copied and transferred at that time. The story of Seller's *English Pilot*, then, is an extreme, rather than an unrepresentative, example of the making of sea atlases. The history of cartography in early-modern Europe is almost without exception a history of copying. Cartographers drew on many sources, including the journals and oral testimony of mariners and the work of other mapmakers. Sometimes access to geographical information about particular coasts was so restricted that sources could be highly prized. It was for this reason that when an English buccaneering vessel captured a Spanish ship off the Pacific coast of South America in 1681, the officers counted a set of manuscript charts and directions as being among the treasures they took back to England. In London, they were translated from Spanish into English, and the maps were copied by William Hack, a prominent cartographer of the Thames School.

It was only at the very end of the seventeenth century that someone was commissioned to carry out a survey of the coasts of the British Isles, so that existing charts could be corrected by systematic work rather than by more ad hoc gathering of information. In a period of intensifying state concern about navigation, this survey was undertaken by a naval captain, Greenvile Collins. With his assistants, he worked over a period of seven years from 1681, using measuring chains, compasses and lead lines to establish distances, bearings and depths. Supported by the king, Trinity House and the Admiralty, it was seen as a project that would limit future dependence on Dutch charts. The work was published in two volumes as *Great Britain's Coasting Pilot* in 1693. With both Seller and Collins, the protection and support for their work indicate a growing state interest in marine cartography, in a period when the intellectual climate strongly supported improvements to navigation. Like Seller's *English Pilot*, the *Coasting Pilot* was much criticized by contemporaries. Collins's work was judged an 'Ill Performance', much inferior to the French charts of British coasts produced around the same time, which were the ones more frequently copied by other cartographers.[8] Collins's work was possible because of the way in which state and scholarly interest in the late Stuart period was directed towards navigation. This chapter has identified efforts to improve navigation from across the period, but it is clear that earlier efforts tend to be found more in improvised arrangements, often around specific voyages or projects, than in explicit institutional arrangements.

In the previous century there had been some fairly concerted attempts to increase mathematical education with a view to improving navigation, with, for instance, the foundation of Gresham College in Bishopsgate, London in 1597. The college provided free lectures on a range of topics, including astronomy and mathematics. However, it was not until the 1670s that there was a major state-backed effort to provide formal navigational education. Samuel Pepys, as Clerk of the Acts of the Navy, persuaded Charles II to endow a Royal Mathematical School at Christ's Hospital, to admit 40 boys to be 'taught the art of Arithmatique and Navigacon',[9] and who would then be examined at Trinity House, the body set up by Henry VIII to oversee matters relating to the safety of navigation. The high political and scholarly interest that led to the creation of the Royal Mathematical School was also at work in the foundation of another institution that further welded astronomical and navigational ambition: in 1675 John Flamsteed was appointed the first Astronomer Royal, and in 1676 the Royal Observatory, established at Greenwich, was completed. Over the next 40 years, Flamsteed and his assistants (some of whom were recruited from the Royal Mathematical School) observed the stars and compiled astronomical data to create what would become the most highly regarded star catalogue of the day.

The Royal Observatory from Crooms Hill. *English school, c.1696.*
*NMM, Caird Fund.* BHC1812.

In England during the sixteenth and particularly the seventeenth century, navigation at sea became a matter of important political and financial interest. With this status came the establishment of institutions for mathematical training and the compilation of astronomical data. At the end of the period, although practical navigation remained an imprecise art in which rule-of-thumb methods were important and effective, and predominantly so in local contexts, the Stuart state lent its weight to its improvement, particularly in the realms of mathematics and astronomy. The growth of long-distance overseas trade and the establishment of imperial interests contributed to navigation's huge scholarly and political prominence.

Indeed, the last act passed by Queen Anne, the Longitude Act of 1714, demonstrates this very point. Offering a reward for a method to determine longitude accurately at sea indicates the great significance navigational matters had by the end of the seventeenth century. The act would, over the course of the eighteenth century, set the tone for much astronomical work and for public discourse around navigation.

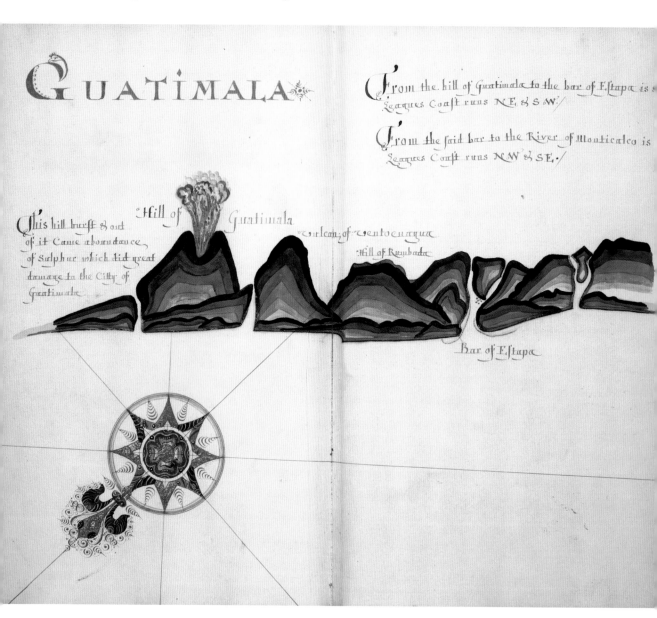

*Map of Guatemala, from* A Wagoner of the South Sea. *William Hack, 1685. P/33(19).*

# Claudius Ptolemaeus

Claudius Ptolemaeus (c.100 CE–c.170 CE), generally known by his Latin name of Ptolemy, was an Egyptian scholar of Greek descent whose work formed the basis of navigation techniques for centuries after. We know little about Ptolemy's life, and his original writings do not survive, but thanks to the translation work of Arab and Byzantine scholars his ideas later spread throughout medieval Europe.

In astronomy, Ptolemy assembled his observations of the stars to create a collection of writings known as the *Almagest* (Arabic for 'the greatest'). Using his star catalogue of over 1,000 star positions, Ptolemy argued that the Earth lay at the centre of the universe while the Sun, stars and planets occupied a series of surrounding nested spheres whose motions could be predicted using trigonometry. This geocentric model of the universe remained the accepted theory until it was overturned by Nicholas Copernicus's Sun-centred theory of the universe over 1,400 years later. In addition to his astronomical work, Ptolemy used mathematics to develop theories of music, optics and astrology.

For navigators, Ptolemy is also remembered as the author of the *Geographia*, in which he compiled all the known geography of the period, complemented by a section on map-making. He listed 8,000 places according to their latitude and longitude, based on a prime meridian of zero degrees longitude passing through the Fortunate (Canary) Islands. These data enabled scholars to reproduce maps based on these coordinates, ensuring that Ptolemy's work continued to influence geographical studies throughout the Renaissance.

Novissima totius terrarum orbis tabula *showing Ptoelmy's prime meridian passing through the Fortunate (Canary) Islands.* John Seller and John Darby, 1675. PBE6862(1).

119

*Coloured engraving of the town of Secota. Theodor de Bry after John White,*
1590 *North Carolina Collection, UNC.* FVCC970.1 H28w. © *University of North Carolina Libraries.*

# Encounter and Exploitation: The English Colonization of North America, 1585–1615

## Laura Humphreys

Rumours and half-truths about the real 'discoverer' of North America have existed for centuries, and continue to endure. Stories persist that the Romans reached the coast of Canada in the first century AD, and there is a plaque on the Alabama coast commemorating the voyage of Madoc, Prince of Wales, whose ten ships are suggested to have crossed the Atlantic in 1170. More widely accepted is the voyage of Leif Erikson, the Icelandic navigator who in the thirteenth century came to 'Vinland', now generally believed to be L'Anse Aux Meadows, Newfoundland.[1] The first transatlantic voyage officially recorded from England was that of John Cabot in 1497 (see Chapter 1), but even this is open to debate. It seems likely that British cod fishermen knew of the abundant waters off Newfoundland for decades, trading with the coastal Beothuk and Mi'kmaq communities, but fiercely protecting the location of their livelihoods.[2] For most of the sixteenth century, England remained an inward-looking state, its focus firmly domestic and European, and it would be almost a whole century after Cabot's voyage before an English colony was successfully established in North America.

This did not mean that individuals refrained from advocating imperial expeditions. While the English state concentrated its attention elsewhere, numerous private investors who believed that England's economic future depended on overseas expansion began to push for a more ambitious overseas strategy. One of these was Richard Hakluyt, whose *Discourse Concerning Western Planting* (1584) was one of the key texts that promoted English overseas colonization. Hakluyt, like many of his equally enthusiastic contemporaries, never went to America, but devoted much of his career to encouraging others to risk their lives doing so. In light of such persuasive texts, and the riches looted by Spanish and Portuguese explorers, English investors slowly came around to the idea that the Americas were potentially a lucrative business opportunity.

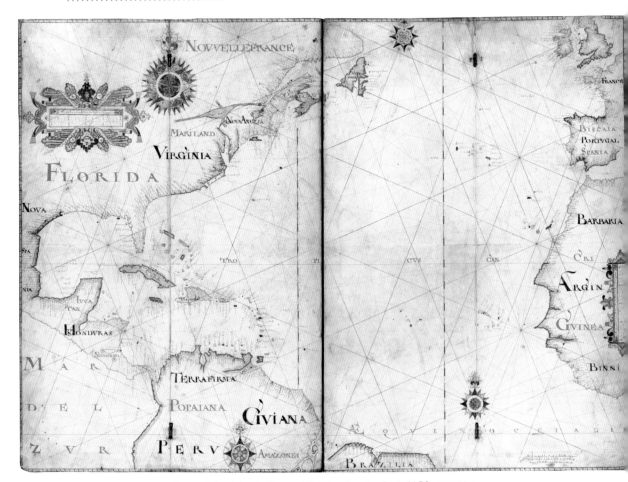

*Chart of the Atlantic Ocean. Nicholas Comberford, 1650. G213:2/·2.*

But what of the people who lived there? Cabot's voyage had discovered a deserted Beothuk camp near the beach, and further engagement with the region revealed a land populated by many Indigenous peoples. Knowledge that the English were not, after all, the first people to set foot in this 'New World' did little to halt imperial projectors; on the contrary, writers like Hakluyt found further cause for advocating the establishment of colonies. Not only would acquiring land in America provide space for the unemployed masses of England to settle and secure new sources of goods for trade, it would also allow the English to Christianize its inhabitants. As he wrote, 'America crye oute unto us, their nexte neighboures, to come and helpe them, and bringe unto them the gladd tidings of the gospell.'[3] Spreading Christianity became a common justification for settler colonialism in the Americas. The captains John Smith and Thomas Harriot also called for widespread evangelism. Harriot argued that 'no Christian Prince hath any possession or dealing' in Virginia that it was ripe for settlement and profitable exploitation of natural resources.[4] This belief in their own spiritual

Engraved for Middleton's Complete System of Geography.

SIR WALTER RALEIGH ordering the STANDARD of Queen Elizabeth to be erected on the Coast of VIRGINIA.

Print depicting Sir Walter Ralegh ordering the standard of Queen Elizabeth to be raised in Virginia, c.1780. PAG7944.

*Portrait of Sir Walter Ralegh, engraved by Philip Audinet after George Vertue. PAD4684.*

and moral superiority blinded the English to their inexperience: were they encroaching not only on long-established Indigenous territories, but on a society with intricate politics, culture and history that pre-dated European arrivals by centuries? In their early colonization attempts, such ignorance cost them dearly.

The first instance of sustained encounter between English settlers and Indigenous peoples followed the creation of the first English colony in North America at Roanoke. This settlement on Roanoke Island, in present-day North Carolina, is primarily famous for its spectacular and mysterious failure. Frequently referred to as 'The Lost Colony' because it was abandoned in uncertain circumstances, for centuries it has fascinated historians and conspiracy theorists alike. The expedition that led to its creation was the brainchild of Sir Walter Ralegh, a driving force in early English colonization attempts, but who himself never travelled to Virginia, the colony he named in honour of Elizabeth I. Instead, he sent seasoned mariners Philip Amadas and Arthur Barlowe on a reconnaissance voyage to Roanoke in 1584. Barlowe was responsible for bringing back to England one of the first eyewitness accounts of North America and of the people who lived there. He recalled their first meeting, when, after three days anchored in the Pamlico Sound, they were approached by a group of Secotan and Croatoan people. Barlowe went to meet them on land and brought one man back to the ship, where they gave him food, wine, a shirt and a hat. In return, this man immediately caught enough fish to equal these gifts, gave them to the English and left.[5] Barlowe's account of this gift exchange is the start of a detailed journal of meetings with the people of the Pamlico Sound. After one of several visits to a local town, Barlowe declared that 'a more kinde and loving people there can not be found in the worlde, as farre as we have hitherto had trial'.[6]

He was as effusive in his praise of the land as he was of the people who lived there, and did much to advance the cause of advocating for further colonization.

Having completed their scouting mission, Amadas and Barlowe returned to England without the much-hoped-for gold, but with tobacco, the crop that would eventually make England's American colonies profitable. They also brought with them two Indigenous Americans: Wanchese, a werowance (i.e. a chief) of the Roanoac, and Manteo, a werowance of the Croatoan. Both of these communities belonged to the wider Carolina Algonquian group of peoples, who were united by mutually intelligible Algonquian languages as well as by geography. This language, brought to sixteenth-century London by Manteo and Wanchese, was of vital importance to the establishment of profitable trade in America. Both men were installed at Walter Ralegh's London home, Durham House. Ralegh tightly controlled access to them, eager to protect his trading advantage in America. He assigned Thomas Harriot, a young

*Detail of a map of Virginia. Roanoke Island sits directly east of Dasamotiquepeue.*
*After John Smith, 1613. PBD7666.*

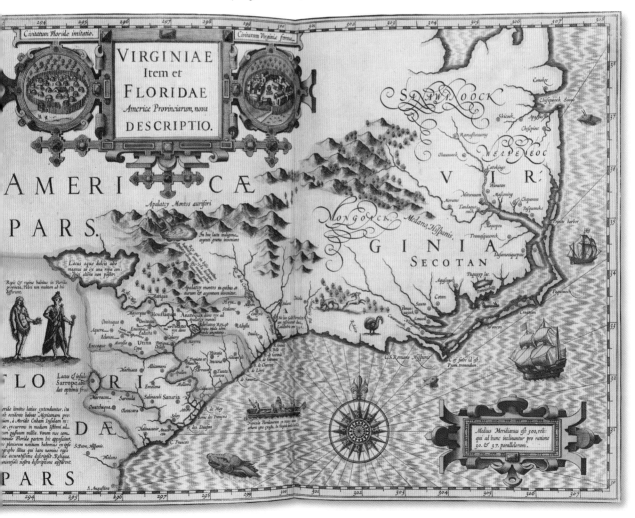

Oxford graduate, to learn and codify their language, and by the end of their eight-month stay, their conversations in English and Algonquian were more or less fluent.[7] Oddly there is no record of Manteo or Wanchese meeting Elizabeth I. This could be a quirk of history, although it seems unlikely that these men, staying in the London home of one of the queen's enduring favourites, would not have been presented at court. It is possible that Ralegh did not dare risk introducing Manteo and Wanchese to the only person who could revoke his exclusive trading rights in Virginia. To him, the two werowances represented a considerable investment on which he had yet to see a return.

Manteo and Wanchese are often characterized as representing two opposing Indigenous views of English colonizers. Manteo, like the people whom Barlowe wrote about, was receptive to their arrival and saw opportunities for trade and the exchange of knowledge, and perhaps for a military alliance for his people. Wanchese, however, was deeply sceptical and saw opportunities only for conflict. On their return to Roanoke in 1585, Wanchese immediately abandoned the English. Manteo, however, remained with them, and made the

A Chieff Lorde of Roanoac. *Theodor de Bry after John White, 1590. PBE7817, plate 7.*

return journey to England again in 1585. He returned to Roanoke with the final voyage of colonists in 1587, when he was baptized a Christian and named Lord of Roanoke, the first American peer. Despite this prolonged relationship with the English, very little is known of Manteo, of his life before and after his transatlantic voyages, or even of his lengthy stays in England. He and Wanchese did go sightseeing regularly, but nothing of their opinions of London and its people has survived.[8]

The second voyage to Roanoke in 1585 was very different from Barlowe and Amadas's scouting mission: this time, Ralegh sent soldiers to build a fort on Roanoke Island. He sent them under the command of Sir Richard Grenville, a military veteran with a ruthless

Portrait of Richard Grenville. British School, nineteenth century. NMM, Caird Fund. BHC2726.

reputation. The voyage was poorly equipped to establish a settlement, indicating that the English believed the local population, who had previously supplied them, would continue to do so. Barlowe and Amadas had stayed for less time with fewer men, and the arrival of an all-male military party probably raised concern in local communities.[9] The site of the Roanoke colony was chosen for its defensive advantages, but it sat on boggy and infertile ground, unsuitable for permanent settlement. Attacks by the Spanish – much feared during expedition's planning – never materialized, but the settlers were incapable of feeding themselves. The werowance of the local Secotan people, Wingina, initially provided for Grenville's men, but as time went on it became hard to feed his own people, let alone over 100 soldiers, so he stopped. The English used violence to try and force the Secotan people to continue to supply them. In a much-disputed event, Grenville claimed a silver cup had gone missing, torching the Secotan village of Aquascogoc and slaughtering its inhabitants in revenge. This violence set the pattern for English soldiers in America who did not get their way.

Less than two months after their arrival, Grenville departed for England to fetch supplies, leaving 107 men behind. However, he did not return in April 1586 as planned and the situation became desperate. The English continued trying to terrorize the Secotans into compliance, killing Wingina and many others, and stealing the supplies they needed. The Secotans responded by retreating, leaving the isolated garrison to starve. Sir Francis Drake visited the colony in 1586, en route back to England from the Caribbean, and found the colonists in such dire straits that he took them with him. In 1587, Ralegh again dispatched over 100 colonists, this time

*The Indian Village of Secoton.*
*John White, 1585–93.*
*© British Museum. 1906,0509.1.7*

including women and children, to establish a settlement on Chesapeake Bay, led by Governor John White. The ships arrived at Roanoke Island to check on the small garrison that had been left behind by Grenville, but found no survivors. The captain who had sailed the Chesapeake Bay colonists to Roanoke, Simon Fernandez, was keen to return to more lucrative privateering, and refused to take them any further. Roanoke was thus an English colony once again.

John White was neither a soldier nor a politician and had no experience of exploration, but he was a talented artist. When Martin Frobisher returned to England with three captive Inuit,

*Engraving of the town of Secota. Theodor de Bry after John White, 1590. Theodor de Bry's engravings greatly embellished John White's watercolours of early Virginia, adding layers of extra detail.*
PBE7817, Plate 20.

a man, a woman and a child, in 1577 after failing to find a north-west passage, it was White who painted their portraits.[10] Ralegh's military approach at Roanoke had been a waste of time, money and human life, and had critically damaged relations with the local peoples. Perhaps White could begin to repair those relations as he captured America's likeness in watercolour; his work would provide important aids for Ralegh to sell America to European investors. White's skill in capturing the 'New World' on paper and Harriot's knowledge of the Algonquian language allowed the two men to document life in sixteenth-century Virginia in great detail. White depicted animals, plants, towns and people. Harriot wrote about the great werowances,

*Print depicting the town of Pomeiooc. Theodor de Bry after John White, 1590.*
*PBE7817, plate 19.*

# Theodor de Bry (1528–98)

Born to a long line of jewellers and engravers in Liège, Theodor de Bry learned the family trade from his grandfather and father. He inherited the family business and successfully practised in the city of his birth until 1570, when he converted to Protestantism, leading to the seizure of his business and his personal property, and to his lifelong banishment from Catholic Liège.[11] This exile led to an itinerant 20 years, which saw the de Bry family (and business) move from Liège to Strasbourg, on to Antwerp, then to London, a nd finally to Frankfurt.

It was during his time in London (1585–88) that he met Richard Hakluyt, who turned his thoughts towards the Americas. Hakluyt and de Bry came to an agreement about the reproduction of John White's Roanoke watercolours alongside John Harriot's account of the same voyage. Like Hakluyt and many other artists and writers who made their living from reproducing the New World in print, de Bry never set foot in America; instead, and in line with the practices of the time, he copied his engravings from the works of others, and distributed them in great numbers across Europe.

In 1588, when he relocated to Frankfurt, he established himself as a publisher, and in 1590 produced the first illustrated edition of John Harriot's *Briefe and True Report*, including 28 illustrations based on White's watercolours. It was enormously successful, and published in five languages within the year. For many Europeans, this was their first and only 'encounter' with the peoples of North America, albeit in de Bry's second-hand, Europeanized style.

*Self-portrait of Theodor de Bry. Theodor de Bry.*
*© British Museum.* 00132713001.

farming and daily life in different communities. The Flemish engraver Theodor de Bry acquired the rights to produce engravings based on White's drawings and published them, alongside Harriot's account. In 1590 the first illustrated *Briefe and True Report of the New Found Land of Virginia* was a tremendous success, and was published in Latin and four other European languages within the year.

It was de Bry's images that had a far wider reach than White's originals in the sixteenth and seventeenth centuries. Although the White watercolours are now an important original source, they were not published until the twentieth century, by which point the de Bry engravings of Indigenous Virginians were ubiquitous.[12] Versions of the engravings adorned

books, prints, maps and charts as recognizable symbols of America for centuries after the Roanoke colony failed. The de Bry engravings, however, take considerable liberties with their source material. The figures of Roanoac and Secotan people retain the poses of the White originals, but are altered to resemble muscular classical figures with European facial features. Their tattoos are rarely accurate and background features are added randomly. For example, the image of the Indian woman and child of the Pomeiooc was altered by de Bry to show a child holding not only an English doll, as in the White version, but also a rattle: both figures are heavily Europeanized, and the woman's tattoos are very different. In the background – blank in the original – details of a different White watercolour showing fishing boats are reproduced to fill an imagined coastal lagoon.

A chief Herowans wife of Pomeoc and her daughter. *John White, 1585-88.*
*British Museum, © Trustees of the British Museum.*

A Cheiff Ladye of Pomeiooc. *Theodor de Bry after John White, 1590.*
*PBE7817, plate 8.*

The reason that White's watercolours and Harriot's account of life in Virginia survived is, somewhat ironically, rooted in the mysterious loss of the Roanoke colony. By the winter of 1588, only months after their arrival, the colonists were starving. Facing many of the same problems as the two parties before them, they elected to send White back to England on a supply mission. White reluctantly agreed, but on arrival in England he discovered that all outbound shipping had been halted, in preparation for conflict with the Spanish Armada. All vessels were requisitioned for national defence and even Ralegh could not persuade the queen to spare a ship for a distant colony. When White finally did make it back to Roanoke Island in 1590, the colony was deserted. There was no sign of a struggle or a hasty departure, but inscribed on a post was the word 'CROATOAN'. White and the colonists had agreed that this would be the sign if they were to move, with a Maltese cross if they left under duress, but there was no cross. He and the supply ships left for Croatoan Island to the south, but encountered dangerous weather that drowned several crew members. They had to abandon the search for the colonists and returned to England.[13]

*Print depicting fishing in Virginia. Theodor de Bry after John White, 1590. PBE7817, plate 13.*

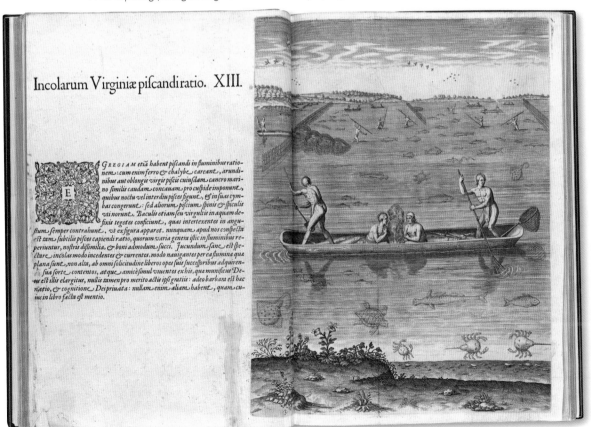

White never again returned to America and no concrete evidence for the fate of the colonists has ever been found. For his part, White believed that his family and the surviving colonists had indeed gone to Croatoan. In his writings he noted that it was Manteo's home, and he hoped that the Croatoan people would have taken in his family.[14] He finally returned to England in 1590 and the century would turn before there was another attempt to colonize America. Elizabeth I died in 1603 and the Tudor dynasty with her. Walter Ralegh fell quickly from favour after her death, and was in the middle of a 13-year imprisonment in the Tower of London when the Virginia Companies of London and Plymouth were founded by James I in 1606. This royal action marked a small but significant return towards a more expansionist foreign policy.

*Sketch of the James Fort, sent in secret to Phillip III of Spain in 1608. Don Pedro de Zúñiga, 1608. © España. Ministerio de Educación, Cultura y Deporte. Archivo General de Simancas. MPD,04,066.*

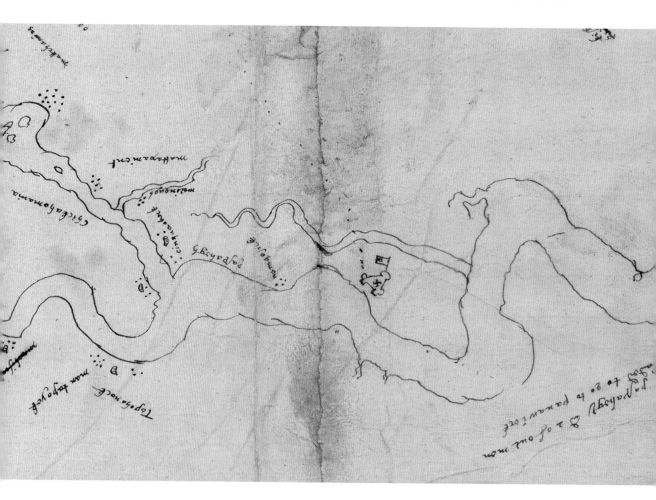

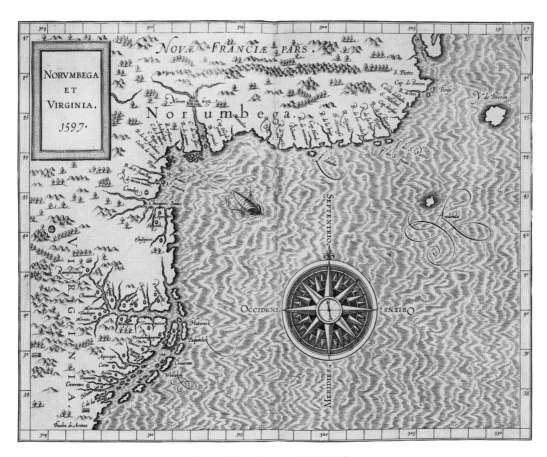

*Map of Norumbega and Virginia from*
Descriptionis Ptolemaicae augmentum sive occidentis notitia. *Cornelius van Wytfliet, c.1597.* PBE9597.

The Plymouth Company was the first to attempt a settlement, Popham Colony, in 1607, but this lasted less than a year before being abandoned. The London Company sent two ships of men, largely soldiers, and they settled on the banks of the James River in the same year, at a site initially known as the James Fort. As at Roanoke, they were instructed to find a spot that could be easily defended against other European powers that were also colonizing the Americas, for English investors remained far more preoccupied with politics in Europe than with the reality of survival in Virginia. These attacks never came, but starvation and illness followed in short order, along with conflicts with local groups who used the land around Jamestown seasonally, and who had encountered dangerous Europeans before. The London Company was explicit in ordering the colonists to establish friendly relations with the Indigenous population, although this proved difficult. Language barriers hampered the settlers' early attempts at diplomacy with their immediate neighbours, the Paspahegh, and sporadic feasts were interspersed with attacks. The Paspahegh were tributaries to the

Map of Virginia, incorporating aspects of de Bry's engravings, 1637. Gerardus Mercator after John Smith. NMM, MacPherson Collection. PBD7674.

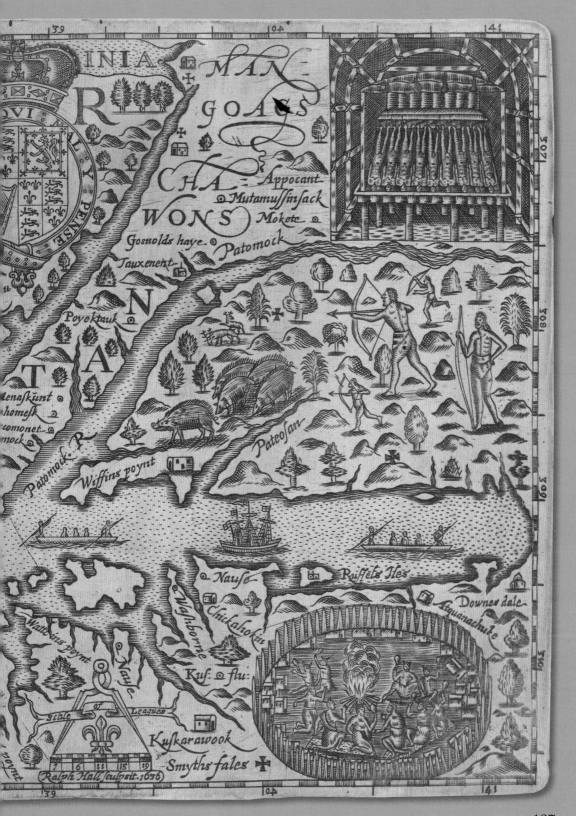

Powhatan Confederacy, a powerful alliance of peoples around the James River and the Chesapeake Bay area, which they called the Tsenacommacah. The paramount chief of the Confederacy, Wahunsenacawh (or Powhatan, the title by which he is often known), was the leader of somewhere between 20,000 and 30,000 Indigenous Americans when the Jamestown colonists arrived, and was a force to be reckoned with.[15] It was only through his intervention that clashes with the Paspahegh ceased.

One of the first Jamestown colonists, John Smith, proved instrumental in the colony's early survival. The son of tenant farmers and a noted military veteran, Smith was not popular with his aristocratic colleagues, but he had the most success in establishing relations with

*Portrait of John Smith, Simon van de Passe, 1616.* PAD2459.

the Powhatan Confederacy. Initially, however, he was taken prisoner when his hunting party was discovered by a Powhatan group led by Opechancanough, the werowance of the Pamunkey and brother of Wahunsenacawh. Smith and his companions were forcibly taken to the town of Werowocomoco, the Powhatan capital. Although no one else of his group survived this skirmish, Smith was able to ingratiate himself with Wahunsenacawh, who was keen to control the English colonists in the same fashion as he controlled the rest of his Confederacy: to the Powhatan, the English were no different from his other tributary nations.

It was at Werowocomoco that Smith first encountered Wahunsenacawh's daughter, Pocahontas. He claimed in later memoirs that she saved his life at this meeting, but this story is widely disputed, not least because she was a small child at that point. Whatever happened, this meeting led to relatively friendly relations between the Powhatan peoples and the colonists for some time, and a thriving trade economy (largely to the advantage of the well-provisioned Powhatan), in which Pocahontas would play an important role as an intermediary between the two peoples.

Years later, Smith wrote about the Indigenous population as a kind and accommodating people with inexhaustible land and resources, and argued for wide-scale settlement of

# Pocahontas (around 1596–1617)

Perhaps the most famous Indigenous American of all time is Pocahontas. The daughter of Wahunsenacawh, the ruler of the Powhatan Confederacy, Pocahontas supposedly saved the life of John Smith by laying her own head over his as he was about to be executed by her father. This story is almost certainly untrue; Smith's accounts are notoriously unreliable and elsewhere he tells the same story about a different princess. Nevertheless, it is one of the myths that has cemented Pocahontas's place in popular imagination.

Pocahontas did serve as an important diplomatic intermediary between the Powhatan and the colonists of Jamestown. During the First Anglo-Powhatan war (1609–14) Pocahontas was captured and held hostage at Jamestown, where she met John Rolfe, an English tobacco planter. They married in 1614, though little is known about the nature of their relationship. Rolfe himself wrote of his love for Pocahontas, but also about the supposed moral transgression of marrying a non-Christian; Pocahontas's experiences bear some of the features of Stockholm syndrome, whereby a kidnapped victim develops feelings of trust or affection for their captor, while Mattaponi oral history holds firm that she was raped in captivity. What is known is that their marriage had political ramifications: the subsequent pause in Anglo-Powhatan hostilities was known as 'The Peace of Pocahontas'.

Pocahontas and Rolfe travelled to England in 1615. Their trip was paid for by the Virginia Company, and had a commercial impetus. Pocahontas was presented to court and society as the 'civilized savage', and like the Indigenous Americans who had come before her, she was used to sell America to risk-averse investors. The couple were due to return to America in March 1617 but she died before the voyage could be made.

*Portrait of Pocahontas, Simon van de Passe, 1616. © Library of Congress.*

their land. Attempting to persuade those who felt uneasy about displacing North America's inhabitants, he wrote:

> *Here in Florida, Virginia, New-England, and Cannada, is more land than all the people in Christendome can manure, and yet more to spare than all the natives of those Countries can use and culturate ... If this be not a reason sufficient to such tender consciences; for a copper kettle and a few toyes, as beads and hatchets, they will sell you a whole Countrey; and for a small matter, their houses and the ground they dwell upon; but those of the Massachusets have resigned theirs freely.*[16]

Smith's writings show an enduring misunderstanding of property and gift exchange in the Americas. It was one that he shared with many of his compatriots and that often led to conflict. Powhatan territory was communal, while private property was an English concept that did not account for seasonal hunting and agricultural movements.[17] This kind of misunderstanding led to many gift-giving transgressions by the English, and to culturally acceptable acts by the Indigenous community being perceived as theft by English standards.[18] This meant that peace was never quite complete and relations remained troubled.

Despite trading with the Powhatan, Jamestown still struggled with a shortage of food and supplies, and relied on regular supply missions from England. The first arrived in January of 1608, bringing some provisions but also more settlers, who put further strain on already stretched resources. When the supply ships left for England, Wahunsenacawh sent Namontack, one of his advisers, with them, instructing him to meet King James and

*ABOVE AND RIGHT Nueva Cádiz beads from Jamestown made in Europe. They were highly prized by Indigenous communities and vital for trade. Seventeenth century. © Jamestown Rediscovery.*

*BELOW Two pipes, the left made by an indigenous American, the right made by a Jamestown colonist. © Jamestown Rediscovery.*

*Medal commemorating the tercentenary of the settlement of Jamestown, showing a bust of Pocahontas, 1907. MEC2295.*

find out all he could about the English. This kind of reconnaissance was a preferred tactic of the Powhatan: Wahunsenacawh was as curious about the 'Old World' as the English were about the 'New'. Namontack returned with the second supply in October 1608, with news of population, climate and aristocratic protocols. There is no record of his meeting the king, but Wahunsenacawh's subsequent knowledge of England, its customs and its people suggests he was successful in gathering intelligence.[19] Jamestown limped on into 1609, but during the summer Smith was badly injured in an explosion and returned to England for treatment. The precarious peace between the English and the Powhatan owed much to Smith's relationship with Wahunsenacawh, and his departure hastened the worsening of relations. Skirmishes progressed into open conflict, and by the winter of 1609, the First Anglo-Powhatan War had begun. One of the most effective Powhatan weapons against the English was hunger. Following a drought, the English did not have sufficient food to feed the increased number of colonists, and the cessation of almost all trade with the Powhatan (who were also suffering crop failures) crippled them. The winter of 1609–10 became known as the 'Starving Time': of around 500 colonists, over 400 died. Archaeological evidence has since suggested that in their desperation, some of the Jamestown colonists turned to cannibalism.[20]

In June 1610, two ships, *Deliverance* and *Patience*, arrived in Jamestown; they already carried a small number of survivors from an earlier supply ship, the *Sea Venture*, which had been driven to Bermuda in a tropical storm and wrecked there, resulting in the establishment of the first sustained settlement there. Finding the survivors of Jamestown in equally dire straits, the decision was made to abandon that colony entirely too and set off for England. However, before they got to the mouth of the James River, they met a large supply mission led by Thomas West, Baron De La Warr. Another severe military veteran, he had been sent to their aid by the Virginia Company, and forced the reluctant colonists to turn around. Had they left earlier and missed De La Warr's arrival, it is quite possible that the Jamestown colony would have failed there and then.

De La Warr imposed martial discipline on both the colony and the Powhatan Confederacy, and, echoing Richard Grenville's tactics from decades previously, demanded that Wahunsenacawh return English prisoners or face total war. Wahunsenacawh declined and countered that if the English did not remain within the walls of Jamestown, he would retreat further inland and abandon them entirely, effectively starving them as the Secotans had done to the colonists at Roanoke. Furious that Wahunsenacawh was negotiating and thereby implying that he considered the two of them equals, De La Warr cut off the hand of a Pasphegh captive in retaliation, and sent him back to Powhatan with another demand for prisoners and a threat of extreme violence against nearby Indigenous towns. Wahunsenacawh did not respond. This led to an English massacre of the Paspahegh – not only of warriors but also of women and children, including the wife and children of the chief, which was considered a severe crime. As a community, the Paspahegh did not survive this attack, and the few who remained alive were assimilated into other Powhatan groups, spreading the word of De La Warr's brutality.[21]

The conflict was relentless, exhausting both the isolated colonists and the Powhatan under the leadership of the ageing Wahunsenacawh. It rose to a peak around 1613, when Pocahontas was kidnapped and her father ordered to pay a ransom for her. Despite his meeting the demands of her captors, she was not returned to him. Eventually she converted to Christianity and married John Rolfe, a rich tobacco planter. The marriage served a diplomatic purpose, with the 'Peace of Pocahontas' beginning in 1614, but this bond between the two peoples was broken by Pocahontas's death, in England, in 1617. Her father died the following year and the Powhatan Confederacy passed into the control of his formidable younger brother, Opechancanough. The peace disintegrated, and relations between the colonists and the Indigenous population never recovered. These early encounters were profoundly significant for both cultures, and left deep and enduring scars.

Tobacco eventually made Jamestown a profitable venture, cementing English commitment to the continent. The *Mayflower* reached the coast of Massachusetts in 1620 with the first group of colonists looking for a new life rather than a business opportunity in North America. They landed in Wampanoag territory and renamed the already thriving local town of Patuxet 'Plymouth'. Within two years, the Patuxet Wampanoag had been wiped out by European diseases. From that point on, numbers of European settlers in North America continued to increase, at great cost to the local inhabitants. America's pre-encounter Indigenous population has been estimated at around 15 million: today it is less than three million.[22]

However, neither this decimation nor England's imperial success was a fait accompli in America. The idea of manifest destiny is a powerful one in the history of the United States, but the Indigenous peoples were politically, tactically and commercially superior to the often-desperate early English colonists at many junctures. Surviving records of early America also reflect a distinctly English point of view, while the lack of written sources in Indigenous societies is still starkly reflected in European museum collections and their interpretation of the past. Although some oral traditions, such as that of the Mattaponi people, have been written down, the imbalance privileges a Eurocentric version of events, which often minimizes, misunderstands or misrepresents Indigenous American histories. But even through such a narrow lens, the stories of travellers like Manteo and Wanchese, leaders like Wahunsenacawh and diplomats like Namontack and Pocahontas demonstrate that the peoples of the North Atlantic coast were active and important players in the early Atlantic world.

*An exaggerated depiction of an attack near Jamestown at the outbreak of the second Anglo-Powhatan war in 1622, from Johann Ludwig Gottfried's* Neue Welt Und Amerikanische Historien, *1655. Prints such as these were used to legitimise European colonial violence in the Americas.* PAG7943.

Ships Trading in the East (detail). Hendrick Cornelisz Vroom, 1614. NMM, Palmer Collection.
Acquired with the assistance of H.M. Treasury, the Caird Fund, the Art Fund, the Pilgrim Trust
and the Society for Nautical Research Macpherson Fund. BHC0727.

# Of Profit and Loss:
# The Trading World of
# Seventeenth-Century England

## Robert J. Blyth

Walter Ralegh, once a favourite of Elizabeth I, was arrested in July 1603 and charged with treason for plotting against her Stuart successor, James I During his long captivity in the Tower of London he wrote extensively, producing, among many other works, *A Discourse of the Invention of Ships...*.[1] In this text, he considered not only the development of ship technology from the building of Noah's Ark, but also the relative maritime strength of leading European powers. Ralegh famously concluded that 'whosoever commands the sea commands the trade; whosoever commands the trade of the world commands the riches of the world, and consequently the world itself'.[2] Such a vision had obvious appeal for an island nation of nascent merchant-adventurers. But compared with its continental rivals, in the first decades of the seventeenth century England's command of the sea and global trade was merely a pipe dream of the imprisoned Ralegh.

Nevertheless, upon his release in 1616, Ralegh seized the opportunity to assert English maritime power. He made immediate plans to sail to the Orinoco River, find the fabled El Dorado and claim its fantastical wealth for England. The scheme gained royal blessing: James I pardoned Ralegh and granted him permission to proceed on his quest for gold and glory. The ensuing expedition was, in every respect, a disaster. El Dorado's location proved frustratingly elusive, while the bloody destruction of Spanish settlements in Guiana not only exceeded Ralegh's orders, but also resulted in his son's death. Moreover, these actions severely strained English relations with Spain and met with James I's disapproval. In the end, Ralegh's men lost faith in the enterprise and they abandoned him in the Caribbean with a single ship crewed by a mutinous company. Humiliated, he limped home in 1618 and was promptly sent back to the Tower. The king, more than happy to comply with pressure from the Spanish ambassador, ordered the adventurer's execution: he was beheaded later that year. As Ralegh's failure helped to show, England's rise to some form of seaborne greatness would be a gradual affair resulting from a series of small, uncertain and largely unremarkable achievements. In other words, an English El Dorado was to be found not in a singular and wondrous discovery at the end of a voyage to Guiana, but as a consequence of decades of risk, disappointment and hard-won gain.

One such incremental change took place at the dawn of the seventeenth century. On 31 December 1600, Elizabeth I signed a new royal charter, granting 'The Governor and Company of Merchants of London Trading into the East Indies' a monopoly on English trade with Asia via the Cape of Good Hope. The East India Company (EIC), as it became known, was established to tap Asia's extraordinary riches, an activity already undertaken with success by continental rivals. Before this venture, England's Asian trade consisted of a series of raiding voyages in the 1590s and the activities of the Levant Company, operating in the eastern Mediterranean. The former did little to advance the country's commercial interests in the Indian Ocean, and the latter could not easily access the wider variety of Asian cargoes promised by the new EIC.

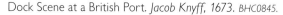

Dock Scene at a British Port. *Jacob Knyff, 1673.* BHC0845.

James Lancaster, an experienced mariner, commanded the first EIC fleet that sailed from Woolwich in February 1601, bound for modern-day Indonesia. He had five ships, procured and fitted out at the extraordinary cost of £40,000; the *Ascension*, the *Hector*, the *Red Dragon* and the *Susan* all made the full round voyage, but the *Gift*, a small victualling tender, was abandoned on the outward leg. The purpose of Lancaster's mission was twofold: first, to acquire lucrative commodities, principally pepper, for sale on the London market; and second, to establish a commercial network in the East Indies that would form the basis of the EIC's future business. The voyage out was long and arduous. Contrary winds meant the fleet took more than two months to leave English waters. Lancaster's ships were then becalmed in the Doldrums and did not reach Table Bay at the southern tip of Africa until September. During this first leg, at least 107 of the 480–500 crew who left England were lost, principally to scurvy, the deadly curse of long-distance voyages. (Lancaster's own ship,

Sir James Lancaster, 1554/5–1618. *English School, 1596.*
*BHC2828.*

the *Red Dragon*, suffered fewer deaths thanks in part to the regular doses of lemon juice given to his crew.) After extended stays in Madagascar and the Nicobar Islands, where refreshment and new stocks of fruit were sought, the plucky fleet sailed for Sumatra to begin trading. The ships finally anchored off Aceh in the north of the island on 5 June 1602.

Having taken 16 months to reach their destination, what did the English have to offer the wily traders of cosmopolitan Aceh? The answer was very little. Lancaster's cargo largely consisted of England's main export commodity, heavy woollen broadcloth – popular in the chilly and wind-lashed climes of northern Europe, but hardly a viable staple in the steamy heat of tropical Sumatra. Consequently, pepper was bought with silver rather than exchanged for English products, although Lancaster's trading efforts were helped by the Asian goods he had plundered from a Portuguese ship. The *Ascension* and the *Susan* were sent back to London laden with pepper. Lancaster sailed on to Bantam in Java, where trade proved easier thanks to much more plentiful spice stocks. It was here that men were left to establish an EIC presence, thereby providing a rendezvous for subsequent English fleets. With his work complete,

147

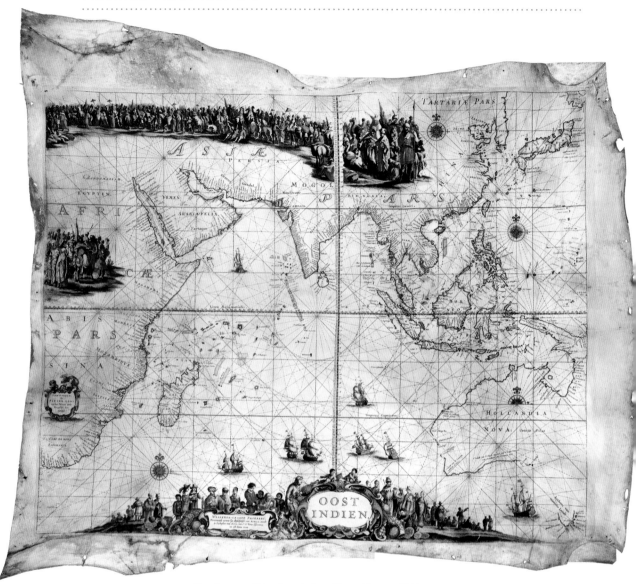

*Dutch map of the East Indies. Pieter Goos, c.1666. G250:1/2.*

Lancaster set off for home on 20 February 1603, arriving back in London that September. Upon returning, he thanked God for his safe delivery from the 'infinite perils and dangers in this long and tedious navigation':[3] more than 60 per cent of the crew had died. Despite all the challenges and difficulties, the EIC's first trading voyage showed the commercial potential of the East Indies. But it also emphatically demonstrated the need to diversify the returning cargo: the sudden arrival of more than a million pounds (nearly half a million kilograms) of pepper swamped the market and depressed prices for several years. Later voyages called at the Spice Islands, India and as far away as China and Japan in an effort to access more profitable produce.[4]

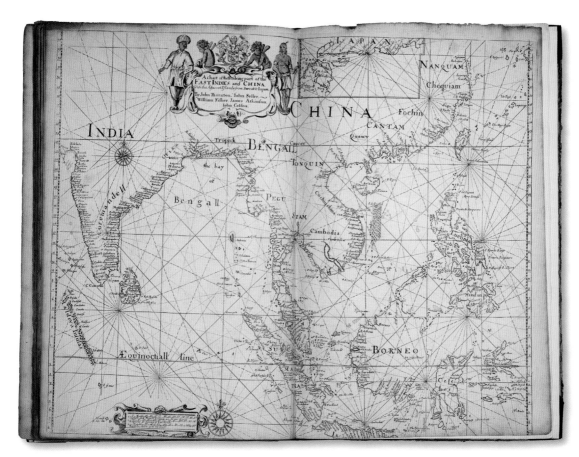

*A chart of the East Indies and China.*
*John Seller, John Thornton, William Fisher, James Atkinson and John Colson, 1677. PBE6858(11).*

Almost from the very start, however, the EIC faced stiff competition from its larger, better-organized and more securely funded Dutch rival, the Vereenigde Oost-Indische Compagnie (VOC). The VOC employed aggressive tactics to protect and expand its trading interests in Asia. In 1623, for example, ten EIC employees were beheaded by the Dutch at Ambon Island in what became known as the 'Amboina massacre'. Yet despite this sustained pressure, the English continued their activities in the Indonesian archipelago. Nevertheless, by the late seventeenth century, the Dutch position had strengthened still further, forcing the closure of the English trading establishment, or factory, at Bantam in 1682. While this was a setback of sorts, the EIC was now more firmly established in India. Its ships first called there in 1606, and factories were set up at Masulipatam on the east coast in 1611 and at Surat on the west coast in 1613. England's position in India was enhanced as a result of Charles II's marriage to the Portuguese infanta, Catherine of Braganza, in 1662. As part of Catherine's dowry, Charles received the port of Bombay. It was transferred to the EIC in 1668 and became an important

Portrait of
an East India
Company Captain.
*English School,
c.1690.
NMM, Caird
Collection.
BHC3126.*

# Jahangir

Jahangir was the fourth Mughal emperor, coming to the Indian throne in 1605. He expanded the borders of his father's empire, bringing more of India under Mughal control and living up to his name, which translates as 'conqueror of the world'. But Jahangir was not simply a warrior-king – he was also a highly cultured man, greatly interested in art, architecture and the natural world. When, for example, Sir Thomas Roe presented him with a portrait miniature, he had five copies produced to demonstrate the skills of Indian artists. Jahangir then challenged Roe to identify the original among the copies – and the ambassador had to admit defeat, to the emperor's delight. Other gifts, presented each year on the annual arrival of the East India Company's fleet, stimulated Jahangir's curiosity and kept him favourably disposed towards England. He certainly appreciated the English coach presented by Roe, commissioning two others from Indian craftsmen for his use.

base of operations, eventually eclipsing Surat. The East India Company also acquired the island of St Helena in the mid-Atlantic, which became an important port of call for ships on the long homebound voyage, providing water and other essential supplies.

From its posts in India, the EIC worked closely with local merchants, officials and rulers. This diplomacy was essential to securing long-term access to Indian goods. In 1615, Sir Thomas Roe was sent to India as the first English ambassador to the Mughal court. At Agra, he obtained a firman, or edict, from the emperor, Mirza Nur-ud-din Beig Mohammad Khan Salim (known as Jahangir, Persian for 'conqueror of the world'), granting the EIC a right to trade. Roe's success was a vital step towards opening avenues to the new commodities offered by the subcontinent. Of primary interest were light, colourful textiles, such as calico and chintz. These 'exotic' fabrics, both fine and washable, delighted English consumers, shaped fashion and sparked a voracious demand for Indian goods that soon provided the profitable core of the EIC's business. Tapping into this trade led to further minor territorial acquisitions in India, including the purchase in 1639 of a small strip on the east coast that became the fortified enclave of Madras and the principal port for the EIC's trade in Coromandel calicos. From Madras, English merchants ventured north to Bengal, accessing another vast textile-producing region, specializing in cottons and silks. Here, in 1690, the EIC alighted on Calcutta as the site for another new fort, settlement and entrepôt. Although textiles dominated the Company's imports in the second half of the seventeenth century, they were also used to barter for other commodities in Asia, such as spices. It extended its range of products further, especially through the gradual reopening of trade with China at the end of the period and by purchasing Chinese goods in other Asian centres. The arrival of tea, and with it blue-and-white porcelain, created a chinoiserie craze that fuelled the next phase of the EIC's development in the eighteenth century.

# Sir Thomas Roe

Sir Thomas Roe was intimately connected to England's expanding overseas commerce, being an investor in the Virginia Company and the commander of an expedition looking for riches in South America. He was, therefore, an ideal choice as England's first ambassador to the Mughal court. When he arrived at Surat in western India on 18 September 1615, Roe learnt of a troubling agreement between Portugal and the Mughal Empire. As part of this deal, England was to be excluded from India. The new ambassador's relationship with the emperor, Jahangir, was now critical. Fortunately, despite the barrier of language, the two men took to each other when they met at Ajmer in Rajasthan. Careful diplomacy gave the East India Company the access to India it desired. Sailing for England in 1619, Roe commanded the ship himself. His efforts in India won him the favour of the EIC and a £1,500 bonus.

Ships Trading in the East. *Hendrick Cornelisz Vroom, 1614.*
*NMM, Palmer Collection. Acquired with the assistance of H.M. Treasury, the Caird Fund, the Art Fund,*
*the Pilgrim Trust and the Society for Nautical Research Macpherson Fund. BHC0727.*

The EIC helped to transform English consumer habits and the marketplace. Essentially
a wholesale importer, it auctioned commodities at regular sales in London to merchants,
who then sold them on at a profit, spreading Asian goods across the country. Importing in
bulk produced economies of scale. As the price of, say, spices and cotton textiles fell, they
ceased to be expensive luxuries affordable only to a small, wealthy elite and became, instead,
commonplace essentials within the reach of an ever-expanding section of society. As a result,
demand boomed and volumes increased. The EIC also responded rapidly to prevailing fashions,
adjusting its orders from Indian textile producers, for example, to ensure that fabrics sold
in London were of the right colour, pattern and quality for English customers. The arrival
of spectacular quantities of such commodities in London was noted by the diarist and naval
administrator Samuel Pepys. During the Second Anglo-Dutch War of 1665–67, he was taken on
board a captured Dutch ship moored in the Thames off Erith. He recorded the captivating sight
before him in the ship's hold: 'the greatest wealth lie in confusion that a man can see in the
world – pepper scatter[ed] through every chink, you trod upon it; and in cloves and nutmegs,
I walked above the knees – whole rooms full – and silk in bales ... [It] was as noble a sight as
ever I saw in my life.'[5] Exotic Asian goods were available in England as never before.

As the EIC grew, it became more important to the wider English economy. Customs duties on Asian imports helped government finances, and the EIC's need to hire ships, secure capital and arrange insurance all boosted the City of London and many trades across the country. The success of this commercial juggernaut was, in large part, dependent on maintaining its monopoly status. Major interlopers (merchants operating in defiance of the EIC's charter) were relatively rare because of the risks, distances and expenses involved in Asian trade. However, during the deregulations of the English Civil War, private traders proliferated, and in 1698, a new company was established with royal support. This rival threatened to undermine nearly a century of activity, but after a short period of fractious coexistence the two merged, creating the United East India Company in 1709. With its domestic arrangements now finally resolved on a surer footing, both politically and financially, the EIC expanded rapidly in the eighteenth century, becoming a significant territorial and military power in Asia as well as a major global commercial enterprise.[6]

The trading monopoly provided by the East India Company's royal charter safeguarded its business interests in Asia, but circumstances were rather different for those seeking similar

Two Views of an East Indiaman of the Time of King William III. *Isaac Sailmaker, c.1685.* BHC1676.

*Teapot. Late seventeenth century. AAA6188.*

success in the Atlantic world. Shorter voyage times and lower capital outlays made the Atlantic a much more open commercial arena than the Indian Ocean, meaning that various trading companies faced far greater competition from interlopers. While the prospect of individual or collective gain might override a chartered company's monopoly, English trade was subject to other forms of regulation. From the mid-seventeenth century, the activities of merchant ships were controlled by the Navigation Acts, a series of legislative attempts to bolster England's trading advantage by denying opportunities to rival powers. Essentially the acts required that English trade be carried in English ships, or 'bottoms', with a majority English crew. England's colonies were to trade directly only with each other and with the mother country, meaning that exports to foreign markets were directed from English home ports. But over time the legislation restricted the access of colonial merchants to potentially profitable export markets, often on their doorstep, and to cheaper and more plentiful imports. As a result, contraband trading became a significant problem for the English authorities and a convenient outlet for colonial enterprise. Nevertheless, the acts certainly prevented the Dutch from carrying significant quantities of English goods and provided a major boost to English merchant shipping and shipbuilding. They were not fully repealed until 1849.

The growth of transatlantic trade was largely bound up with the development of English colonies in the Americas. Following a series of earlier failures, outlined in Chapter 6, England began to establish permanent settlements along the eastern seaboard of North America in the first decades of the seventeenth century. These fledgling outposts were almost wholly reliant on goods from home, including foodstuffs, agricultural equipment and even basic building materials. In times of need, additional assistance was received, or often forcibly taken, from Indigenous Americans, underlining the precarious existence of the early colonies. Further south, England joined the ferocious competition among the European powers for islands in the Caribbean. The settlement of Bermuda began in 1612, providing an Atlantic bridgehead for additional territorial acquisition. Barbados and other islands followed, including, most significantly, Jamaica, which was seized from Spain in 1655.

With labour in short supply and vast swathes of land to be cleared for settlement and farming, it took time to realize the full commercial value of the North American colonies. In this respect, the embryonic colonies were regarded as 'plantations', with the settlers as saplings putting down roots in a new land. Like any newly planted forest, it would take

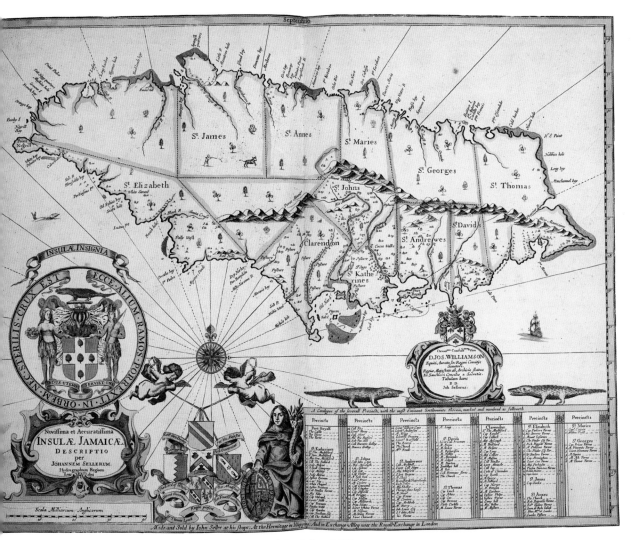

*Map of Jamaica. John Seller, 1675.* PBE6862(26).

a colony several generations to reach maturity and play its part in English enterprise. Unsurprisingly, commerce was dominated by exploitation of the continent's natural resources – through forestry, fur trapping, fishing and whaling – and trading with Indigenous Americans. Initially, agriculture was purely an essential means of survival, but cash crops quickly followed. In Virginia, for example, tobacco became a major export commodity. John Rolfe, a Jamestown colonist, reaped his first harvest of 'brown gold' as early as 1612 and sizeable plantations grew up around Chesapeake Bay to meet growing demand. Annual Virginian exports eventually rose to more than 30 million pounds (13.6 million kilograms) by the end of the century: the saplings were bearing fruit.[7]

155

By contrast, in the forests and wildernesses beyond the Great Lakes, England and France competed for land and the profitable trade in furs. To spearhead the English push to the north, the Hudson's Bay Company (HBC) was founded in 1670 by a group of courtiers and financiers headed by Charles II's cousin, Prince Rupert. As elsewhere, the company received a royal charter, which granted it a trading monopoly over the geographical basin that drained into Hudson Bay. Named Rupert's Land, this vast territory formed much of modern-day Canada and checked French ambitions in the region. The company operated from remote outposts, its trappers hunting beaver and other animals, while agents forged trading links with Indigenous

*Map of the Atlantic Ocean from the* Atlas Maritimus. *John Seller, c.1675.* PBE6862(22).

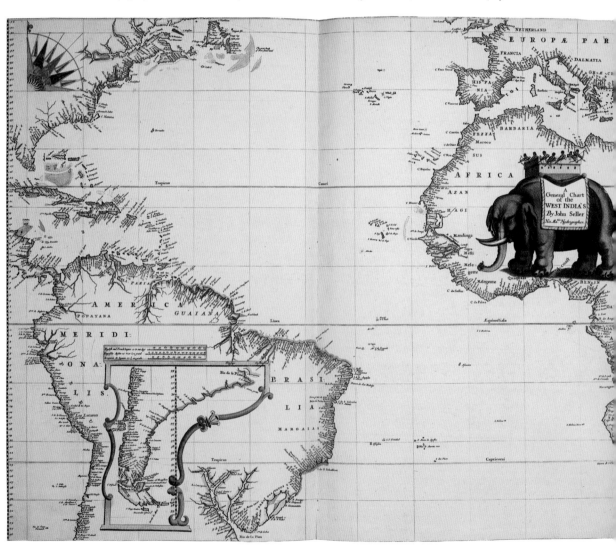

Americans, exchanging goods (most famously woollen blankets) for yet more pelts. In Europe, beaver fur was felted and used in hat making: demand was enormous. Through the HBC large tracts of land were opened up to gradual European settlement as trappers and traders expanded their operations. However, unlike the other great trading companies of the period, the HBC still survives, having diversified its interests away from fur and into a multifaceted retail empire that continues today.

Trade with the Caribbean was closely bound up with Africa. In 1660, Charles II signed a royal charter granting the Company of Royal Adventurers Trading with Africa (later reorganized as the Royal African Company) a thousand-year monopoly over English trade with West Africa. Headed by the king's younger brother, James, Duke of York, the company's merchants initially sought to exploit the region's gold deposits. From 1663, this was used to produce gold coins bearing an elephant, the company's symbol: these were the origin of the 'guinea' in English currency. But gold was only one component of its activities, which were centred on a series of forts along the West African coast, each leased from local rulers. There

Views of Forts and Castles along the Gold Coast, West Africa. *Jan Kip, 1707.* PAH2826.

was also a trade in ivory, tropical woods and other commodities, as well as intense competition from Dutch merchants. In addition, the company became involved in the transatlantic slave trade. By the 1680s, it regularly transported 5,000 Africans a year to the Americas to meet some of the seemingly insatiable demand for plantation labour. Unlike the situation concerning trade with the East Indies, successful interlopers abounded and in the second half of the seventeenth century England began to emerge as a major slave-trading power, with private traders far outstripping the Royal African Company. The monopoly, which proved impossible to enforce, was formally ended in 1698. As a result, the number of slaving voyages increased significantly, presaging the near-industrial scale of trade in the mid-to-late eighteenth century. While this horrific level of activity was still in the future, the dreadful conditions on board slave ships and the inhuman cruelty of plantation servitude were already a grim reality for the growing African population of the Americas.

The appalling rise of the slave trade was driven by the demand for colonial produce, especially sugar and, to a lesser extent, tobacco. The acquisition of island colonies in the Caribbean provided the ideal location for sugar plantations. However, clearing the land for cultivation and then tending and harvesting the crop required considerable labour. This could not be met by the limited supply of indentured workers from the British Isles, who were typically bound to their master for seven years before gaining freedom. As the consumption of sugar grew and profits rose, more land was brought into production and thus the need for labour soared. This shortage required the ever-increasing forced migration of Africans. In 1660, for example, the European population of Jamaica was about 3,000 and the African population only around 500, but by 1713, these figures were 7,000 and 55,000 respectively. The expansion of the African population was the direct result of the sugar boom that would continue through the eighteenth century, but this huge growth masked the grisly truth of high plantation mortality rates. A combination of hard physical labour and malnutrition, together with the violence associated with resistance and repression, meant that the colonies needed to import thousands of Africans every year simply to maintain populations. Moreover, the rapid colonization of Caribbean islands also placed the indigenous inhabitants under considerable strain. Already ravaged by western diseases, islanders were displaced from land turned over to plantations and were then subjected to sustained and systematic assaults from European settlers, who sought to purge the new colonies of their local habitants. The human toll of England's sweet tooth was shocking and shameful. The profits from Caribbean trade made many Englishmen wealthier and a few became fabulously rich. This financial gain, large and small, was built on the bones of countless enslaved Africans, whose loss amid the brutal, unremitting toil was conveniently obscured by the dazzling growth of the empire's balance sheet.

The major long-distance English trading networks in the North Atlantic and the Indian Ocean were not separate complexes, but interconnected systems. As the seventeenth century progressed, more goods, people and capital moved around the globe to advance England's

East India Company Ships at Deptford. *English School, c.1683. NMM, Caird Collection.* BHC1873.

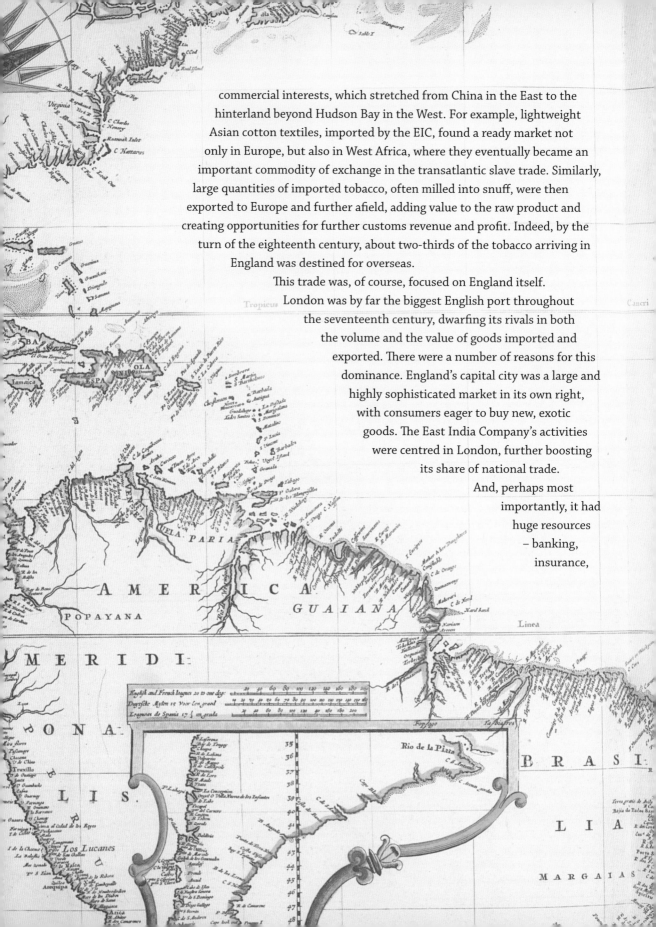

commercial interests, which stretched from China in the East to the hinterland beyond Hudson Bay in the West. For example, lightweight Asian cotton textiles, imported by the EIC, found a ready market not only in Europe, but also in West Africa, where they eventually became an important commodity of exchange in the transatlantic slave trade. Similarly, large quantities of imported tobacco, often milled into snuff, were then exported to Europe and further afield, adding value to the raw product and creating opportunities for further customs revenue and profit. Indeed, by the turn of the eighteenth century, about two-thirds of the tobacco arriving in England was destined for overseas.

This trade was, of course, focused on England itself. London was by far the biggest English port throughout the seventeenth century, dwarfing its rivals in both the volume and the value of goods imported and exported. There were a number of reasons for this dominance. England's capital city was a large and highly sophisticated market in its own right, with consumers eager to buy new, exotic goods. The East India Company's activities were centred in London, further boosting its share of national trade. And, perhaps most importantly, it had huge resources – banking, insurance, ship brokering and warehousing, among others – making the city attractive to other commercial concerns. However, the growth of Atlantic trade did give a certain geographical advantage to west-coast ports in terms of voyage lengths. By the middle of the century, Bristol, for example, was second only to London in the scale of its trade; and West Country merchants seized the opportunities presented by colonial imports, the Newfoundland fisheries and the slave trade.[8]

While trade with the rest of the world increased in volume and relative importance, European commerce continued to dominate. Throughout the period, England's medieval staple of woollen cloth was its key export commodity and northern Europe remained its most important market. In 1714, as the Georgian era began, Britain's import and export trade with Europe was worth nearly three times as much as its combined trade with the rest of the world. But the trend was emphatically upward for transoceanic trade in the eighteenth century: by 1800, nearly

*Coat of Arms of the South Sea Company. Robert Jones, 1711–12. HRA0043.*

half of British exports were bound for non-European markets, and the wider world produced almost two-thirds of Britain's imports.[9] Ultimately, though, trade was a matter of profit and loss. Risks were manifold. Ships, cargoes and crew might be lost at sea, victims of weather, accident or war. Commodity prices could shift during a voyage, bringing unexpected fortune or unwelcome ruin. Overall, the English gained from trade, but further afield this commerce had negative effects. In the Americas, production relied heavily on enslaved labour and the dispossession of indigenous populations. In Asia, the growing power of the EIC began to move the terms of trade in England's favour, allowing the greater exploitation of local producers that would be the hallmark of its dominion over parts of the Indian subcontinent in the years to come. In the final analysis, the commercial impact of long-distance trade remained limited in the seventeenth century, but it did provide the necessary foundation for eighteenth-century expansion. Nevertheless, it certainly fired the imagination: England and its merchants were beginning to think and act globally.

Portrait of a Royalist. *William Dobson, c.1643. NMM, Caird Fund.* BHC3133.

# The British Civil Wars, 1638–53

## Elaine Murphy

The civil wars of the 1640s were, together, one of the most divisive and destructive conflicts in British history. Approximately 7 per cent of the population of the British Isles died, amounting to 3 per cent of the population in England, 6 per cent of the Scottish people, and an extraordinary 15–20 per cent in Ireland.[1] This devastation occurred mostly on land, and so our collective memory of the wars that engulfed Charles I's kingdoms remains fixed on the terrestrial campaigns that ravaged the British Isles. In particular, the mind turns to popular visions of dashing, mounted Cavaliers facing off against the severe Roundhead troops of Oliver Cromwell. As a result, the role of naval affairs in the outbreak, course and outcome of the war has been neglected. This chapter will demonstrate that we should not overlook the events that took place at sea between 1638 and 1653. Not only did the sea play a crucial part in deciding the outcome of this wide-ranging conflict, but the developments that occurred during the civil wars made an important contribution to the emergence of Britain as a powerful maritime nation.

From the outset, maritime issues were to play a significant role in the breakdown in relations between Charles I and his subjects. The king's interventions in conflicts in Europe led to a series of ill-conceived and costly amphibious operations in the late 1620s. Seaborne expeditions to aid the besieged Huguenots at La Rochelle in 1627 and 1628, for example, ended in failure and the assassination of George Villiers, Duke of Buckingham, who was at the time the Lord High Admiral and the king's favourite. Paying for these campaigns also caused increased hostility between Charles and the House of Commons, which resulted in the king dissolving Parliament in 1629. Peace with France in the same year and with Spain in 1630 enabled Charles to rule for the next 11 years without recourse to Parliament, in a period known as the 'Personal Rule'. In order to raise revenue during this period, the king resorted to a series of financial expedients, the most infamous of which was 'Ship Money'. This was a traditional levy on maritime communities to pay for ships in a time of emergency, but from 1634 onwards Ship Money was levied each year, and eventually expanded to include inland counties. As a means of funding the navy, building new ships and setting out a strong

Portrait of Oliver Cromwell
(1599–1658), British general
and statesman. *Samuel Cooper,
date unknown. DEA Picture Library,
Getty Images. 163239501.*

naval guard each year, Ship Money was successful: ships such as the *Sovereign of the Seas*, the *Henrietta Maria* and the *James* were built in this period. However, the high-handed manner in which it was assessed and collected alienated many.

The king's questionable financial policies, combined with his unpopular political and religious reforms, pushed his subjects towards rebellion in the late 1630s. Religion provided the spark that led to open warfare. In 1637 discontent with the king's attempts to impose religious uniformity and a new English-style prayer book on the Presbyterian Scots led to rioting in Edinburgh. In January 1638 the Scots drew up a National Covenant that called for the withdrawal of the prayer book. Rather than appease his Scottish subjects, Charles prepared to wage war against them, writing in June 1638 that he intended 'not to yield to the demands of those traitors'.[2] The king's plans to subdue the Scots in the First Bishops' War contained a strong maritime element – he planned to use his navy to transport soldiers from Ireland and England to fight for him in Scotland – but in the end Charles's naval superiority counted for little. After a series of humiliating minor defeats on land, Charles signed the Treaty of Berwick, which ended the war, on 18 June 1639. Instead of pacifying his Scottish subjects, the king began to plan a second campaign to reduce them to obedience. In order to fund his army for

Charles I, 1600–49 King of Great Britain and Ireland. *Studio of Daniel Mytens the Elder, c.1631. NMM, Caird Collection.* BHC2606.

the Second Bishops' War against the Scots, he was forced to recall Parliament in April 1640 to seek taxation. Following 11 years of Personal Rule, the 'Short Parliament' was reluctant to grant Charles the revenue he needed and he dissolved it in May. The navy could do little to help the king's cause, and the Scottish army defeated his forces and occupied Newcastle in August. Following this defeat, Charles had little option but to call a second parliament, known as the 'Long Parliament', in November 1640. Over the following months tensions between the king and Parliament remained high.

The situation came to a head in October 1641 with the outbreak and spread of a bloody rebellion in Ireland brought about by long-term religious, political and economic grievances. The Irish rebels gained control of most of the country, including key port towns such as Wexford and Waterford. In the summer of 1642 the insurgents established their own government, the Confederate Association, with its capital in Kilkenny. Issues relating to command and control of the military, as well as the naval forces being prepared to suppress the rebels in Ireland, led to an escalation of tensions between the king and Parliament. Many seamen were discontented with Charles due to their pay arrears and his political dealings with the Scots, and Parliament flouted the king's authority by ignoring his selections for naval

*Commonwealth Standard, 1652–54.* AAA0800.

commanders, appointing the popular Robert Rich, second Earl of Warwick, as seagoing admiral in place of Sir John Pennington. Attempts by Charles to reassert control and remove Warwick proved futile. In July, the majority of the seamen and officers of the fleet chose to obey Warwick rather than the king. This secured control of the navy for Parliament even before the formal outbreak of war in England, when the king raised his Royal Standard at Nottingham in August. The Earl of Clarendon later described the defection of the navy to Parliament as an act of 'unspeakable ill consequence to the King's affairs'.[3]

For much of the 1640s three distinct naval forces operated in the seas around the British Isles: Confederate, Parliamentarian and Royalist. Parliamentarian control of the navy meant that the Confederates and Royalists turned to private enterprise to fight for their cause. In Ireland the Confederates established their own admiralty and appointed Donough MacCarthy, Viscount Muskerry, as Lord High Admiral. Irish agents in Flanders and France issued letters of marque to captains and shipowners who were willing to set out private men-of-war to operate from Irish harbours. In turn, merchants, nobles and clergymen invested in privateers to fight for the Confederate cause. Randal MacDonnell, the Marquis of Antrim, owned four frigates, while Antonio Vanderkipp, a Flanders merchant, supplied arms and deployed two vessels for the Confederates. Most ships were owned by syndicates, such as the *Mary and John* of Wexford, set out by a group of five merchants from that town. From surviving records, at least 84 named Confederate warships can be identified over the course of the war. These ships ranged in size, and some Confederate supporters invested in specially designed warships, known as 'Dunkirk frigates', among the most advanced warships of the period. They sat low in the water and were heavily manned and armed to overwhelm merchantmen or escape quickly if they encountered a superior enemy man-of-war. The *Paul* of Dunkirk used its speed to flee when two Parliamentarian warships pursued it in 1645.

These privateers were certainly threatening. In July 1642 two frigates, *St Peter* and *St Francis*, arrived on the Irish seaboard from Dunkirk and reportedly caused the English to 'quake for dread of them'.[4] Over the course of the war Confederate privateers captured in excess of 450 known prizes and probably seized many more. One contemporary estimate put the figure at 1,900. The sale of captured merchantmen and their cargoes, such as the *Adventure* of London, which was seized in 1643 and valued at £14,000, provided considerable

# Henrietta Maria

Henrietta Maria was born in Paris in November 1609, the youngest daughter of the French king, Henri IV. May 1625 she married the English king, Charles I, and they developed a close and affectionate relationship; in 1633 the *Henrietta Maria*, named in her honour, was launched. The new queen's first voyage – across the English Channel to meet her new husband – was hardly auspicious as she was quite seasick. However, she subsequently grew accustomed to seafaring. During the civil wars she made a number of hazardous voyages to and from Europe to aid the Royalist cause, not least that of 1643, when she sailed with Parliamentary forces in close pursuit. She remained in France for the remainder of the war, never to see her husband again. Despite the dangers she faced at sea during the 1640s, Henrietta Maria made a number of voyages between France and England following the restoration of the monarchy. She died in France in September 1669.

Queen Henrietta Maria, 1609–69.
*Studio of Sir Anthony van Dyck, c.1638.*
*NMM, Caird Collection.* BHC2761.

financial assistance to the Confederate cause. Parliamentarian supporters in England decried their losses, with John Pine of Weymouth complaining that 'the cellars and storehouses of Waterford are full of Englishmen's goods'.[5] Confederate frigates terrorized English ports and merchant shipping, with reports from places like Ipswich complaining that 'there is great lamentation in this Town, for the loss of many Ships taken by those pilfering vessels call'd Irish Frigots'.[6] Most of the known sailors on Confederate men-of-war came from Ireland, but there is also evidence of men being recruited from England, France, Flanders and the Dutch Republic. The crew of 109 on the *Mary* of Antrim included mariners from Ireland, Dunkirk, Holland and England. Antonio Vandermarche, the captain of the *Mary*, came from Flanders, and James Gott, the lieutenant, from Waterford.[7]

By autumn 1642, with the bulk of the navy committed to Parliament, Charles and his supporters adopted a variety of measures to create a 'substitute navy' to harass the Parliamentarians at sea. Charles even sent his wife, Henrietta Maria, to the Netherlands in 1642 to raise funds to purchase munitions. The dangers posed by storms and the Parliamentarian navy made the queen understandably apprehensive about her return voyage, and she wrote to Charles that 'I dread the sea so much, that the very thought of it frightens me'. Her fears proved well-founded when in February 1643 she barely evaded a pursuing Parliamentarian squadron. After Henrietta Maria's ship landed and the arms were unloaded at Bridlington, the Parliamentarian ships opened fire on the house in which the queen was spending the night, forcing her to flee from her bed.[8] During the war the Royalists nevertheless managed to acquire a considerable naval force. The capture of towns such as Dartmouth, Falmouth and Bristol in 1643 saw the seizure of many ships, greatly adding to the king's naval strength. Sir John Pennington captured 40 ships at Dartmouth, and by early 1644, reports claimed that the king could deploy 260 ships. The Venetian Secretary in England, Gerolamo Agostini, wrote that the Royalist fleet 'is now more numerous than that of Warwick'.[9] In reality, the comparison was illusory, as most of the captured ships were merchantmen and of little military use against the mighty Parliamentarian warships.

Charles also bought or hired ships to fight against his enemies, many of which were sourced from the continent. He also licensed his supporters to set out private men-of-war against Parliament. In 1645 he issued commissions to Sir Nicholas Crispe and John van Haesdonck, the latter a Flemish merchant based in England. Crispe sent out between 10 and 25 ships, and 11 vessels served under Haesdonck. Details about the service of these ships are sketchy but some were clearly substantial and active men-of-war, such as a 22-gun frigate commanded by Captain Bowden. Charles also tried to persuade Parliamentarian sailors to change their allegiance, issuing a proclamation in 1643 that promised pardons and arrears of pay to those who switched sides. Some mariners and their ships did defect to the king, such as the *Tenth Whelp* in 1643, but attempts by others to join the Royalist cause ended in failure or proved to be short-lived. The crew of the *Providence* discovered the plot by Captain Brook to change sides and promptly 'clapped their captain under deck'.[10] Holding on to his own seamen proved as much of a problem for Charles. Many sailors abandoned the king's service because of poor

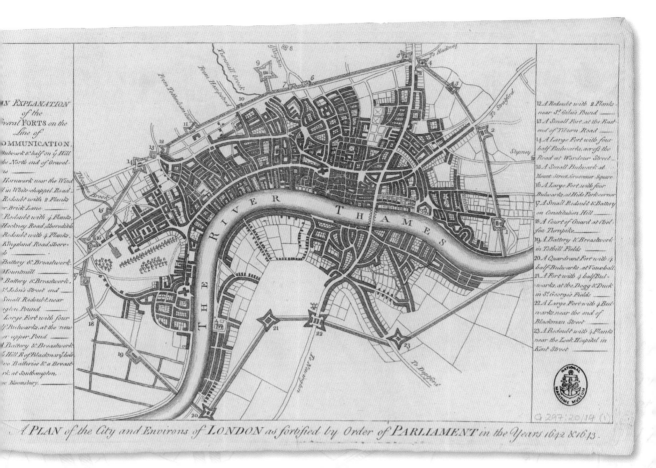

A plan of the city and environs of London as fortified by order of
Parliament in the years 1642 and 1643. c.1643. G297:20/14(1).

pay and conditions: in 1645, for example, the crew of the *Swan* surrendered without a fight
and agreed to serve Parliament, since they had been unpaid for so long.

Indeed, inheriting the naval administration that oversaw sailors' pay and rations was one
of many advantages enjoyed by Parliament at the start of the conflict. It had secured the bulk
of the naval fleet, while its control of London gave it access to the financial machinery that
underlay naval strength. Throughout the conflict, the House of Commons was able to approve
strong squadrons of men-of-war and armed merchantmen to put to sea each summer and
winter: between 1642 and 1648, the number of active parliamentary warships never fell below
29, and was sometimes as high as 65. It quickly became clear that massive 'prestige' vessels
such as the *Sovereign of the Seas* were largely redundant for the patrolling and small-scale
fighting that became the core day-to-day activities of Parliamentarian men-of-war. Parliament
was able to hire a number of 'private' armed merchantmen, and granted licences to privateers:

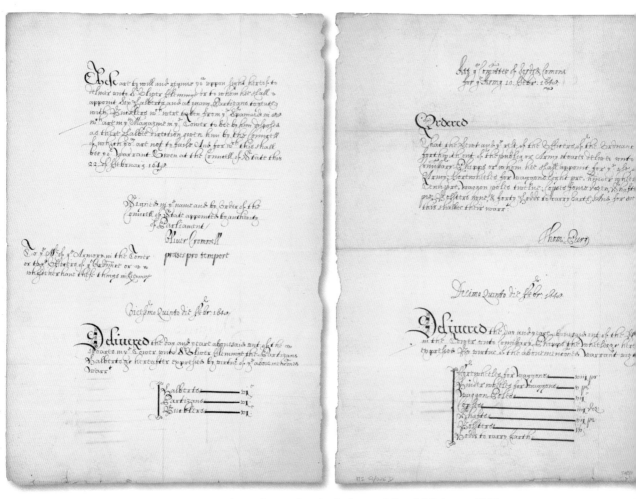

*Copy of order issued by Oliver Cromwell to the Ordnance Office, 22 February 1648. ADL/H/10.*

at least 156 ships received letters of marque (licences to privateer) during the war. It was also able to embark on a new shipbuilding programme that began to deliver smaller, faster frigates. They quickly proved their worth, with three of the new vessels – the *Adventure*, the *Assurance* and the *Nonsuch* – seizing 14 prizes on the Irish seaboard in their first year of service. Parliament's final advantage was its greater ability to draw from the large pool of experienced officers and men from the wider maritime community, especially in London, to command its ships and administer naval affairs. Many of those who rose to prominence as admirals and officials were veterans of the merchant service or of privateering expeditions, including the Earl of Warwick (appointed to the position of Lord High Admiral in December 1643), William Batten, Richard Swanley, Robert Moulton, Richard Cranley and Squire Bence.[11]

At first glance, with no major battles taking place in the waters around the British Isles, it may seem as if little fighting took place at sea during the 1640s. In reality, the naval theatre

*Painting of the* Fairfax, *the* Assurance, *the* Tiger *and the* Elizabeth.
*Attributed to Isaac Sailmaker, c.1680. NMM, Caird Collection.* BHC3334.

of the war was very active and at times extremely bloody, with hostilities continuing at sea even after the end of the First English Civil War and the king's surrender to the Scots in 1646. Many of the most important sieges during the conflict were of coastal towns, with naval involvement. Parliamentarian squadrons deployed considerable resources to transport fresh supplies and soldiers to strategic outposts by sea, support that proved vital for key

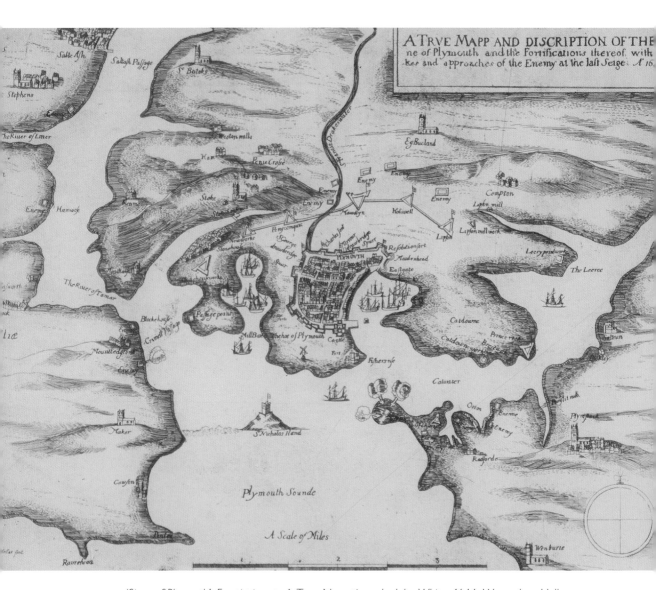

*'Siege of Plymouth'. Frontispiece to* A True Narrative... *by John White, 1644. Wenceslaus Hollar. Royal Collection Trust/© Her Majesty Queen Elizabeth II, 2017.*

Parliamentarian garrisons at Hull, Lyme, Pembroke, Plymouth and Youghal. Captain Thomas Rainborowe led mariners from the *Lion* in an attack that drove the Royalists from their entrenchments at Hull in 1643.[12] Enabling these places to withstand Confederate and Royalist attacks often gave the Parliamentarians a foothold in areas dominated by their enemies, and this helped to tie the enemy forces down. Plymouth, for example, remained a thorn in the side of the king's army in the south-west, for Royalist soldiers were needed there and so could not be sent to campaign elsewhere. Sea power alone was not enough to help every besieged Parliamentarian garrison hold out: a number of places surrendered, including Bristol and Exeter in 1643, Duncannon fort in 1645 and Bunratty Castle in 1646, as the navy alone could not get enough relief through to them, while shore-based Royalist artillery damaged and sank a number of Parliamentarian vessels. A determined and well-equipped besieging army could always drive men-of-war away from a besieged coastal outpost. Nonetheless, naval strength would play a crucial role in these amphibious operations.

Subterfuge became a common element of the war at sea. Men-of-war on all sides made use of false flags to lure in unsuspecting prey, while merchant captains regularly carried falsified papers to try to avoid seizure if stopped by hostile ships. The *Magdalen* and the *Lorne*, two Parliamentarian privateers, successfully used the ruse of flying Bristol colours to intercept Royalist ships. Some captains resorted to torture to compel captured seamen to admit that their ship was bound to an enemy port and therefore a legitimate prize. Captain Thomas Plunkett placed lit match-cord between the fingers of some prisoners and executed others to terrify their crewmates into confessing what he wanted to hear. During the war, a number of prisoners were executed at sea. The most notorious occasion occurred in April 1644 when Captain Richard Swanley tied 70 Irish men and women back to back and threw them overboard at Milford Haven. The large numbers of mariners held captive by each side during the war meant that atrocities like this were uncommon, as a culture of reciprocity became the norm between the opposing naval forces. In October 1644, for example, Warwick ordered the release of 24 Irish sailors in exchange for the return of 27 English mariners.[13]

Attempts to reach a settlement between the king and Parliament in 1647 came to nothing. The king's duplicitous negotiations with the Irish and Scots, combined with grievances over pay and conditions, convinced many in the New Model Army of the need for a more radical settlement. The New Model Army was created in January 1645 to reorganize and professionalize Parliamentarian military forces, and from the beginning its soldiers took a strong interest in the religious and political settlement of the war. But by 1648 many people in England were becoming increasingly alienated from the army's radicalism and the increasingly hard line in their position on dealing with the king. In the spring, a series of uprisings known as the Second Civil War broke out in a number of areas, including Kent and South Wales. This unrest spread to the Parliamentarian ships stationed in the Downs. A large proportion of the sailors on board those and other ships favoured a political accommodation with Charles, and in May they rejected the authority of Captain Thomas Rainborowe, the newly appointed vice-admiral who was noted for his radical affiliations. The mutineers petitioned the Earl of Warwick, seeking a treaty with the king and the disbandment of the army. Fearing the spread of further military uprisings, Parliament chose to adopt a hard line with the seamen and began to prepare a fleet to move against the king. In June a number of ships crewed by the mutineers sailed to Holland and submitted to Prince Charles, Charles I's son living in exile. Some prominent Parliamentarian officers, such as Captain William Batten, also defected.

From a Parliamentarian perspective, the situation then took a turn for the worse in Ireland.

[WYN/2/3]

Instructions given by the right hono:<sup>ble</sup>
the Comittee of Lords and Comons for
the Admiralty and Cinque ports to
be duly observed by all Captaines and
Officers whatsoever and common men
respectively in this Fleete provided, to
the glory of God, the hono<sup>r</sup> and service
of the Parliam<sup>t</sup> and the Safety of the
these Kingdomes of England Scotland
and Ireland

First and above all things you must provide y<sup>t</sup> God be
duly Served publiquely twice every day in the Ship
under your Comand

You are to take Care That all men imployed under
your Comand (in this Expedicon) live orderly and
peaceably together and performe the Duty of theire
places And if any Seaman or other person in your
Ship shall comitt Murther or Manslaughter you
are to give notice thereof to the Sheife of y<sup>e</sup> Squadron
that he may be sent in Safety to the next Gaole &
receive Triall according to Lawe And if any shall
raise ffaction, Tumult, or Conspiracy or shall
quarrell fight, or drawe blood or weapon to that ende,
or be a common Swearer Blasphemer Drunkard
Railer Pilferer or Sleepe at his Watch, or make
noyse

Prince Rupert, 1619–82, Count Palatine of the Rhine, Duke of Cumberland. *Samuel Cooper, 1660-72.* NMM, *Caird Collection.* MNT0122.

There the Confederates, Royalists and disaffected Parliamentarians formed an alliance that placed most of the country and a large number of privateers under the king's control. For the first time in the war the Royalists found themselves with a considerable fleet at their disposal. Over the next 18 months, however, they largely squandered the potential of their naval forces. Prince Charles attempted to use his newly acquired navy to put pressure on London's economy by blockading the Thames in July and August 1648. The Royalist squadron achieved little and returned to Hellevoetsluis in Holland in September.[14] Warwick, having pacified the mutinous Parliamentarian mariners, followed and established a blockade at Hellevoetsluis. Financial problems and mutinies bedevilled the Royalists as sailors, including Batten, and some of the revolted ships, like the *Constant Warwick*, re-submitted to Parliament. In November, Prince Charles named his cousin Prince Rupert as the new admiral. Warwick, believing Rupert would not put to sea that winter, returned to England with most of his ships. This proved to be a major miscalculation as Rupert's fleet sailed from Holland to Kinsale in January 1649.

Having defeated the Royalists for a second time in 1648, many in the army and in Parliament believed that there could be no negotiated settlement with Charles I, who by that time was in Parliamentary custody. In December, Colonel Thomas Pride and the army removed the less radical members of the House of Commons in what became known as 'Pride's Purge'. This allowed the remaining radical MPs, known as the 'Rump', and the army to put the king on trial. On 20 January 1649 the trial began and Charles was sentenced to death on 27 January. The execution of the king on 30 January 1649 changed everything. Parliament faced enemies at home and overseas, with opponents in Ireland and Scotland posing the most immediate military threats. Oliver Cromwell was appointed to command the army to subdue Ireland in March. In February three generals-at-sea, Robert Blake, Richard Deane and Edward Popham, were appointed to command the navy. In the following months they successfully reorganized the fleet, and in May, Blake put to sea with a flotilla of ten ships. Financial problems and political disagreements meant that Rupert's fleet remained largely inactive at Kinsale. On arriving there in late May, Blake was able to blockade the Royalist ships in the harbour and

# Richard Deane

Richard Deane was an army officer, a general-at-sea and one of the regicides. At the beginning of the civil wars, Deane was part of a Parliamentary force that captured Woolwich Dockyard. At the trial of Charles I in January 1649, he was one of the signatories of the death warrant that resulted in the king's execution. Later that year he was appointed as one of the generals-at-sea. He also played a prominent role in the Battle of Worcester in 1651, routing the Royalist army led by Charles II. The First Anglo-Dutch War followed, and on 3 June 1653, during the Battle of the Gabbard off the Suffolk coast, Deane was hit by a Dutch cannonball, which nearly sliced him in two. His body was taken to Greenwich, where he lay in state at the Queen's House. Deane was buried in Westminster Abbey, but following the Restoration, his remains, like those of other regicides, were dug up and thrown into a common pit.

*Portrait of Richard Deane. Robert Walker, c.1653.*
*NMM, Caird Collection. BHC2646.*

ensure they could do nothing to prevent the Parliamentarian army crossing the Irish Sea in August. Cromwell did not enjoy the voyage, with one report describing him as being as 'sea sick as ever I saw any man'.[15] In the following months and years the navy played a major logistical role in the campaigns of Cromwell and his successor to subdue the country. Men-of-war transported the artillery train and supplies for the army that enabled Cromwell to move quickly against, and capture, Royalist garrisons along the Irish east coast, such as Drogheda and Wexford. In October, as Cromwell advanced south, Rupert seized the opportunity of a storm to flee from Kinsale with a number of his ships. The capture of these towns and others such as Waterford in the following year, together with the departure of the prince's fleet, removed the most pressing Royalist naval threats from the British Isles.

Over the next four years Rupert's squadron sailed to Portugal, into the Mediterranean and across the Atlantic to the West Indies, with the Parliamentarian navy in relentless pursuit. The Royalists were reduced to little more than a band of roving privateers as enemy action, bad weather and a lack of funds led to the gradual depletion of their fleet. In September 1652 Prince Maurice, who was Rupert's brother and the vice-admiral, was lost with his ship the *Defiance* in a hurricane in the West Indies. Rupert and two ships finally returned to France in March 1653. The prince's fleet remained a thorn in the navy's side, but after 1650 it never really threatened to undermine the final Parliamentarian victory. It was in the seas around the British Isles, and not pursuing the Royalists, that the navy made its most important contribution to victory in the civil wars in the early 1650s. The navy played a key logistical role in Cromwell's conquest of Scotland in 1650 and 1651. Naval support ensured that the vast array of supplies and money that the army needed to campaign in the country arrived safely. In 1651 and 1652 Parliamentarian men-of-war combined with the army to force the surrender of the remaining outlying Royalist outposts, including the Isle of Man, the Channel Islands, the Isles of Scilly and Barbados. In April 1652, the surrender of Galway, the last major Royalist-held port town in the three kingdoms, marked the end of the naval element of the civil wars. By this point the focus of the navy was shifting as tensions with the Dutch escalated to open warfare.[16]

*LEFT AND ABOVE Naval reward medal commemorating the service against six ships, 1650. NMM, on loan from a private collection. MEC0841.*

*Map of Kinsale. John Mansell, 1649.* P/49(16).

*Proceedings of a Royalist fleet, extracted from a ship's journal, 1648–52. AND/45.*

The fighting at sea during the civil wars can seem insignificant in comparison to the campaigns on land, and in many respects the naval war was a secondary concern for the protagonists fighting in the 1640s. But for the mariners who fought at sea this was a fast-paced, innovative and often bloody theatre of the war and not just a sideshow. The navy was a vital component in the ultimate Parliamentarian victory in the civil wars. Naval superiority allowed Parliament to support isolated garrisons, attack Confederate and Royalist merchantmen and privateers, and campaign effectively in Ireland and Scotland. The civil wars also had longer-term consequences for British naval history, as much of the groundwork for future developments was laid during this conflict.

*Journal of Edward Barlow, 1659–1703.* JOD/4.

# CHAPTER 9

# Life at Sea

## Richard J. Blakemore

A ballad from the early seventeenth century, 'Saylors for my Money', opens with these lines:

> *Countrie men of England,*
> *Who live at home with ease:*
> *And little thinke what dangers*
> *Are incident o'th Seas,*
> *Give eare unto the Saylor.*

This dramatic contrast between the 'ease' of life ashore and the challenges faced by seafarers is a theme that runs throughout the rest of the song, which celebrates the 'valiant heart' and 'noble courage' of men whose 'calling is laborious / And subject to much woe'.[1] This same idea was expressed by John Smith, sometime seafarer and governor of Virginia, in a book published just a few years before the ballad: 'the labour, hazard, wet and cold is so incredible I cannot expresse it', because 'Men of all other professions in lightning, thunder, stormes and tempests … may shelter themselves, and [have] good cheare; but those are the chiefe times, that Sea-men must stand to their tackelings'.[2] Edward Barlow, another seafarer, struck a similar refrain in the journal he kept during the second half of the same century. 'There are', he wrote, 'no men under the sun that fare harder and get their living more hard and that are so abused on all sides as we poor seamen … never will I wish any of my friends to go to sea'.[3]

The oceans held little romantic charm for people in the sixteenth and seventeenth centuries: the sea was a hostile place, the site of raging storms like the one depicted in Shakespeare's famous play *The Tempest*, the abode of the monsters that luridly decorated sea charts, and the haunt of pirates and other potential enemies. Yet this image of toil and turmoil is not the whole picture. If the working lives of sailors were hard, so too was life ashore for the majority of people at this time, and seafaring could also offer great promise. This was because shipping – whether in the fisheries, in coastal and short-distance trade, or in the burgeoning intercontinental traffic which began to transform the world in these centuries – was vital to early-modern Britain in various ways. It was the mainstay of many communities, supporting not just mariners but also their families, as well as many labourers and craftsmen in docks

*Barlow's depiction of a storm. Journal of Edward Barlow, 1659–1703. JOD/4.*

*Barlow's image of a shark. Journal of Edward Barlow. 1659–1703. JOD/4.*

and shipyards. This industry, which expanded continually in scope and scale throughout this period, certainly demanded hard work, but it also created opportunities. The number of people employed in shipping rose steadily with the increasing tonnage of the naval, mercantile and fishing fleets. Mariners might engage in trade themselves, bringing home their own small cargoes to supplement their wages. If they were both skilled and fortunate, they might also rise in their career in a way that was not possible in many other areas of Tudor and Stuart Britain. Life at sea presented many risks but could also yield considerable rewards.

Contemporary labels for maritime workers, like 'seaman' or 'Jack Tar' (which first appeared during the seventeenth century), obscure a considerable amount of variety. The experiences of a man working on a small fishing boat or a Newcastle collier running down the east coast to London would contrast greatly with those of a sailor on a privateer destined for the Caribbean, on a whaling vessel heading to Greenland or on an East Indiaman. Yet it is still worth considering the stereotypical idea of a 'seaman', since it had definite cultural purchase during the period and was applied to all who worked at sea. Outsiders certainly thought seamen were distinctive. Seafarers wore different clothes, walked with a different gait and talked in a practically impenetrable jargon that set them apart. Nor were these the only characteristics

*Barlow leaving home. Journal of Edward Barlow, 1659–1703. JOD/4.*

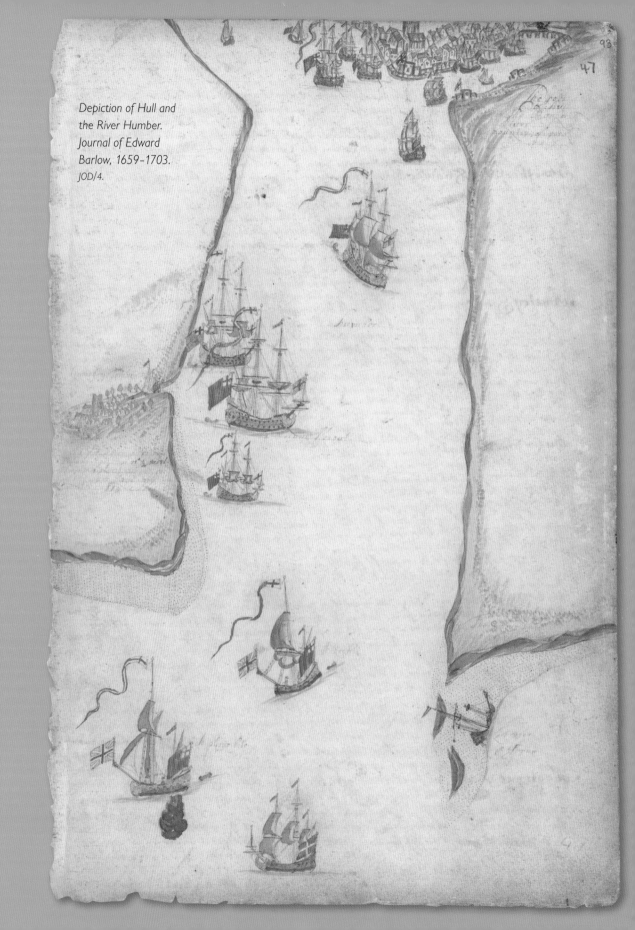

Depiction of Hull and
the River Humber.
Journal of Edward
Barlow, 1659–1703.
JOD/4.

that contemporaries noticed. Shakespeare's depiction of an unruly and disrespectful boatswain in the opening scene of *The Tempest* is a well-known, but by no means unique, caricature of the seamen of the time: when told to 'be patient', he replies he will be 'When the sea is', and declares, 'What cares these roarers / for the name of king?'[4] A seaman, wrote Richard Brathwaite a few decades later, 'was never acquainted much with civilitie ... [he is] more *active* than *contemplative* ... though his hand is strong, his head-peece is stupid ... He ever takes worst rest when he goes to bed most sober'.[5]

Yet there was another side to the idea of the 'seaman', and this celebrated their skilful and diligent nature. Some seafarers, at least, saw themselves in this way, as men following a 'calling' or craft – men with considerable and valuable expertise. They were not the only ones to think so. It was widely recognized throughout the sixteenth and seventeenth centuries that these workers were essential, both to man the navy (the 'wooden walls' that secured the British Isles from threatened invasions) and for trade and fishing. Literary wits might mock, and aristocrats and naval officers might condemn the behaviour of seamen, but they also accepted that they were professionals, and that their skills and experience were absolutely necessary.

Seafarers – especially shipmasters – might belong to local maritime guilds such as the Trinity Houses of Deptford, Hull and Newcastle, but there were no official regulations or qualifications that determined who could and who could not be a seaman. William Ball, a privateer, noted that 'it is an ancient proverb and true, the sea and the gallows refuseth nobody'.[6] Each ship's commander was appointed by its owners, or by the naval administration for royal ships, and these commanders were then responsible for recruiting the rest of the crew. Men signed on for a single voyage, and at its end, they could decide whether to ship again with the same vessel or to go elsewhere. Throughout the Tudor and Stuart period these contracts were largely unwritten and agreed individually between mariner and master.

Not everyone who signed up for a ship's voyage was the same. Some were novices, young men who moved into and out of seafaring quite easily, alternating it with seasonal work ashore. The backbone of the workforce, however, was what might be termed 'career' seafarers: men who spent their lives in this 'calling', and who acquired the know-how to manage ships (which were, after all, the most complicated, advanced and expensive machines of the age). While seafaring was predominately a young man's profession, a few career seamen kept sailing into their later years, and some at 70 or 80 years old. From about the middle of the seventeenth century, the navy began to refer to men who had some experience at sea as 'able seamen', distinguishing them from 'ordinary seamen'. Even then, there was no paperwork involved; neither able seamen nor shipmasters had certificates, so they were judged by the ability they could demonstrate and by their reputation in the maritime community. Some may have served an apprenticeship – by no means a required path into seafaring but still a common arrangement at this time. Apprenticeships were regulated, as they were in other trades, by the Statute of Artificers of 1563, and coastal parishes could confirm apprenticeship indentures and also place pauper boys as maritime apprentices.

the making of that Breech which Syr Ffeller that day gaue mee at Billingsgate was
Earnest Mney & that wcase and the first Money that Euer J took to My Remembrance out J am
shure not the [...] So being bound for Seuen years and all things being Redey J took my Leaue of my
frendel and and as wee Came to the water side and takeing water at sant tobes Stairer wee Came
Downe to Ratelife Crose where My Master and Mistris Liued where my Mistres Carring Me to there hous
and Staying there that night and the next Day wee were to goe Doune to Chatham where the ship lacke
that My Master was in Called the Nasbey Morning being Com to billingsgate wee Came and takeing
water for to goe to graues end and leaueing that famos Citey of London where So Many
doth Rich and yore haue taken a farwell both of there frends and Contrey J wel thinking that wold
bee the last time that the shold see them here hath the husbond parted with the wife the Children
from the Parentes and one frend from a nother which haue neuer Enioyed the sight of one another again
som finding there Dayes in on foran land and som in another and som by war and som in year and som by
one Jorin Weauer and som by another and Nob knowing what Dangers Might befal mee as J was now going
to seeke my fortune in the oran seas and in foran landes and Departing from ordney gate J thought good
to Describe you the Riuer of thames from London brig to the boy of the nore where the Riuer of Chatham
welch J and both runeth into the main sea and also all the towne es on the riuer on both sise as you pase
from London and up to Rochester

Depiction of London and the River Thames.
Journal of Edward Barlow, 1659–1703. JOD/4.

# Edward Barlow

The mariner Edward Barlow was present at many of the seventeenth century's defining moments and was a participant in England's remarkable maritime expansion. Born near Manchester in 1642, Barlow got his first taste of the maritime world serving as a master's mate on board the *Naseby*, and he was aboard this ship (hastily renamed the *Royal Charles*) when it carried Charles II back from the Netherlands at the Restoration. He served in the navy throughout the Second Anglo-Dutch War, fighting in many of the major engagements, and then sailed in East India Company ships, to Bombay, Bantam and Taiwan, among other places. He learned how to write after becoming a sailor, and his journal is probably the most important first-hand account of seafaring in the early-modern era. Beautifully illustrated, and written with characteristic candour, it remains one of the most important objects in the National Maritime Museum's collections.[7]

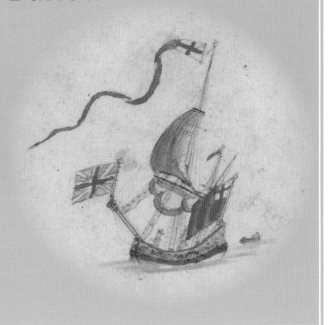

Two detailed accounts of how young men first went to sea survive in the autobiographies of Edward Barlow and his contemporary Edward Coxere. Barlow came from Prestwich, near Manchester, and had no maritime connections. He remembered the initial impact of 'seeing so many things upon the [Thames] with long poles standing up in them and a great deal of ropes ... not knowing that they were ships', and how soon 'my mind was to see ships and boats upon the River Thames ... taking great pleasure therein ... as often as I had spare time, I would be gone to the waterside to see the ships'. Barlow insistently persuaded his uncle, for whom he was then working at the Dog and Bear tavern in Southwark, to arrange a maritime apprenticeship for him, but he was later quite scathing of his seven years as an apprentice, writing, 'I would have gone and learned as much in two or three voyages'.[8] Coxere, meanwhile, came from Dover, and his father and brothers were mariners. After spending his first trial voyage 'mostly very sea-sick', he went as boy on his brother's ship, and then as servant to the Irish captain of a Dutch vessel.[9] He never had any formal training, but nevertheless learnt quickly (in Dutch, however, and when he later transferred to an English ship, he had to learn the technical terms all over again). Both men spent their lives as seamen. Their accounts show the diverse paths into seafaring, and underline how being a seaman was a matter of experience and perspective rather than of strict rules. You were a seaman if others accepted you as one.

*Bantam. Journal of Edward Barlow, 1659–1703.* JOD/4.

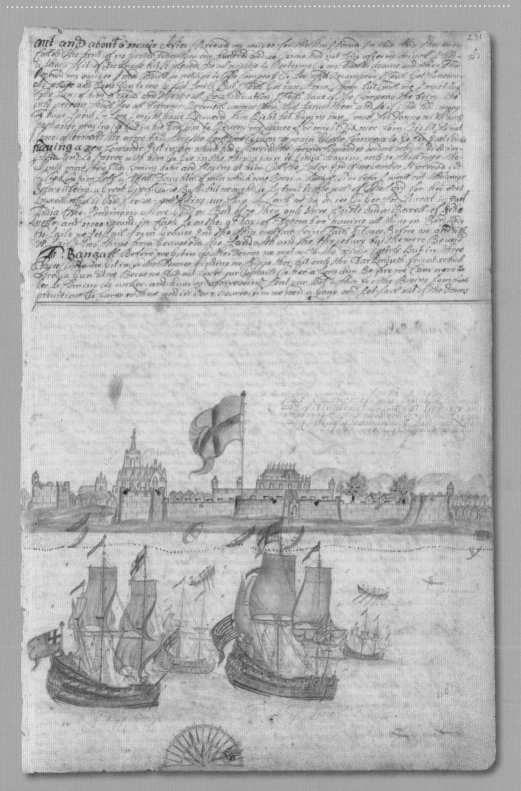

*Madras. Journal of Edward Barlow, 1659–1703.* JOD/4.

*Banks of the Ganges. Journal of Edward Barlow, 1659–1703.* JOD/4.

Once a man was signed on to a ship, whether for the first time or as an old hand, life at sea would depend very much on the vessel and the voyage in question. Some mariners did specialize in particular regions or routes, and acquired considerable experience by doing so, but many sailors moved between different sectors during the course of their maritime careers. The Elizabethan government, while abolishing many Roman Catholic practices, still enforced 'fish days' to preserve and stimulate the fishing sector, precisely because fishermen were often recruited into the navy. Barlow served in the navy and as a merchant sailor voyaging to Scandinavia, Europe, the Mediterranean, the Caribbean, China and India; Coxere served on Dutch, English and Spanish ships, mostly on commercial voyages, including to the Caribbean and the Mediterranean. There was, therefore, a degree of continuity in both personnel and experience that spanned the shipping industry as a whole, and some conditions were universal in seafaring.

One important dimension was food, a logistical concern for all but the shortest of voyages. In the navy, mariners were entitled to a set diet: in 1565 it was ordered that every man should receive each day a gallon of beer and a pound of bread, plus either salt beef, bacon or fish with butter and cheese. Naval rations were often rotten and ruined, however, since victuallers, captains and pursers cut corners in order to make themselves a profit. Seamen in commercial

*Iron chest, or portable safe, sixteenth century. AAA3309.*

*Tin or pewter medieval boatswain's call, c.1500.* PLT0457.

ships were also entitled to food on board, but here too some complained of the fare they received. John Smith described 'a little poore *Iohn*, or salt fish, with oyle and mustard, or bisket, butter, cheese or oatemeale pottage on fish days, salt beefe, porke and pease and sixe shillings beere ... is youre ordinary ships allowance'.[10] Yet the picture may not have been so entirely bad: the very presence of complaints suggests that seamen had expectations, and spoke out when these were not met. Food also provided a social basis for ships, especially larger vessels, where men were organized into messes of four who ate together. Similarly, crews were split into watches (Smith suggested that there were usually two, a 'Starreboord' and a 'Larboord' watch), and each day at sea was organized according to these, except for those occasions when all hands were needed. Some efforts were made to continue the religious observances that were a regular part of life ashore: in naval ships, where there was often a chaplain on board, services were held on Sundays, and on both naval and merchant ships a psalm might be sung or recited together at the changing of the watch.[11]

When mariners were not on watch, they slept or amused themselves below deck; for example, a backgammon set was found in the wreck of the *Mary Rose*.[12] John Smith writes of paired '*Comorados*', one in each watch, who alternately slept in a shared berth, and many sources mention cabins, which might imply no more than a space of deck divided by canvas screens, though on larger ships permanent cabins were available, especially for the officers.[13] These spaces were very

*A 60-minute ship's glass, c.1630.*
*NMM, Caird Collection. AST0080.*

important to seafarers: one ship's pilot was punished by being 'turned [out] from lying in his cabbin … and out of his messe'.[14] Seafarers slept on straw palliasses, sometimes placed in 'wainscot beds', although the navy also purchased large numbers of 'hamaccoes'. There are other occasional hints about material life aboard ship: sailors' wills mention 'sea beds' and 'sea clothes', presumably hard-wearing canvas suits.[15]

Sleeping arrangements reflected and enforced the social hierarchy on board ship – the existence of which was a key part of seafaring life. Most voyages represented a large investment by the ship's owners, and success and safety required coordinated work by the crew. It is therefore hardly surprising, especially given the generally hierarchical nature of society at the time, that the organization of a ship's crew involved distinctions of rank and power. The officers had their quarters towards the aft of the ship, while the crew slept in the forecastle or forward on the lower decks. The ship's boys were the lowest rank and above them were the 'common men', also known as 'foremastmen'. Most large ships had a few quartermasters, who were more experienced seamen, after which came those with specific responsibilities. The boatswain's job was to supervise the mariners and set them to work, and he was also in charge of the 'boatswain's stores' – the rigging and sails. Another common specialist was the carpenter, who kept the ship's hull in working order. Both military and commercial vessels usually carried a gunner, who had charge of the ordnance, shot and powder, and oversaw the ship's gunnery during a fight. On larger ships these specialists often had their own mates, or several of them. At the top was the master, the owner's representative, who held ultimate responsibility for navigation and command over the crew. He was assisted by master's mates, with the senior mate in line to take over command should the master die or be incapacitated.[16] In naval ships, and in some privateers, there was also a captain who had general command and directed the ship in military actions (although the master still carried out navigation and piloting of the ship).

This stratification was reflected in the wages paid to different crewmen, with those higher up receiving correspondingly higher pay. Specialists received roughly half as much again as mariners, and master's mates were paid about twice as much as mariners, while masters earned four or five times the amount. However, remuneration was a complex business in the maritime world. First of all, there were different kinds of pay: fishermen and privateers received a share of the catch or the plunder, while sailors on short commercial voyages were often paid a single lump sum. Men on longer voyages and in the navy were paid in monthly wages, at a rate set by the government for naval sailors; merchant seamen earned double or more what the navy offered, but naval sailors received prize money if they seized an enemy vessel in wartime. Besides wages, mariners had the opportunity to conduct small-scale commerce, and many carried goods to trade, including those who sailed in naval ships. Robert Rumes, for instance, carried 'soape Bibles & pepper' on a voyage to Maryland, which he traded for tobacco.[17] This was known as a 'venture', highlighting how, in a sense, mariners were speculators as well as paid labourers.

In principle, the social structure of a ship was rigid and strictly imposed. On naval vessels the captain held authority from the state and was empowered to punish any disobedience, with the penalty of death for serious offences. Although privateers did not have the same legal status, their on-board discipline was also notoriously harsh, probably because the prospect of plunder, or indeed the conspicuous lack of it, could make crews unruly. On merchant and fishing vessels, customary maritime law entitled masters and boatswains to chastise any transgressing crewmember in a variety of ways. These included fines and physical punishments like flogging and beating, the 'bilboes' (a kind of shipboard stocks), and binding a mariner to the capstan with a basket of shot hung around his neck. These rules suggest a picture of brutal and cruel treatment for sailors, and there are certainly examples where this happened, but it was not always the case. Shipmasters who mistreated their sailors found themselves sued for loss of earnings, and soon became notorious, finding it hard to recruit men. Moreover, there was a strong tradition of consultation on board ship. Sailors protested, for example, when the length or destination of their voyage was changed, when they felt their ship or provisions were dangerously faulty, or when the circumstances of the voyage seemed too threatening. Masters often acquiesced to these demands, and those who did seek to prosecute their men for 'mutiny' in court found that maritime judges frequently ruled in favour of the mariners' rights.

Indeed, mutiny was not actually a felony under English law during this period, and even in the navy, where mutiny was punishable by death under martial law, sailors were rarely executed. Moreover, dramatic and violent mutinies were rare: Sir Francis Drake's trial and execution of Thomas Doughty during his circumnavigation of the globe in 1578, and the mutiny during Henry Hudson's 1611 voyage in search of the North-West Passage, which led to Hudson's abandonment and death, were exceptional incidents on exceptional voyages. Cooperation among seafarers was therefore just as common as conflict. One likely reason for this was that many commanders began their careers as 'foremastmen'. Luke Foxe, a shipmaster from Hull, wrote, 'I doe not allowe any to be a good Sea man, that hath not undergone the most

*Flintlock pistol, c.seventeenth century.* AAA2394.

Offices about a Ship.'[18] Edward Barlow spent about 15 years as a seaman and apprentice, two as a gunner or boatswain, and the next 25 years as a master's mate. Coxere, too, was promoted to gunner and then to mate and finally master, purchasing his own 'hoy, to use a home-trade', meaning coastal trade and trips to France or Holland. Thomas Trenchfield, whose unusually detailed will describes him as 'not of Eminent yet of honest and Religious Parents', ascended further and more rapidly: of his 37 years at sea, he spent 30 as a shipmaster, ending his life a landowner in Kent and appending 'Esq.' to his name.[19]

Serving an apprenticeship, as discussed earlier, probably helped in this sort of progression, as did having the right contacts. This was particularly crucial for the step from master's mate to master, which required the trust and support of a ship's owners or of naval administrators. Barlow bemoaned that he 'had very few friends or acquaintance ... in helping me thereto';[20] Trenchfield's progress may have been assisted by just such 'friends'; and Coxere's certainly was. Many masters were, or became, owners in shipping, and it is therefore no surprise to find that throughout this period there were some maritime dynasties whose younger members could expect to attain their own command in due course. As Barlow's career shows, some advancement (and with it greater wages and opportunities) was possible even without such connections – but not everyone was so successful. If there were opportunities in seafaring, there were also considerable risks: some ships did not return, and many men died by accident, injury or sickness, especially on longer voyages. The arrangements made by the government and by local guilds to care for wounded or 'decayed' seamen, and for their widows, shows some concern for their welfare but also indicates the perils that sailors faced. Yet mariners were also resourceful: for example, in 1697 Scottish sailors living in Rotterdam established a 'seamen's box', or communal fund, to support members in times of distress, and other similar societies may have existed elsewhere.[21]

Considering the hazards of life at sea, the economic insecurity of maritime labour and the length of time spent away from their homes, it is not surprising that seamen also depended on help from their families and neighbours. Many popular ballads of the time depicted the tearful farewell between a sailor and his sweetheart, followed by a joyous reunion at the end of the voyage which celebrated the attachment and constancy between the two lovers. It is impossible to say with certainty how many mariners would have entered into such relationships. A large proportion of seamen's wills that survive from this period do mention wives, although a married seafarer was far more likely to make a will in the first place. For those who did marry, it clearly mattered a good deal, and married men were allowed to sleep ashore when in their home port, while single men stayed with the ship. Barlow and Coxere both married, and for them their wedding was a significant moment (though, curiously, neither recorded their wife's name in their journal). Other mariners left provision in their wills for their children, and Thomas Trenchfield sent his two sons to Oxford and Cambridge. Thus, although distance from their families may have been a common feature of seafarers' lives, that did not diminish the strength of these relationships.

On a more practical level, too, neighbours and families were important. Mariners often needed their support during time spent ashore between voyages. Coxere wrote about how his wife 'with her own industry kept me out of debt',[22] and Barlow described his wife as a 'meet help … agreeable and industrious; and it doth much behove all seamen's wives to be

The Loyal Seaman's Happy Return. *English Broadside Ballad Archive.*

the same'.[23] Mariners granted these relations or neighbours power of attorney to act for them, including the right to collect their wages, and the East India Company allowed part of their wages to be collected in England while their voyage was still underway.

Nevertheless, for the families of seamen, and especially for their wives, making ends meet could be challenging. Like Coxere's wife, most worked and combined their earnings with the income brought in by their husband's labour. Some ran lodging houses or taverns. Magdalena Hendricx, who was born in Amsterdam but moved to London after marrying an English sailor, reported when appearing in court as a witness that she 'getts her living with and by the winding of silke', but nevertheless, 'she and her husband are very poore persons and in a very wanting condition'.[24] Losing their husband's income could prove disastrous for these women, and uncertainty defined their lives; Coxere recalled a homecoming where his wife, 'being surprised, could hardly speak to me, for she knew not before whether I was dead or alive'.[25] They also had to contend with negative attitudes about mariners' wives, encapsulated in one ballad that ridiculed a 'witty Seamans wife' who 'play[ed] at Venus Game' during her husband's absence.[26] However, marrying seafarers may well have given some women more freedom to act as the de facto head of their own household, and sometimes mariners' widows chose to remarry within the maritime community. Some women even went to sea themselves, either accompanying their husbands or dressed as men. Elizabeth Watson, from York, travelled to Amsterdam in her early twenties and from there sailed to Brazil with the Dutch West Indies Company, 'in man's clothing for a soldier', spending about nine weeks in this disguise; in Pernambuco she then married a ship's surgeon.[27]

The stereotype with which we began, of seamen as totally different from people ashore and immersed in a miserable and perilous profession, has a grain of truth, but is in many ways misleading. As Barlow wrote, 'the calling is not altogether so bad … [Mariners] may live indifferently well, as well as many ordinary tradesmen, yet they must go through many more dangers.'[28] Seafarers certainly worked in an environment and an industry that not only was dangerous but was very different to life ashore, and they embraced this difference, celebrating their own professional culture. Yet they were also deeply embedded in Tudor and Stuart society. Their activities were essential to Britain's economy and security, and although both naval and commercial ships had their own hierarchical and legal arrangements, these were still regulated – and challenged – in Britain itself. Just as importantly, mariners belonged to families and communities, and their lives were shaped by these connections, even as the range and duration of voyages continually expanded.

The Battle of the Texel, 11 August 1673 *(detail)*.
*NMM, Caird Collection.* BHC0346.

# The Seventeenth-Century Anglo-Dutch Wars
## Rebecca Rideal

On the afternoon of 19 May 1652, Robert Blake, one of England's Generals at Sea, sailed with a flotilla of warships from his anchorage at Rye towards an approaching fleet of Dutch vessels, controlled by Lieutenant-Admiral Maarten Tromp. The opposing commanders were the same age (53), but Tromp was by far the more experienced seaman. The son of a merchant sailor, he had been captured by pirates at the age of 11 or 12, had spent his entire life at sea, and 13 years earlier had rocked Europe when he spectacularly defeated a Spanish fleet during the Battle of the Downs (1639). Blake, on the other hand, had only been General at Sea (the parliamentary equivalent of Admiral) for three years and his appointment owed more to his military success on land during the British and Irish Civil Wars than it did to seamanship. Nevertheless, under Blake's supervision, the rival Royalist and Parliamentarian factions within the navy were united and the strong fleet he had inherited was expanded further. By May 1652 it was preparing to fight the opening action of what would become known as the First Anglo-Dutch War.

*Miniature of Robert Blake.*
*Possibly Samuel Cooper, early 1650s.*
*NMM, Caird Collection. MNT0192.*

Relations between the Commonwealth of England and the Dutch Republic had rapidly deteriorated since the end of the civil wars. While Oliver Cromwell expressed his personal ambition to form a grand Protestant alliance, there was justifiable concern on the part of the Dutch about English economic ambitions. Diplomatic discussions between the two nations were marred by mistrust and miscommunication. The English believed that the Dutch were dragging their feet; by contrast, the Dutch feared that England's hunger for wealth would

Maarten Harpertszoon Tromp.
*After Jan Lievensz, early nineteenth century.*
*NMM, Greenwich Hospital Collection.* BHC3062.

lead to their subordination. Indeed, when Cromwell introduced the first of a series of Navigation Acts in October 1651, he boldly set out England's mercantile ambitions. Crucially, the regulations restricted imports into England and stipulated that all trade goods from outside Europe had to be transported in English ships. For the Dutch, the world's foremost maritime trading nation, this had obvious consequences as they gazed warily on their commercial rivals across the North Sea.

Despite these long-standing tensions, when the war broke out in May 1652 it was for reasons that might seem ridiculous by today's standards. On board his 60-gun flagship, the *James*, Blake received word that Tromp's ships were making something of a nuisance of themselves. The Dutch fleet had been out since April to safeguard returning Dutch merchant ships, but bad weather forced it to seek refuge near Dover. Tromp's seamen used their free time to perform noisy musket practice, much to the chagrin of English locals. Exacerbating the situation was a tradition whereby any foreign ships passing through 'English' waters (the Dover Straits and the Channel) had to salute English warships in recognition of their sovereignty of the seas. Failure to do so ran the risk of a fight. Foreign captains largely indulged the archaic English custom. However, as diplomatic relations worsened, the Dutch government (the 'States General') left the decision of whether to salute English warships up to Tromp's personal discretion. Despite cannon being fired from Dover Castle as a reminder, the Dutch commander refused to salute. This failure amounted to an act of war.

What happened when the English and Dutch fleets met in the Channel the following day is blurred by the respective commanders' opposing testimonies. According to Blake, the *James* fired a series of three shots to remind Tromp's flagship, the *Brederode*, to salute – all of which were ignored. After the third reminder, however, Tromp fired his broadside and a battle commenced. Conversely, Tromp claimed that not only did the English fire their broadside first, but their fleet was arranged in such a manner that he could not tell if the English were holding Dutch merchant ships against their will (although, in fact, there were no merchant ships present). Whichever way the conflict began, it was followed by a fierce five-hour engagement that came to be known as the Battle of Goodwin Sands. Then, on 10 June 1652, for the first

The Battle of the Texel, 11 August 1673. NMM, *Caird Collection*. BHC0346.

time in history, England officially declared war on the Dutch Republic.

Very rarely is a war triggered by a single issue, but nothing exposes the root of the mid-century conflict between England and the Dutch Republic better than this microcosmic moment between Tromp and Blake. At a rudimentary level, on the one side, there was a Dutch merchant's son driven to the sea to defend his country's belief in free trade; on the other was an English military antagonist defending his nation's perceived ancient right to dominion of the Narrow Seas. Furthermore, the Battle of Goodwin Sands was fast, brutal, expensive and avoidable. It proved to be the harbinger of three costly wars – the Anglo-Dutch Wars of 1652–54, 1665–67 and 1672–74. Curiously, despite their enormous contemporaneous importance, not just to the protagonists but all across Europe, the Anglo-Dutch Wars have failed to enter public consciousness to the degree that other historical conflicts have done (in England at least). This oversight may have something to do with the complex nature of the conflict.
At a logistical level, however, the objectives were simply to gain control of the two major trade routes. The first was the route along the North Sea to the Baltic; the second was the route along the Channel towards the Iberian coast, the Mediterranean and beyond.

An opportunity first presented itself in June 1652 with the expected return of a cargo-rich Dutch East India convoy via Scotland and the North Sea. The Commonwealth navy split

*Portrait of Sir George Ayscue.*
*Sir Peter Lely, 1665–66.*
*NMM, Greenwich Hospital*
*Collection. BHC2522.*

in two, with Blake taking the largest and best ships north to intercept the Dutch convoy and his fellow General at Sea, George Ayscue, remaining with ten warships to guard the Channel. It was Ayscue who saw action first. On 2 July, he attacked a group of 30 or so Dutch merchant ships, destroying three and capturing seven. In response, Admiral Maarten Tromp assembled 82 Dutch warships and nine fireships, and approached Dover to attack Ayscue's grossly outnumbered squadron. Unfortunately for Tromp, bad weather forced his fleet back and the clash was averted. Instead, the Dutch regrouped and headed north to safeguard their East India ships from Blake's expected assault.

Blake had already captured several Dutch North Sea fishing vessels and was positioned ready to attack the East India ships. On 24 July, he was stationed at Fair Isle and the Dutch had him in sight, but once again bad weather scuppered Tromp's plans. A fierce storm raged for three days, scattering and wrecking many of the Dutch ships. Blake's fleet, although damaged, managed to find shelter. There was no battle and it proved to be a disaster for both sides. Although Blake successfully disrupted the Dutch trade route, he failed to capture the Dutch East India ships. For Tromp it was even worse: he had lost control not only of the North Sea but also of half of his fleet to bad weather. After the storm, both commanders returned to their respective homes, and Tromp resigned his commission.

By the summer, Ayscue's squadron had grown to around 40 warships. On 16 August it met an outbound convoy of Dutch merchant vessels, escorted by 31 warships, resulting in the Battle of Plymouth. Tromp had been replaced as commander by Witte de With, but it was a 45-year-old sea captain (or vice commodore, as he was known) named Michiel de Ruyter who led the Dutch fleet in shepherding the merchant vessels through the Channel, the occasion also being his first time in sole command. Ayscue attacked first and broke the Dutch line, but failed

intelligence and on the acquiescence of an uncertain ally – namely, the King of Denmark and Norway, Frederick III. The idea was that the English fleet – now under the active command of the Earl of Sandwich – would attack the heavily laden Dutch vessels at anchor. The 'neutral' town of Bergen was to comply and the prizes would be split between the Danes and the English. Unfortunately, messages from Frederick III were slow to reach Bergen and letters warning Sandwich that the town's governor might not comply did not reach him in time. With the winds against the English, and with the town showing support for its Dutch guests, it was a bloodbath. There were no gains, 500 men were killed (including many notable captains) and dozens of ships were badly damaged.

It marked a real turning point in the direction of the war. In the Dutch Republic, it was celebrated as a great victory. In England, it was seen as an abject failure. To make up for the failure, Sandwich spent most of the summer and early autumn capturing stray Dutch merchant ships, with considerable success. The prizes, however, were not logged in the correct way.

*Print depicting the Battle of Lowestoft, 3–13 June 1665. Willem van de Velde, the Elder, c.1674. NMM, Caird Collection. PAJ2436.*

Instead, the valuable goods were divided between fleet officers. The whole debacle became a huge scandal and cost Sandwich his position. On top of this, a combination of plague and lack of funds left many seamen disgruntled and desperate: in Portsmouth there were reports of unpaid seamen being 'turned out of doors by their landlords' and dying 'more like dogs than men'.[4]

It was not until June 1666 that the fleets met in action once again in what came to be known as the Four Days' Battle. This time, the Royal Navy was under the joint command of Prince Rupert and George Monck, now Duke of Albemarle. With plenty of time to prepare, new ships were commissioned and old vessels repaired. In addition, seamen had been recruited, albeit with some difficulty. A couple of weeks before the battle, the government received erroneous intelligence that the French (who had entered the war on the Dutch side in January 1666) were on their way to attack from the west. In response, a decision was made to split the fleet in two, with Prince Rupert sailing with 20 or so ships to Plymouth, while Monck remained with just under 60 ships near the Kent coast. The Dutch fleet of 84 ships, under the command

Dutch Ships in the Medway, June 1667. *Willem Schellinks, late seventeenth century.* BHC0294.

*Four-pounder bronze muzzle-loading smoothbore cannon. J. Browne, 1640. KTP0023.*

of Michiel de Ruyter, along with Cornelis Evertsen and Cornelis Tromp (Maarten's son), had been at sea for weeks. When the English scouts spotted them, Monck made the decision to engage despite being significantly outnumbered. What followed was four days of carnage. The arrival of Prince Rupert on the third day could do little to sway the inevitable. The English lost a total of 23 ships, including the prestigious *Royal Prince*, and just under 5,000 men were either killed, wounded or captured (including commanders Christopher Myngs and William Berkeley, who died, and George Ayscue, who was taken). Dutch losses were much smaller, consisting of four ships and just under 3,000 men, including Cornelis Evertsen. It was a messy victory, albeit a substantial one, for the Dutch.

Observing the fleet after the battle, John Evelyn lamented 'the sad spectacle, more than half that gallant bulwark of the kingdom miserably shattered, hardly a vessel entire, but appearing rather so many wrecks and hulls, so cruelly had the Dutch mangled us'.[5] Blame for the disaster was levelled at the dockyards for not supplying the new ships in time, at some of the fleet's captains for retreating from the fray, and also (though much more quietly) at George Monck for his overconfidence. Nevertheless, in remarkable time, the navy was back on its feet and out at sea gunning for another fight. It came on 25 July and this time the weather was on the English fleet's side. Evenly matched, the English and the Dutch engaged in battle close to North Foreland off the Kent coast. The action – a clear English victory – became known as the St James's Day Fight and was followed in August by 'Holmes's Bonfire', an English attack on the islands of Vlieland and Terschelling that was conceived by a Dutch turncoat and orchestrated by Captain Robert Holmes. It resulted in the destruction of an estimated 150 Dutch merchant ships and the torching of the town of West Terschelling. In London, the incident was celebrated with bells and bonfires, but the Dutch were appalled and rioting broke out in Amsterdam.

The damage inflicted by the Great Fire of London in September 1666 forced the war to take a back seat and by early 1667 the conflict seemed as good as over. Despite the start of peace

*Full hull model of the* Naseby, *later the*
Royal Charles. *Robert Spence, 1943.* SLR0001.

negotiations, however, there was to be one final incident that worked to strengthen the Dutch hand at the negotiating table: their raid on the Medway. This audacious attack was masterminded by the Dutch Grand Pensionary Johan de Witt, and saw admirals Michiel de Ruyter and Willem van Ghent navigate the tricky River Medway, break through English defences and set fire to and capture several great ships, including the navy's flagship the *Royal Charles*, which was towed back to Amsterdam as a prize. It was to prove one of the most embarrassing moments in English naval history, and recriminations aimed at the navy's management would continue for many years. Just over a week after the raid, the Treaty of Breda, which ended the Second Anglo-Dutch War, was completed. The Navigation Acts were revised to be more favourable to the Dutch than before, and while the English retained New Netherland (which would later become New York and New Jersey), the Dutch Republic retained the lucrative colony of Surinam. The silent guest at the negotiating table was Louis XIV of France, who anxiously watched the growing confidence of the English, who were at that time uneasy allies of the French.

The Third Anglo-Dutch War, fought between 1672 and 1674, formed a small but significant part of a larger geo-political conflict between France and the Dutch Republic. Louis XIV had his sights set on conquering the Netherlands, but he needed Charles II's support. A clandestine agreement was reached in 1670 between the two monarchs, called the Treaty of Dover. It carried huge risks for Charles II but also the lure of massive financial gain – 'two millions of crowns' to be precise. In it, Charles agreed to support a French war against the Dutch by providing 6,000 soldiers for the land attack and 50 warships for the inevitable battles at sea. In exchange, he was promised Walcheren and the isle of Cadzand, both at the mouth of the River Scheldt. The other part of the treaty stipulated that Charles II was to announce his conversion to Catholicism at some later point. If discovered, the terms of the agreement would have been utterly explosive and could very well have cost Charles II his crown; but it would take over 100 years for the details to emerge.

*Painting depicting the* Royal Charles *being towed back into Dutch waters. Ludolf Backhuysen, 1667. NMM, Caird Fund.* BHC0292.

Unable to reveal the truth, Charles needed a proxy reason to go to war. He found it in August 1671, when the royal yacht *Merlin*, carrying Dorothy Osborne, the wife of Sir William Temple (an English statesman), sailed through a line of Dutch warships and they failed to salute in the proper manner. This provided a pretext for a deliberately more aggressive English attitude to the Dutch, which became conflict when, in March 1672, Sir Robert Holmes was allowed to attack the Dutch homebound annual trade convoy from Turkey in the Channel. The English formally declared war on 7 April 1672, the day after the French had done the same. The French were rapid in their land attack, advancing along the Rhine towards Betuwe in the Dutch Republic. The first action at sea was swift to arrive too: the Battle of Solebay, which took place on 28 May 1672. George Monck had died in 1670, but several figures from the previous wars returned to action, including the Earl of Sandwich, Prince Rupert and Edward Spragge. Overall charge of the fleet – which consisted of a combined English and French force of 93 ships – fell to the Duke of York in his flagship the *Prince*. As the disunited allied fleet engaged with Michiel de Ruyter's Dutch warships, the French component fled. The battle proved

*Miniature of Charles II. Samuel Cooper, c.1660–65.*
*NMM, Caird Collection.* MNT0188.

inconclusive, with gains and losses on both sides. Perhaps the most notable loss for the English was the Earl of Sandwich, whose body was found washed up on shore, only identifiable by the Garter ribbon on his clothing.

The Battle of Solebay was a huge blow to English morale, which was further undermined by Dutch propaganda. Throughout all three wars the power of print media was used to attack the other side. By the Third Anglo-Dutch War propaganda had become so fierce that the English physician Henry Stubbe remarked, 'The *Tongues*, the *outrages* and *insolences* of the *Dutch*, have done *England* more *prejudice*, than *Their Ships* and *Canons*.'[6] Yet there was more failure to come. Following the Test Act of 1673, which prevented Roman Catholics from holding government office, the Duke of York was replaced in active command by Prince Rupert. In late May 1673, the prince instigated two attacks on the Dutch fleet at anchor, which came to be known as the Battles of Schooneveld. Despite their inferiority in numbers – 64 Dutch ships to 86 English and French ships – the Dutch managed to defeat the allied attack, proving once again the naval superiority of their commander, Michiel de Ruyter. The allied forces' subsequent attempts to draw out de Ruyter resulted in the final engagement of the war, the Battle of Texel, in August 1673. With the weather against them, the allied navies struggled to overpower de Ruyter's attacking Dutch forces and the overall conflict, for the English at least, came to an embarrassing end. Homegrown opposition, combined with another defeat, ensured that the English bowed out under the 1674 Treaty of Westminster.

# Damaris Page

Referred to by Samuel Pepys as 'the great bawd of the seamen',[7] Damaris Page was a famous brothel keeper and property developer with intimate connections to the navy. Born into poverty in Stepney in 1620, Page became a sex worker in her teens and a successful madam by her twenties. She operated two London brothels: one for naval officers, and one for lower-ranking seamen. She bolstered her profits by press-ganging clientele, which was deeply unpopular, and in the 1668 Bawdy House Riots, she was one of the first to lose her establishment to rioters. She died the following year a wealthy woman, having built a small property empire in the East End. According to her biographer, Page continued her lifelong charity in her will, leaving money to 100 poor seamen's widows.

On the surface, the Anglo-Dutch Wars of the seventeenth century appear to have produced few tangible achievements. Yet they would prove to be revolutionary: naval tactics were radically redefined, highly significant territories were conquered and the architecture of the warship was re-sculpted and perfected for broadside battle. The process of recruiting seamen through 'pressing' became entrenched, while print media were utilized to wage propaganda wars both within and outside the respective combatant nations. Administrative systems were substantially improved, creating a bureaucracy that would serve as the backbone of the Royal Navy for centuries to come. The legacy of these wars can perhaps be found in a popular pamphlet from 1652, depicting Oliver Cromwell with the tail of a fox scrambling up the wheel of fortune as General at Sea Robert Blake tries to keep him aloft. The image is tagged with the Dutch phrase '*hebben is hebben, krijgen is kunst*', which translates as, 'having is having, but getting is an art'.[8] The Anglo-Dutch Wars of the seventeenth century gave both the English and the Dutch the perfect arena in which to refine the art of 'krijgen'.

*Portrait of Prince Rupert. Sir Peter Lely, c.1665. BHC2989.*

*Painting of the Battle of Texel. Abraham Storck, late seventeenth century. NMM, Palmer Collection. Acquired with the assistance of H.M. Treasury, the Caird Fund, the Art Fund, the Pilgrim Trust and the Society for Nautical Research Macpherson Fund. BHC0307.*

*Engraving of Edward Teach, or 'Blackbeard'. Joseph Nicholls, 1734.* PAD2732.

# A Sea of Scoundrels: Pirates of the Stuart Era

## Aaron Jaffer

The world's oceans have known many pirates. It is the period covering the late seventeenth and early eighteenth centuries, commonly called the 'Golden Age of Piracy', that is most prominent in the public mind. Historians cannot agree on when exactly this 'Golden Age' began, but the ten or so years that followed the accession of Britain's first Hanoverian king in 1714 are widely acknowledged to be its climax. The 1710s and early 1720s are associated with a collection of pirates whose names have become legendary for their daring and often violent exploits. Chief among these was Edward Teach (c.1680–1718), whose fierce appearance, nickname of 'Blackbeard' and decapitation by a Royal Navy officer have done as much for his lasting fame as his somewhat short piratical career off the eastern seaboard of the Americas. The famous Welsh pirate Bartholomew Roberts (1682–1722) was far more successful: he reputedly captured over 400 ships and disrupted Britain's expanding slave trade in West Africa. Also active at this time were Anne Bonny (c.1698–1782) and Mary Read (c.1695–1721), two female pirates known for dressing in men's clothes, who have been viewed both as perplexing anomalies and as feminist icons. Sensationalized biographies of these men and women and of many of their contemporaries appeared in *A General History of the Robberies and Murders of the Most Notorious Pyrates* (1724). Published under the name of 'Captain Charles Johnson' – the author's true identity remains disputed – this bestseller is perhaps the most influential book on piracy ever written.[1]

These flamboyant figures from the 1710s and early 1720s come closest to the popular notion of a pirate. They attacked indiscriminately, not limiting themselves to the vessels of a particular nation. They ranged long distances in ships capable of spending weeks or months at sea. They used black flags bearing skulls, hourglasses, bleeding hearts and other morbid motifs to terrorize their victims. They would later serve as inspiration for Robert Louis Stevenson's adventure novel *Treasure Island* (1883), J. M. Barrie's blockbuster play *Peter Pan* (1904), several generations of Hollywood swashbucklers and innumerable other works of fiction.

*Engraving of Henry Morgan. Joseph Nicholls, 1734. PAD2637.*

*Engraving of Bartholomew Roberts. Joseph Nicholls, 1734. PAD2721.*

Scholars, meanwhile, have expended much ink arguing over whether they should be seen as glorified rogues or misunderstood rebels.[2]

Stripping away the layers of myth and romance is essential to understanding the complex and violent realities of piracy, a problem which of course continues to trouble the oceans to this day. The so-called Golden Age of Piracy was a chaotic and unsustainable phase that ended in the 1720s, when its most prominent captains and crews were captured or killed. It was, moreover, the conclusion of a much longer period during which robbery at sea was widespread and, in many cases, encouraged by monarchs, officials, landowners and others in positions of authority. This chapter will introduce some of the countless people who were labelled as 'pirates' during the Stuart era. This group included family men who engaged in

*Engraving of Anne Bonny from Charles Johnson,* Historie der Engelsche zee-roovers, beginnende met de geschiedenisse van capiteyn Avery, en zyne makkers. *Amsterdam, 1725. PBB0231.*

*Engraving of Mary Read from Charles Johnson,* Historie der Engelsche zee-roovers, beginnende met de geschiedenisse van capiteyn Avery, en zyne makkers. *Amsterdam, 1725. PBB0231.*

part-time piracy, aristocrats in search of glory, English converts to Islam, pirates who doubled as explorers and ruthless crews who were backed by respectable investors ashore. These examples serve to remind us that piracy has taken many different forms and that our understanding of it need not be preoccupied with its most famous chapter.

We often associate piracy with tropical settings, but it was rife around the cold and rainy coastlines of the British Isles throughout the Middle Ages and Tudor period.[3] It was still a problem in 1603 when James VI of Scotland became James I of England. The king condemned piracy as loudly as he condemned witchcraft and tobacco, but it was not until the 1620s that it ceased to be a major problem in the waters around his kingdoms. These part-time pirates typically ranged short distances from convenient bases like Studland Bay in Dorset, living on

An English Ship in Action with Barbary Corsairs.
*Willem van de Velde the Younger, c.1685.*
*NMM, Palmer Collection. Acquired with the assistance of*
*H.M. Treasury, the Caird Fund, the Art Fund, the Pilgrim Trust*
*and the Society for Nautical Research Macpherson Fund.* BHC0323.

*A painting of a Dutch merchantman attacked by an English ship. Cornelis Claesz van Wieringen, 1616. NMM, Caird Collection. BHC0723.*

land and frequently holding other jobs when not at sea. They often enjoyed the support and protection of local magnates, to whom they paid huge shares. Their motivations were similar to those that drive people into piracy today: poverty, a lack of alternative occupations, membership of communities that considered their actions justifiable and the inability of the central authorities to exert control over coastal areas.[4] The Thames was a particularly lawless waterway, with the impoverished men and women living along its banks eager to rob passing trade going in and out of London. They stole everything from expensive cargoes of wine and textiles to more mundane items like fishing tackle and butter. Names such as 'Black Will' and 'Dick of Dover' were associated with numerous acts of riverine piracy but, as with rural outlaws, it is impossible to know whether they referred to individuals or whether they were used by more than one person.[5]

Women played important roles in domestic piracy. Pirates relied on wives, mistresses, mothers and daughters to aid them in their illicit business, as well as on women who ran shops, alehouses and brothels. The records of the High Court of Admiralty are littered with examples of women who provided alibis for pirates, received their stolen goods and even helped them escape from prison. These women have not received the same attention as Bonny or Read but their cases provide fascinating examples of ingenuity, defiance and violence during fraught encounters

# Gráinnie O'Malley (c.1530–c.1603)

Gráinnie (Anglicized to 'Grace') O'Malley provides a rare but fascinating example of a sixteenth-century woman who was directly involved in piracy. Most of what is known about her comes from official sources, often hostile towards this 'most famous femynyne sea captain' who outlived two husbands. As the daughter of a chief based in Clew Bay on Ireland's western coast, her family claimed customary rights over surrounding waters. After her father's death, she continued the tradition of attacking passing ships and launching short-range coastal raids using swift and highly manoeuvrable vessels known as 'galleys'. O'Malley lived during an era of growing Tudor power and struggles within Gaelic society. She was implicated in uprisings against the English, one official even claiming that she was 'nurse to all the rebellions in the province [of Connacht]', but her overall approach was to compromise with them. She famously journeyed to Greenwich Palace in 1593 to petition Elizabeth I for the release of imprisoned family members and to claim her property rights as a widow, the first of two such visits. Like Anne Bonny, that other celebrated piratical Irishwoman, O'Malley and her exploits have been romanticized and exaggerated by novelists, illustrators, musicians and scriptwriters. Often portrayed as a rebellious 'pirate queen', she is better understood as a resourceful leader who used piracy to survive in a volatile political environment.[7]

with the law. A pirate named Edward Edmondes, for example, escaped arrest near Bristol in 1604 thanks to the help of three female family members. A Frenchman sent to apprehend him complained of being menaced by his 'wife and her sister, the one with a rapier & the other with a dagger'. Another report alleged that his mother had advised throwing scalding water at those trying to arrest her son.[6]

One of the reasons many seafaring communities condoned piracy was because it existed alongside lawful forms of violence at sea. There were various circumstances under which Stuart rulers and their representatives authorized subjects to plunder or seize foreign vessels. Merchants who became embroiled in armed disputes with their competitors were allowed to engage in reprisal action to recover losses. Private individuals, meanwhile, were encouraged to take part in naval warfare during conflicts – a cheap and effective way of attacking the shipping of hostile nations. 'Privateering', a term coined in the mid-seventeenth century, also licensed the seizure of enemy vessels as potential prizes. These practices were, of course, highly vulnerable to unscrupulous captains, legal ambiguities and the vagaries of international politics. Unsurprisingly, the word 'pirate' was often used as a term of abuse by those on opposing sides.[8] Sir Kenelm Digby's (1603–65) contentious voyage of 1628 provides a particularly colourful example of the muddy waters in which state-sanctioned plunder flourished. This young aristocrat was desperate to redeem his family's honour after his father's execution as a Gunpowder Plot conspirator. The English were at war with both Spain and France, so he secured a royal commission and set out to attack enemy shipping. Digby sailed to the Mediterranean, taking with him two ships and around 250 men, all paid for from his own purse. His eventful expedition culminated in a skirmish at the Turkish port of Iskanderun. Digby's eagerness to seize French vessels caused him to attack those belonging to Venice,

which was not at war with England.[9] He was greeted as a hero
when he returned home, but the Venetians declared,
with some justification, that his actions were unlawful.
Their indignant ambassador questioned why Charles
I should protect 'a man whose father was a traitor ...
and himself a pirate'.[10]

Digby's voyage had also taken him to what
Europeans called the 'Barbary Coast', a blanket
term covering the regencies of Algiers, Tunis
and Tripoli – all nominally part of the Ottoman
Empire – as well as the independent kingdom of
Morocco. The rulers of these states sanctioned
attacks on their northern neighbours as part of
a long-running conflict between Christianity and
Islam, providing themselves with a useful source
of income and a means of maintaining political
stability in the process. The sailors who issued
forth to harass European shipping have often
been called 'pirates' and, as we shall see, their
actions certainly bore many piratical hallmarks.
It is more proper, however, to describe them
and their Christian counterparts as 'corsairs'
since both were engaged in the *corso*, a system
of warfare unique to the Mediterranean that
takes its name from an Italian word for 'chase'
or 'hunt'. This was, in effect, a form of state-
sanctioned raiding based on traditional religious
rivalries rather than individual licensing.[11]

Miniature of Sir Kenelm Digby. John Hoskins, c.1645.
NMM, Caird Collection. MNT0135.

The most lucrative commodity that the Barbary corsairs sought was people, whom they
obtained by what an English consul at Tripoli grimly described as going out 'a Christian-
stealing'.[12] Corsairs could sell men, women and children for handsome profits in North Africa's
numerous slave markets. Ships crossing the Mediterranean, sailing to the Americas or returning
from Atlantic fishing grounds all fell victim to corsair attacks. More terrifying still were forays
against coastal settlements, in which heavily armed men would come ashore and abduct people
from their homes. Spanish, French, Italian and Portuguese communities bore the brunt of
these attacks, but corsairs also attacked the British Isles during the seventeenth century.
The worst raid took place at the Irish village of Baltimore in 1631, when one group carried off
over a hundred settlers originally from Cornwall, Devon and Somerset. Estimating the number
of Europeans enslaved by the Barbary corsairs has proved a difficult and controversial task.
One historian has put this figure at over a million between 1530 and 1780.[13]

*Painting of shipping off Algiers. Reinier Nooms, seventeenth century.*
*Palmer Collection, NMM. Acquired with the assistance of H.M. Treasury, the Caird Fund, the Art Fund,*
*the Pilgrim Trust and the Society for Nautical Research Macpherson Fund. BHC1766.*

Europeans taken back to North Africa could escape slavery by various means, including arranging for a ransom to be paid or setting up an exchange for one of the many enslaved Muslims held in Christian lands. Digby, for example, paid £1,650 to redeem 50 captives during his visit to Algiers. Another much more dangerous option was to run away. Those lucky enough to return home often wrote accounts of their captivity. Containing a heady mix of adventure, piety, bitterness, travel writing and tirades against Islam, the appeal of such texts to early-modern readers is easy to understand. John Rawlins gave a blow-by-blow account of a violent struggle between Christian captives and Muslim captors in his 1622 narrative, which he self-deprecatingly labelled 'an unpolished work of a poor sailor'.[14] William Okeley, another seafarer, declared that he and his fellow escapees looked 'not like captives broke from the chains of Algiers, but like persons raised from the dead' after escaping using a homemade boat in 1644.[15] These narratives were one of the many ways in which the sea, and the violence wrought upon it, left a cultural mark on the nation. Those who had never seen a pirate, privateer or corsair were introduced to them via books, ballads, songs, sermons, pamphlets and plays.[16]

*Bust of a North African Seafarer, seventeenth or eighteenth century. ZBA5063.*

*Cartouche from a chart of the Levant and the Mediterranean. John Seller, 1675. PBE6862(14).*

# Diogo (1595 to sometime after 1615)

During his complicated and unsettled life, Diogo crossed the Atlantic, Mediterranean and English Channel, sailing with Catholic, Protestant and Muslim seafarers. Born in Bahia in Brazil to enslaved Africans, his Portuguese master took him to Lisbon as a child but then ordered him back to South America when he was 12. He was seized by Barbary corsairs during the passage and sold at Algiers, where his new North African master made him convert to Islam and work as a corsair for seven or eight years. He briefly served aboard another corsair ship until its

English commander returned home to obtain a royal pardon and the crew disembarked. Diogo thus found himself in London and emancipated. He used this newfound freedom to return to his original master in Lisbon, where the Portuguese Inquisition interrogated him in 1615 and wrote down his life story. Diogo's traumatic experiences at sea, shaped by the fierce political and religious struggles of the era, may help to explain what today seems like a perplexing decision to return to his captor.[17]

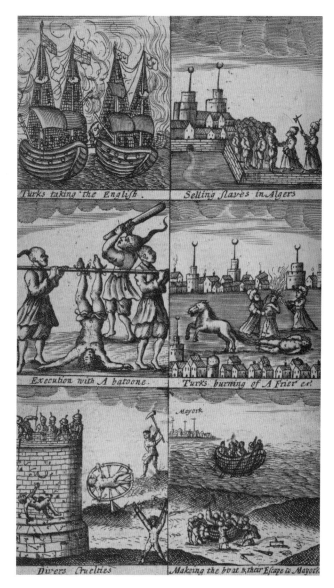

It would be wrong to suggest that all Europeans crossed the Mediterranean as slaves. As Chapter 2 has noted, England had closer contact with the Barbary States than anywhere else in the Islamic World during the Tudor and Stuart era, with the result that diplomats, merchants, soldiers, sailors and artisans travelled south to conduct business. Far more Britons visited North Africa in the early decades of the seventeenth century than set foot in the Americas. This included hundreds of men and women who chose to become Muslims, if only nominally, in order to start new lives in these societies and take advantage of the benefits this might bring. Sailors were so prominent among this group that clergymen

ABOVE *Frontispiece of William Okeley,* Eben-ezer: or, A Small Monument of Great Mercy. *London, 1675.* PBE0647.

RIGHT *Engraving of enslaved Europeans attempting to escape from North Africa from Pierre Dan,* Historie van Barbaryen, en des zelf Zee-Rovers, *Amsterdam, 1684.* PBD154.1.

with seafaring congregations often preached against the temptations of 'turning Turk'. These so-called *renegadoes*, as converts were known, joined other Europeans who used Barbary ports as bases from which to launch attacks.[18]

John Ward (c.1553–c.1623) ranks as England's most successful Muslim pirate. His career is a rags-to-riches tale of mutiny, plunder, conversion and vilification. Supposedly born to a poor family in Kent, he led an uprising on board an English warship in the early seventeenth century. He sailed to Tunis, began plundering ships in the Mediterranean and, according to a man who claimed to have dined with him, eventually took up residence in a house 'beautified with rich Marble and Alabaster stones'.[19] His greatest triumph came in 1607, when he seized the Venetian ship *Reniera e Soderina* and its cargo, valued at £100,000. Ward subsequently tried, but failed, to secure a royal pardon that would have enabled him and his men to return to his native land. Reports that he had converted to

*Miniature of Sir Edward Spragge. Peter Cross, c.1685. NMM, Caird Collection. MNT0190.*

Islam and changed his name to Yusuf Reis earned him widespread condemnation in Europe. Three centuries before Barrie introduced Captain Hook to Edwardian theatregoers, Jacobean dramatists were portraying Ward as an equally contemptible pirate captain. Thomas Dekker's *If This Be Not a Good Play, the Devil Is in It* (1611) featured damned souls anticipating his arrival in Hell, while Robert Daborne's *A Christian Turn'd Turk* (1612) presented him as a lecherous reprobate who ultimately commits suicide. This was wishful thinking since the real Ward would live for another ten years or so after the play was written, probably dying of plague in about 1623. An ambassador to Venice branded him as 'beyond a doubt the greatest scoundrel that ever sailed from England'.[20] A modern reassessment of this skilled sailor and his complicated life might place him in a long line of seafaring scoundrels that also includes Sir John Hawkins, Sir Francis Drake and, as we will see, Sir Henry Morgan.

The European powers were generally too mistrustful of each other to mount joint operations against the Barbary States. Each hoped that the corsairs could be coerced or persuaded into confining their attacks to the vessels of rival nations. It was not until the second half of the seventeenth century that the English and Dutch began asserting their might in the Mediterranean by sending naval expeditions to North Africa. Sir Edward Spragge (c.1629–73), an ambitious English Restoration admiral, earned himself great acclaim and a sizeable pension during one such operation. He destroyed an Algerian squadron at Bugia in 1671 and described the burning vessels as 'our lovely bonfires ... the most glorious sight that ever I saw'.[21] England eventually signed treaties with Algiers, Tripoli and Tunis in the 1680s that ended the Barbary threat to its shipping, until a resurgence following the outbreak of the French Revolution. These campaigns against the corsairs took place at the same time as English officials on the other side of the Atlantic were sponsoring another form of maritime raiding: buccaneering.

Many sailors crossing the Caribbean during the seventeenth century would have tasted wild beef from Hispaniola, which today is home to Haiti and the Dominican Republic. Spain claimed sovereignty over this mountainous island yet consistently failed to stop other Europeans from settling. Living rough, these settlers hunted cattle that had multiplied after being introduced by earlier colonists. One observer likened them to 'the butcher's vilest servants, who have been eight days in the slaughterhouse without washing themselves'.[22] They smoked meat using a technique borrowed from the few remaining Arawak people and the French called them *boucaniers* after the wooden grill, or *boucan*, used in the process. Spanish efforts to remove

An English Ship in Action with Barbary Vessels. *Willem van de Velde the Younger, 1678.*
*NMM, Caird Collection. BHC089.3.*

*A nimcha (Moroccan sword) taken from a North African ship, c.1675. WPN1057.*

these hunters in the 1630s backfired when they fled to the nearby island of Tortuga and started using small boats to attack passing ships.

The former hunters were joined by many newcomers, who also took to piracy. The two groups gradually became indistinguishable, all being labelled with the Anglicized word 'buccaneer'. The buccaneers operated as a loose confederation of raiders – chiefly French, English and Dutch – who came together at sporadic intervals to pillage the towns and villages of the 'Spanish Main', as Spain's territory on the mainland was known. 'Pieces of eight!', the catchphrase of Long John Silver's parrot, referred to the *peso de ocho reales*, or Spanish dollar, that the most successful buccaneers stole by the thousand. The famous Welsh buccaneer Henry Morgan (c.1635–88) took approximately 750,000 of these silver coins after marching his men through the jungle and sacking Panama in 1671.

Buccaneers armed themselves with the sorts of weapons that could be found on board

*A map of Hispaniola. Nicholas Comberford, 1653. G245:8/2.*

warships and merchantmen. This included everything from knives and bludgeons to pistols and blunderbusses. Cutlasses were particularly useful in hand-to-hand combat on the cramped decks of sailing ships. These short and heavy swords could also be used for everyday tasks such as cutting rope or chopping firewood. The buccaneers routinely used violence to frighten people into submission and discover the whereabouts of valuables. It is worth noting that there are no documented examples of buccaneers or Golden Age pirates making people 'walk the plank', although both are known to have tortured prisoners in ways that make this mode of execution seem tame. Such brutality, however, seldom exceeded the levels of violence witnessed on land as part of colonization, enslavement or religious conflict during the seventeenth century.[23]

Oliver Cromwell sent a military expedition known as the Western Design to the Caribbean in 1655. This scheme failed to seize Hispaniola but began English (later British) rule in Jamaica, which was wrested from Spanish control. The island became a major buccaneering centre as governors granted questionable licences to attack the Spanish. Port Royal, its capital, was known as the 'Sodom of the New World' thanks to the riotous behaviour of returning crews. Merchants relied on these consumers not to bury their treasure but to support the local economy by spending it on alcohol, provisions and prostitutes. It would take several decades before sugar replaced piracy as the basis of the island's economy. The presence of so many heavily armed buccaneers also discouraged Spanish attacks against the fledgling colony. This marriage of convenience ended following the Treaty of Madrid in 1670, whereby Spain relinquished all claims to Jamaica and England promised to suppress its buccaneers. Morgan

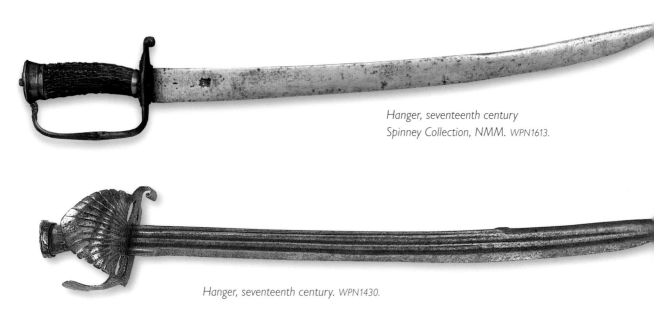

*Hanger, seventeenth century*
*Spinney Collection, NMM. WPN1613.*

*Hanger, seventeenth century. WPN1430.*

*Two pieces of eight minted during the reign of Philip II of Spain, (1557–98). Seville, sixteenth century. OBJ0197.3-4.*

was arrested for piracy – his Panama raid occurred after the agreement was signed – but, in a curious example of poacher-turned-gamekeeper, he was appointed acting governor of Jamaica in 1674 and knighted.

English buccaneers who were eager to continue raiding began venturing into the Pacific. This huge ocean was still almost completely unknown to Europeans despite its being termed a 'Spanish lake'. The 1680s witnessed about a thousand buccaneers travel across the Isthmus of Panama or sail round via the Straits of Magellan or Cape Horn, at the tip of South America. These men described themselves as 'privateers', but most sailed with licences of dubious validity or with none at all, making their attacks along the coasts of what are now Chile, Peru and Mexico acts of outright piracy. It was for this reason that Bartholomew Sharp,

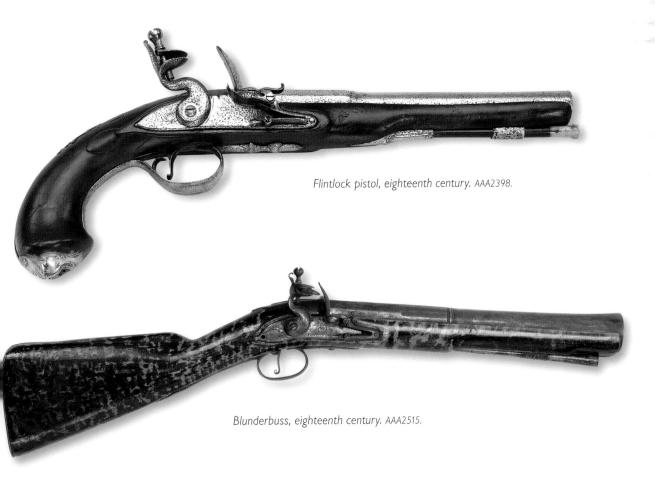

*Flintlock pistol, eighteenth century. AAA2398.*

*Blunderbuss, eighteenth century. AAA2515.*

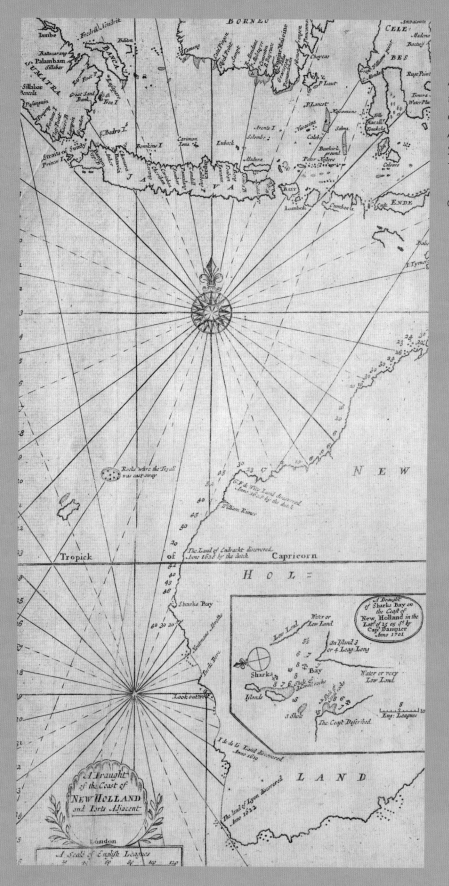

A chart of the west coast of Australia. Samuel Thornton, 1703. G262:11/11.

a skilled seafarer but an unpopular buccaneer captain, was put on trial after returning to England. He was pardoned by Charles II, almost certainly due to his possession of a volume of important charts that his crew had taken from a ship named the *Santa Rosario*, which he presented to the king. 'The Spaniards cried when I gott the book', he boasted in his journal.[24]

These 'South Sea Men', as they were called, produced a remarkable body of logs, diaries, maps, navigational notes, voyage narratives and other writings that vastly expanded England's knowledge of the region.[25] William Dampier (1651–1715), one of Sharp's shipmates, emulated Drake and sailed westwards across the Pacific as part of a long and eventful journey home. He bettered the Elizabethan Sea Dog, however, by becoming the first Englishman to land on what would one day be called Australia in 1688. The account he published helped transform him from buccaneer to best-selling author. He made the now-notorious statement that the Aboriginal men and women he met, thought to be the Bardi people, were 'the miserablest People in the World'. More useful are his descriptions of the words they used and their lack of interest in European clothes, neither of which he was able to understand. Dampier would return to Australia, but British colonization of the continent would not begin for another century.[26]

Pirates from the Atlantic and Caribbean also descended on the Indian Ocean during a short-lived but spectacular series of raids that began during King William's War (1689–97). Spain's power in the Americas, along with its wealth, had declined and many pirates were in search of new hunting grounds. Their targets were Asian ships carrying gold, silver, ivory, spices and other valuable goods, as well as pilgrims travelling to and from Mecca. In the finest piratical traditions of preying upon ships owned by those of different faiths, sailors often justified these attacks on the grounds that their victims were Hindus and Muslims. Many of these pirates were backed by wealthy investors in the Americas, who financed their voyages and provided outlets for the goods they brought back to the colonies. Frederick Philipse, New York's richest merchant, was at the centre of one elaborate trading network that included not only these illegal voyages but also more respectable enterprises.

These lucrative Indian Ocean ventures relied on pirate settlements in Madagascar, the fourth largest island in the world, which provided a convenient base for launching attacks, dividing plunder and refitting ships. English attempts at founding a colony on the island during the 1640s and 1650s were unsuccessful, but pirates succeeded where more conventional settlers had failed. St Mary's Island, off the north-east coast, was said to have had around 1,500 pirates in residence at start of the eighteenth century. Members of this transient population married local women, entered into alliances with local rulers and drank a local liquor made from honey. European writers indulged in wild fantasies about these distant communities, ignoring the fact that life in this Malagasy utopia could be nasty, brutish and short.[27]

Henry Avery (1659 to after 1699) called at Madagascar to resupply his ship before sailing northwards and capturing the Indian ship *Ganj-i-Sawai* in 1695. He had already achieved notoriety as a mutineer but this exploit would soon earn him the title 'King of Pirates' owing to the staggering value of its cargo. His men spent several days plundering the stricken vessel and committing what one would later describe as 'horrid Barbarities'.[28] They raped the ship's female passengers, although this was soon trivialized by fictional accounts that had Avery marrying an Indian princess supposed to be on board. This act of

*A map of Madagascar from Joan Blaeu,* Atlas Maior, *Amsterdam, 1662–65.* PBD8254/1.

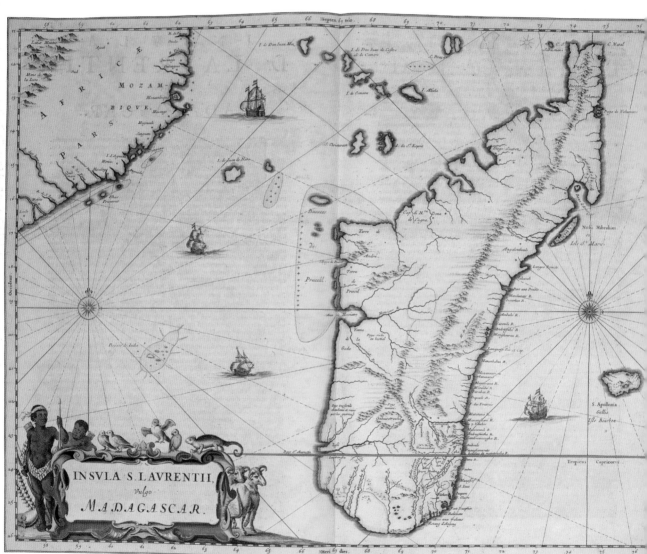

*An engraving of Captain Avery. W. Tett, 1734.*
PAD2666.

piracy, along with those of the Scottish seaman William Kidd less than two years later, angered the Mughal emperor Aurangzeb and threatened the East India Company's precarious position on the subcontinent. Kidd was executed on 23 May 1701 at Execution Dock in Wapping, maintaining until the end that he was merely a privateer. Avery, by contrast, was never caught. How and where he lived out the rest of his days remains a subject of speculation.

Robbery at sea was one of the most lucrative 'exports' of the Tudor and Stuart era, but England's attitude to global piracy hardened in the late seventeenth century. Indicative of this was 'An Act for the more effectual Suppression of Piracy', passed in 1700, which greatly improved the means of prosecuting pirates and paved the way for hundreds of executions over the coming decades. Many pirates conveniently joined naval vessels or privateers during the War of the Spanish Succession (1701–14), but officials soon began to worry about what these men would do once peace came. Sailors like Edward Teach, who appears to have worked as a privateer during the conflict, proceeded to justify these fears by refusing to give up their violent way of life. No longer sailing under national flags or even claiming to serve national interests, members of this new generation of looters were increasingly portrayed as outcasts beyond redemption, both by officials and in print. Some pirates even mocked the new Hanoverian king, George I, by giving their ships names like the *Royal James* or the *King James* in reference to the Stuarts. The climax of the 'Golden Age of Piracy' had arrived.

Elizabeth I, 1533–1603, the 'Armada Portrait'. *English School, c.1588. NMM, acquired with the support of the Heritage Lottery Fund, the Art Fund, Linbury Trust, Garfield Weston Foundation, Headley Trust and other major donors, together with contributions from over 8,000 members of the public following a joint appeal with the Art Fund.* ZBA7719.

# Art and the Maritime World, 1550–1714

## Christine Riding

By 1590, one of the great iconic images of British history, the Armada portrait of Elizabeth I, was created. The work commemorates the most celebrated event of Elizabeth's reign, the failed invasion of England by Philip II's 'invincible' Armada. As such, it can be said to summarize not only the achievements but also the hopes and aspirations of the monarch and the state at a watershed moment. Furthermore, this supremely powerful and confident image has come to represent, anachronistically, the now seemingly irresistible rise of the English navy and thus the making of a maritime superpower. The queen is shown in a richly embroidered and bejewelled dress, as the epitome of royal magnificence, her right hand resting on a terrestrial globe showing the Americas, an imperial crown on the table behind, and beside her a chair of state. The seascapes in the background represent two events from the campaign: on the left, the English fleet in calm waters with fireships approaching the Armada, and on the right, home-bound Spanish ships being wrecked on some remote coast of the British Isles, in a menacing storm. Far from displaying any of the anxiety and vulnerability she undoubtedly felt in the summer of 1588, Elizabeth is shown dominating the composition, her eyes turned towards us, her expression composed, almost otherworldly, and her demeanour commanding.

During the 1570s, portraits of the queen began to utilize the iconography of Empire, such as globes, crowns, swords and columns. At the same time, the representation of globes also became indispensable elements within portraits of Elizabethan imperialist explorers, such as Sir Francis Drake (see page 47). Indeed, Drake may well have commissioned or owned the version of the Armada portrait now in the National Maritime Museum's collection. The idea of Elizabeth as the 'Empress of the World' was complemented by a second layer of symbolism representing her as the Virgin Queen, the destined Protestant defender and protector of her people. This dual emphasis was heralded by John Dee's *General and Rare Memorials Pertayning to the Prefect Arte of Navigation*, published in 1577, which first promoted the notion of a 'British Empire', including expansion into the New World, backed by a strong navy. His argument was given visual form in the accompanying frontispiece, which showed Elizabeth enthroned on board a ship representing

Protestant Europe with the figure of Britannia kneeling on the shore, entreating the queen to fulfil her imperial destiny. The successful defence of the realm in 1588 gave fresh impetus and justification to such representations. Poems and pamphlets extolled Elizabeth as vanquisher of the Roman Catholic threat, of which Philip II of Spain had constituted himself as the leading European military champion. Medals and prints celebrating the Armada's defeat proclaimed it a Protestant victory; the storms that lashed the enemy fleet were evidence of divine

intervention. In this regard, the juxtaposition of 'calm' and 'storm' in the seascapes within the Armada portrait also utilizes the classical 'ship of state' analogy: that is, the effect of good governance under Protestant Elizabeth (left), juxtaposed with that of tyrannical rule under Catholic Philip (right).

*The embarkation of Henry VIII at Dover, c.1520–40. Royal Collection, Hampton Court.*

*Portrait of Charles Howard. Studio of Daniel Mytens the Elder, c.1620. NMM, Greenwich Hospital Collection. BHC2786.*

What is often overlooked in discussions of the Armada portrait, however, is how unusual it is in representing Elizabeth, or indeed any British monarch prior to 1588, in a naval and maritime context. In discussions of the development of European marine painting, for example, art historians have highlighted the Armada of 1588 and the earlier Battle of Lepanto of 1571 – during which the Holy League led by Don John of Austria, Philip II of Spain's half-brother, inflicted a major defeat on the Ottoman Empire – as key moments.[1] In effect, these major fleet actions acted as drivers for the creation of maritime imagery and particularly for the focus on, and eventual dominance of, battle painting from 1600 onwards. However, in representing contemporary or near-contemporary events (as opposed to the maritime world as backdrop to historical, biblical or classical narratives), artists had few examples to look at in European art before the mid-sixteenth century. One of the earliest was painted for Henry VIII (see page 82), showing the king embarking from Dover in 1520 to meet with François I of France at the so-called Field of the Cloth of Gold. Thus, the novelty of the Armada portrait's composition in the late sixteenth century lies primarily in its inclusion of the two marine paintings.[2]

The development of European marine painting as a distinct and specialist artistic genre is closely linked to one of the most luxurious, costly and thus prestigious forms of art at the time: tapestry design. Arguably, the most impressive visual expression of the Armada victory was not painted but woven. The Armada tapestries, ten large-scale battle scenes with

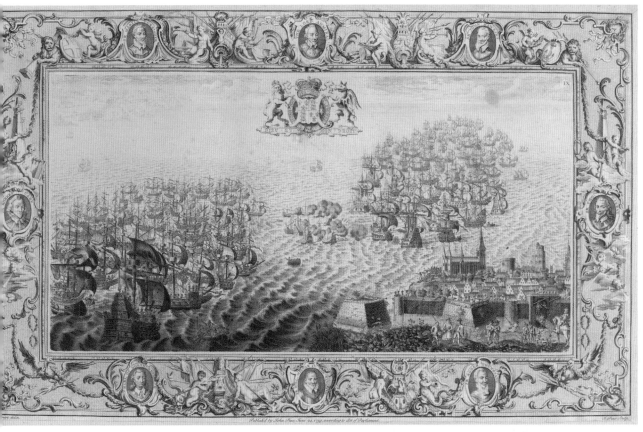

*Print of the Spanish Armada, taken from a series of tapestries that hung in the House of Lords until the whole building was destroyed by fire in 1834. C. Lempriere, 24 June 1739. PAI6238.*

medallion portraits of the English commanders in the borders, were commissioned from the Spiering manufactory in Delft by Charles Howard, Lord Admiral of the Navy, in 1588, and used to decorate the walls of the Howard residence, Arundel House, in the Strand. The designer was Hendrick Vroom, an artist from Haarlem, commonly regarded as the 'father of marine painting'.[3] Vroom based his designs on the maps by Robert Adams and a detailed account of the Armada campaign, also commissioned by Howard. Delivered in 1595 and costing the colossal sum of £1,582, the Armada Tapestries may have resulted from a private commission, but they were in every sense a national statement that came to define not just a historical event but the Elizabethan maritime age for generations to come. Perhaps unsurprisingly, rumours abounded at the time that Howard would present his tapestries to the queen herself.

Elizabeth I's carefully constructed image as a Protestant heroine with an impressive record in military success, imperial endeavour and defending the realm became the standard by which her Stuart successors were judged. This may in part explain why James I acquired the Armada tapestries from Lord Howard in 1616. Furthermore, the king's focus on peace through diplomacy from 1603 onwards was balanced by a concerted effort at court to present his eldest son, Henry, as a potential militant Protestant hero, through portraiture and his participation in elaborate entertainments that included imperial and maritime symbolism, and mock sea battles.[4] One such entertainment, 'Prince Henry's Barriers', performed in 1610, was presented as a rebirth of Arthurian chivalry founded on British military and naval victories, at the forefront of which was the Armada campaign. The same year saw the launching of the *Prince Royal*, named in Henry's honour, which was at that time the largest, most powerful and splendid warship in England. Conceived as a national symbol, the ship was liberally decorated with the Prince of Wales's feathers and the cypher 'HP', and the figurehead represented St George, the patron saint of England, and the Order of the Garter, the nation's highest chivalric order. Henry kept a model of the *Prince Royal* in his cabinet room at Richmond Palace.

Peter Pett and the 'Sovereign of the Seas'. *Sir Peter Lely, c.1645–50.*
*NMM, Caird Collection.* BHC2949.

The launching itself was commemorated in a portrait of Phineas Pett, the earliest of a group of seventeenth-century portraits showing royal shipwrights with prestigious vessels, subsequent examples being Peter Pett with the *Sovereign of the Seas* of 1637 (see opposite) and Fisher Harding with the *Royal Sovereign* (1701).[5]

By his late teens, Prince Henry had a burgeoning role as a Protestant leader and champion of the navy, maritime exploration and colonial expansion. His death in November 1612 was perceived as a blow in every regard. Indeed, the Elizabethan 'Golden Age' of military triumph and lucrative naval raids against Spain was, by the 1620s, an embarrassing point of comparison for the Stuarts. Contemporaries needed only to compare Essex's successful Cádiz expedition of 1596 with that led by the Duke of Buckingham in 1625, or the Elizabethan victory over the Armada with the Caroline fiasco in defence of the Huguenots at La Rochelle (1628–29). The prelude to the second Cádiz foray and La Rochelle was the visit to Spain made by Charles and Buckingham in 1623 to further a marriage alliance between the prince and the Spanish Infanta. Albeit unsuccessful, the attempt was viewed by many as a betrayal of England's ongoing mission against Catholic tyranny. Charles's return from Spain was commemorated in paintings by Hendrick Vroom, with the *Prince Royal* shown leading the fleet home.[6] At the same time, the Dutch artist Adam Willaerts produced paintings showing the departure from Margate and arrival at Flushing (Vlissingen) of the Protestant Frederick, Elector Palatine, and James I's daughter Elizabeth, after their London marriage in 1613. The choice of subject was politically charged, first, because the royal couple had returned to the Netherlands in 1622 as exiles (Frederick was deposed from the Bohemian throne by Hapsburg forces), and second, because of the prominent representation in Willaerts's paintings of the *Prince Royal*, the pride of the English fleet, launched and decorated in honour of a Protestant British prince.

By the 1630s, Charles I was seeking to redefine the Stuart monarchy, not as the prosecutor of war and empire in emulation of the Elizabethans, but as the guardian of peace. The new pacific order was heralded by the termination of the Accession Day jousts, an event instigated by Elizabeth I and continued by James I, and by a significant change in tone and symbolism of court masques, which were performed before the monarch, the court and foreign dignitaries at the Banqueting House, Whitehall. During Thomas Carew's masque *Coelum Britannicum* of 1634, a mock decree from Jupiter, King of the Gods, announced the banishment of trophies and mementoes of past conflicts, including the 'hangings [i.e. tapestries] of the Guard-Chamber of this court, wherein the Naval Victory of [15]88 is to the eternal glory of this nation exactly delineated'.[7] Only three years later, the *Sovereign of the Seas*, which superseded the *Prince Royal* as the most powerful and spectacular English warship, was launched. Decorated with an iconographic scheme – designed by the playwright Thomas Heywood – that combined legendary British history, classical references and royal symbolism (mirroring the language of contemporary masques), the ship propagandized Charles I's claim to rule the oceans using naval power as an instrument of global peace. The supreme irony of that claim is underscored by Peter Lely's portrait of the shipwright, with the ship itself painted by an unidentified assistant – an image probably executed during the English Civil War.

*Portrait of
Sir John Harman.
Sir Peter Lely, 1666.
NMM, Greenwich Hospital
Collection. BHC2750.*

While Charles had sought to remove the Armada tapestries (and the history they represented) from public consciousness, in 1644 they were on display in the Parliamentarian House of Lords, a calculated act by Oliver Cromwell that sought to align the Elizabethan past with Parliament's present-day struggle against popery and absolutism.

Charles II's restoration to the throne in 1660 presented an opportunity to emphasize continuity with his father's reign and to promote the legitimacy and achievements of the new regime in art and culture. The cosmopolitan artistic scene that developed in the capital and beyond was exploited at court, not least by the king's brother James, Duke of York. Importantly, James had a personal investment in the visual culture surrounding the navy, as Lord High Admiral and through his personal command of the English fleet during the Second and Third Anglo-Dutch Wars. Furthermore, the plentiful subject matter that emanated from the bloody encounters between the Dutch and English navies was to result in an unprecedented boom in maritime-related imagery.

In portraiture, the obvious successor to Charles I's principal painter, Sir Anthony van Dyck, was Peter Lely, who had been working in London since the 1640s. Between 1665 and 1668,

*Portrait of
Sir William Berkeley.
Sir Peter Lely, 1665–66.
NMM, Greenwich Hospital
Collection.* BHC2553.

Lely undertook a commission from James, Duke of York, for a series of naval portraits, the so-called Flagmen of Lowestoft (above and left). The 'flagmen' set consists of 13 individual portraits of prominent naval officers, most of flag rank, who had fought at the victorious Battle of Lowestoft against the Dutch in 1665. Generally, Lely worked in emulation of van Dyck, and his portraits of the 'flagmen' follow the standard established by the Flemish artist, above all in the full-length portrait of Algernon Percy, 10th Earl of Northumberland.[8] Northumberland was appointed admiral in charge of Charles I's ship-money fleet in 1636. Painted soon afterwards, the portrait shows him standing on coastal battlements surrounded by various accoutrements that denote his court status and naval responsibilities. He wears a blue Garter ribbon over contemporary military dress, and grasps his sword hilt in one hand and his baton of command in the other, as he glances out towards the viewer with gentlemanly ease, leaning on the fluke of a great anchor with his left foot resting casually on its wooden stock. Behind him, two warships are engaged in battle. Thus, the image melds the conventions of naval portraiture with battle painting.

Unlike the more rigid compositions produced by other court artists during the early Stuart period, such as by Paul van Somer and Daniel Mytens, what van Dyck offered the Caroline court, as well as the painters that followed in his wake, was a highly seductive artistic formula – one that suggested the attributes of power and control in a way that made them appear innate and effortless. Eminently transferable, this approach could enhance the reputations of individual officers within a broader visual culture surrounding the Royal Navy that privileged and glamorized the rights of social and naval rank. While the 'flagmen' portraits operate on these levels, the fact that they were produced concurrently with another series by Lely of female courtiers, known as the 'Windsor Beauties', for James's wife Anne Hyde, Duchess of York, also demonstrates how integrated the image of the naval officer-courtier had become in elite culture.[9] Some measure of the legacy of the 'flagmen' series in establishing a shared or even corporate naval identity in British visual culture can be gleaned from a subsequent series of portraits – nine by Godfrey Kneller and seven by Michael Dahl – commissioned by Queen Anne and her husband and Lord High Admiral, Prince George of Denmark, of the leading admirals of her reign (1702–14).[10]

A group of six fishing people. *Willem van de Velde the Elder, c.1655.* PAE5186.

# The van de Veldes

Willem van de Velde the Elder (c.1611–93) was a marine painter of the Dutch Golden Age. He was born in Leiden, the son of a Flemish skipper, and was said to have been bred to the sea. Based in Amsterdam, Willem the Elder was renowned for his 'pen paintings', monochrome representations that accurately depicted shipping and maritime matters. During the 1650s he became the Dutch Republic's semi-official marine painter, accompanying the Dutch fleet during numerous battles, including the Four Days' Battle (1666) and the Battle of Solebay (1672). His two sons, Willem van de Velde the Younger (b.1633) and Adriaen van de Velde (b.1636) were both painters, the latter specializing in landscape. Willem the Elder and Younger moved to England in 1672 and 1673 and entered the service of Charles II. They established a thriving studio practice based at the Queen's House, Greenwich, before moving to Westminster in 1691. By his death in 1707, Willem the Younger was celebrated as the leading marine painter in Europe. His dramatic compositions and naval imagery shaped the development of British seascape painting throughout the eighteenth century and beyond.

*Miniature of William van de Velde the Younger, c.1675–76. NMM, Caird Collection.* MNT0131.

While naval portraiture was evidently well served, what is surprising is the absence of a major battle painting as part of James's 'flagmen' commission. The tradition of marine painting had developed as a distinct genre in the Netherlands during the late sixteenth and early seventeenth centuries, in parallel with the emergence of the United Provinces as a dominant maritime and imperial power. It was primarily Netherlandish artists who brought a visual culture of ships and the sea to England from the 1590s. Those who came to London include Jan Porcellis (a pupil of Hendrick Vroom), Isaac Sailmaker and Adriaen van Diest. The market for Netherlandish marine paintings and drawings, whether parades of ships, coastal scenes or seascapes, thrived across Europe during the entire seventeenth century.

Although the talented and itinerant artists named above were instrumental in the development of marine painting, none of them achieved the enduring fame of Willem van de Velde the Elder and his son, Willem the Younger, or the same impact on contemporary taste, the development of a British maritime identity and the subsequent history of British art. At the time of their migration to England, probably during the winter of 1672–73, the van de Veldes enjoyed an unrivalled reputation that was closely aligned with the military and

Greenwich. Wenceslaus Hollar, 1642. PAJ2421.

A Royal Visit to the Fleet in the Thames Estuary, 1672. *Willem van de Velde the Younger, probably 1670s–1696. NMM, Caird Collection.* BHC0299.

commercial fortunes of the Dutch Republic. Furthermore, both had a lifelong engagement with maritime affairs and the range and intricacies of naval architecture – factors that greatly enhanced their artistic standing. Over and above assisting his father in a thriving studio practice, Willem the Younger had secured his own reputation from the late 1650s as a painter of 'calms' – sunlit maritime scenes, often shown on the shallow waters of the Zuiderzee, which vividly projected an image of the commercial prosperity and social order of the Dutch Republic that was based on its sea power. He would return to this theme, adapted to suit his English clientele and often on a far grander scale, in his portrayal of royal warships, yachts and other vessels, pre-eminent examples being *A Royal Visit to the Fleet in the Thames Estuary, 1672* (left) and *The English Ship* Royal Sovereign *with a Royal Yacht in a Light Air* (page 261).

While Willem the Younger is now recognized as the more innovative and influential artistically, Willem the Elder forged new ground in his method of researching maritime subjects, above all that of naval conflict: for about 20 years he was the Dutch navy's semi-official war artist. During the 1640s, he was at sea with the Dutch fleet and in 1653 the States-General, provided him with a small craft and skipper so that he could observe the Battle of Scheveningen at close quarters. After the battle, he wrote an account that was sent to the States-General noting that 'at about 2 o'clock in the afternoon I saw 14 or 15 ravaged English ships … One of them sank and two were on fire. All this can be seen in the drawings made, as accurately as possible, in the heat of the battle.'[11] One of the 'pen paintings' that he produced as a result, which portrays the event as a Dutch success with the burning of the English ship the *St Andrew*, was probably owned by Harpert Tromp, the son of Admiral Maarten Tromp, who had died during the battle, commanding the Dutch fleet. Therefore, while Hendrick Vroom had had to rely on verbal and written accounts and charts for his Armada imagery, some 50 years later Willem the Elder could claim that his battle scenes achieved greater accuracy and thus authenticity because of his privileged position as an eyewitness – a point he reinforced in some of his paintings, including the image representing Scheveningen, by depicting himself sketching in his galliot within the composition.

The van de Veldes travelled to England as the Dutch came under attack from Anglo-French forces. Thus in May 1672, Willem the Elder would be observing and sketching as his countrymen engaged the Anglo-French fleet during the Battle of Solebay, and within the year was working under royal patronage from a studio in the Queen's House, Greenwich, using the drawings he had made during the battle as the starting point for tapestry designs representing

OPPOSITE *Portrait of James, Duke of York.*
*Henri Gascar, 1672–73.*
*NMM, Greenwich Hospital Collection. BHC2797.*

LEFT *Miniature of George Clifford.*
*Nicholas Hilliard, c.1590.*
*NMM, Caird Collection. MNT0193.*

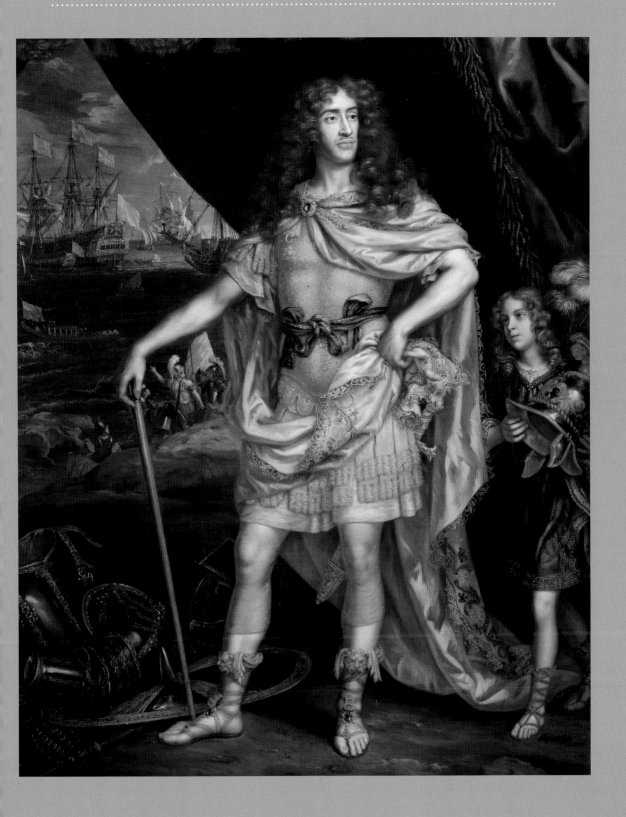

the event from the English perspective. The speed with which the van de Veldes were put to work in the service of the crown and the navy indicates that the arrival of such renowned Dutch artists in London was considered a tremendous coup by Charles II, James and others, not least as a propaganda tool. In fact, the artists' move from one side to the other marks a contemporaneous shift from the Netherlands to England as the artistic hub for ambitious marine painters, as the balance of power between the two rival maritime nations changed.

The royal commission for the tapestries and other works from the van de Veldes is a case in point. Rather than a discrete series of events from the Battle of Solebay, the original commission from Charles II seems to have been more ambitious, involving five or more representations in addition to the Solebay ones, and including fleet actions from 1665 onwards. Drawings by the van de Veldes in the National Maritime Museum's collection representing the Battle of Lowestoft and the Battle of the Texel (1673) suggest that these events were to have been translated into tapestry format.[12] The focus on tapestry design continued in James's concurrent commission from the van de Veldes of large-scale battle paintings executed between 1676 and 1682, which cover events of the Anglo-Dutch Wars

and the ongoing attempts by the Royal Navy to subdue the Barbary corsairs, a subject much favoured by marine painters and naval patrons.[13] Albeit painted, these works of art employ the same high viewpoint and panoramic focus as traditional tapestry design. In this regard, it is worth remembering that the Armada tapestries, which remained on display in the House of Lords, had (post-1660) returned to the ownership of the crown. Hence, it is possible that the van de Veldes were initially employed to create a single, monumental project that sought to represent, writ large, the triumphant rise of the English navy under the restored Stuart monarchy, and, furthermore, using a decorative-art medium that would visually confirm the Stuarts as the heirs to the naval and imperial successes of the Elizabethans. That this was a feature of Restoration psychology is suggested by the inclusion of a suit of armour made at the pre-Civil War royal armoury, Greenwich, in Henri Gascar's flamboyant portrait of James, Duke of York (page 253). Here the prince is shown as the successor, through his classical dress, to the commanders of imperial Rome and at the same time to the military prowess and daring exploits of those who wore Greenwich armour, from Henry VIII, Henry Prince of Wales and other Tudor and Stuart royalty, to Elizabethan warrior-courtiers, such as George Clifford, Earl

The 'Gouden Leeuw' at the Battle of the Texel, 21 August 1673. *Willem van de Velde the Younger, 1687.* NMM, *purchased with the assistance of the Art Fund and the Society for Nautical Research Macpherson Fund.* BHC0315.

of Cumberland, the Queen's Champion and a naval veteran of the 1588 Armada campaign (page 252).

Albeit settled in England under British royal patronage, Willem the Younger did not work exclusively for the English but continued to paint for Dutch clients. One of his acknowledged masterpieces, *The* Gouden Leeuw *at the Battle of the Texel, 21 August 1673* (pages 254-5), is thought to have been painted in 1687 for the Dutch admiral Cornelis Tromp, whose flagship the *Gouden Leeuw* (Golden Lion) is represented in the centre of the composition. The battle itself was the last attempt by combined English and French forces to destroy the Dutch fleet in preparation for an invasion. In van de Velde's painting, the prominence of Tromp's ship, seen firing its guns at the enemy, can be read as a symbol of national defiance. Tromp had visited London in 1675 and was painted by Lely in a similar manner to the 'flagmen' portraits, but with a representation of the *Gouden Leeuw* by Willem the Younger in the background. This artistic collaboration between portraitist and marine painter was conventional in seventeenth-century naval portraiture, as seen in van de Velde's earlier collaboration with Ferdinand Bol for the state portraits of Admiral Michiel de Ruyter (see page 203). The relaxation in Anglo-

William III departs from Hellevoetsluis, 1688. *Style of Abraham Storck.* BHC0325.

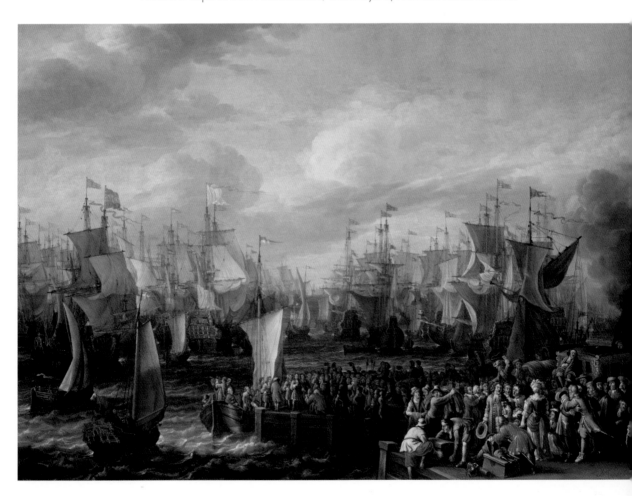

*Tapestry depicting the Battle of Solebay. Thomas Poyntz, c.1672.*
*NMM, purchased with the assistance of the Art Fund, 1968. TXT0106.*

Dutch relations that the above examples represent came after the Treaty of Westminster
(1674) that ended the Third Anglo-Dutch War and saw England withdraw from its alliance
with France and its own war against the Dutch. The direction of political travel was cemented
in 1677 by the marriage of James, Duke of York's eldest daughter Mary to his nephew William
III of Orange (then Admiral-General of the Dutch fleet). This also seems to have resulted in
James's commissioning in 1682, as a gesture of reconciliation, a marine painting representing
the Battle of the Texel, arguably the Dutch navy's finest hour since its audacious raid on
the Medway in 1667.[14] At the same time, work continued on the tapestry commission, now
comprising six large-scale scenes from the Battle of Solebay (above) and woven by the royal
tapestry maker, Frances Poyntz, at Mortlake.

In the event, neither Charles, who died in 1685, nor James, who succeeded him as
James II, ever took delivery of the tapestries. Although Catholic in private, Charles had for
political reasons insisted on the heirs to his throne being raised and/or presented in public as
Protestants. James had converted to Catholicism, however, thus initiating a three-year political

crisis that resulted in the English Parliament inviting William of Orange, by now viewed as the champion of Protestant Europe, to invade England and depose him. William's departure from Hellevoetsluis at the end of October 1688, accompanied by the English and Dutch fleets, and his arrival at Brixham in Torbay on 5 November, were commemorated by numerous artists on both sides of the North Sea (pages 256 and 259). This is unsurprising, given the momentousness of the event for British and European history. While these works of art emphasize the tremendous show of strength that backed William's bid for power – indeed, this is presented as a great *naval* event – the aims and objectives (as shown) are those of peace and stability, not war and aggression. Furthermore, the format employed of royal embarkation and arrival – a long-established theme in marine painting – also self-consciously recalls the works of Adam Willaerts in their depiction of the 1613 departure from England of Frederick, Elector Palatine, an earlier champion of Protestant Europe, as a symbol of hope that had by the 1620s (when the paintings were created) turned into a crisis for the Protestant cause. Consequently, the representations might be said to bookend this protracted struggle for religious autonomy. For the British, the fact that William landed on 5 November, the date associated with the failed Catholic 'Gunpowder Plot' of 1605, and in the centenary year of the 1588 Armada, made the occasion all the more auspicious, if not divinely providential. As a direct result, the late 1680s saw the re-circulation of anti-Catholic imagery of the late-Elizabethan and Jacobean periods and a widespread appreciation (also reflected in visual culture) that linked 1588, 1605 and 1688 as formative moments in the history of the nation's resistance to, and deliverance from, Catholic tyranny.

The 'Glorious Revolution' that placed William and Mary on the English throne from 1689 signalled a new period of conflict across Europe. During this time, the navy and the nation can be said to have met the challenge thrown down by the enduring power of the Elizabethans as represented by the Armada portraits and tapestries. The question of how the extraordinary transformation in the nation's maritime fortunes was to be visually commemorated was answered in part by the continuing success of the van de Velde studio, and by the political poignancy and artistic legacy of images like the *Royal Sovereign* (page 261). At the time of its launch in 1701, the *Royal Sovereign* was unrivalled as the most powerful and prestigious warship in the Royal Navy. The painting was begun in light of England's entry into the War of the Spanish Succession in 1702 and was designed to project an idyllic vision of maritime order, naval strength and commercial prosperity under a Protestant monarch, a vision that the Armada portrait had also confidently projected, but with far less historical justification.

Only a few years after Willem the Younger's painting was completed, an opportunity presented itself on a scale that had not been seen before and that has not been rivalled since in British art: the decoration of the Painted Hall in the Royal Hospital for Seamen at Greenwich.[15] Given that James Thornhill's monumental scheme, executed between 1707 and 1726, represents (on one level) an apotheosis of the Protestant succession, incorporating portraits of five monarchs from the late Stuarts to the early Hanoverians, it is ironic that the idea for such a hospital was first mooted in 1687 by James II, by then exiled. Moreover, the

William III lands at Torbay, 1688. *English School, seventeenth century.*
*NMM, Caird Collection.* BHC0326.

exuberant Baroque style and complex allegorical language employed by Thornhill were long established in European palaces and aristocratic houses and much favoured at the Restoration court. Hence the site-specific decorative history schemes that informed the Greenwich project included early Stuart commissions of the 1630s, such as the ceiling paintings by Rubens for the Banqueting House, Whitehall. Between 1678 and 1688, Antonio Verrio had been employed by Charles II and then James II to decorate some 25 interiors at Hampton Court Palace and Windsor Castle. Tellingly, the Italian artist drew inspiration from Charles Le Brun's much-admired decorative schemes for Louis XIV at Versailles, particularly the ceiling of the Hall of Mirrors, which includes scenes celebrating the Franco-Dutch War (1672–78). Here the correlated themes of royal wisdom, good governance and military success, previously alluded to via mythological figures in other areas of Versailles, now incorporated the French king in person as the epitome of absolute power.

While Thornhill's work at Greenwich represents a royal panegyric to equal anything at Versailles, Whitehall and Windsor, the iconography offers a firm rebuttal to the claims to glorious immortality rooted in autocratic rule that were made in these royal residences. In the centre of the lower hall ceiling at Greenwich, for example, Mary II holds the orb and sceptre of royal power, as William III (in the role of mediator rather than subjugator) hands to Europe the cap of 'Protestant' liberty with Peace looking on. Meanwhile William tramples on Tyranny shown as a vanquished 'French' monarch, as the crown of popery topples. Elsewhere Thornhill alludes to recent British military and naval victories, and in the upper hall he represents William's arrival at Torbay in 1688 opposite another scene showing Queen Anne's successor, George I, landing peacefully at Greenwich in 1714. The triumphal symbolism of the entire

*ABOVE The Painted Hall at the Old Royal Naval College.*
*Photo © Peter Smith, Jigsaw Design and Publishing, 2013.*

*OPPOSITE The English Ship 'Royal Sovereign' with a Royal Yacht in a Light Air.*
*Willem van de Velde the Younger, 1703. National Maritime Musem, Caird Collection. BHC3614.*

scheme, however, goes much further than simply representing the orderly handover of royal power in a Protestant state. Indeed, an exceptional feature of Thornhill's scheme is the use of relatively conventional court portraiture and symbolism within an overwhelmingly maritime-related programme of classical gods, naval trophies, mythological creatures, personifications and historical figures, alongside the almost life-size presentation of the stern of a Royal Navy ship, laden with booty. The result is a patriotic spectacle that above all celebrates British sea power as the prime bastion of national liberty, stability and prosperity.

# Notes

## INTRODUCTION

**1** *A Relation or Journal of the Beginning and Proceedings of the English Plantation Settled at Plimoth in New England by certain English Adventurers both Merchants and others* (London, 1622).
**2** The term 'sea change' was coined by William Shakespeare in his most overtly maritime play, *The Tempest*, written in 1610–11. It remains a perfect phrase to describe the remarkable changes taking place on the world's oceans during the Tudor and Stuart period.
**3** N. A. M. Rodger, 'Queen Elizabeth and the Myth of Sea-Power in English History', *Transactions of the Royal Historical Society*, 6th ser., xix (2004), pp. 153–74.
**4** For a detailed summary of recent historical scholarship, see the bibliography.
**5** John Morrill, 'The British Problem c. 1534–1707', in Brendan Bradshaw and John Morrill (eds), *The British Problem, c.1534–1707: State Formation in the Atlantic Archipelago* (Basingstoke: Palgrave Macmillan, 1996) pp. 1–3.
**6** See Armitage, 'The Empire of Great Britain: England, Scotland and Ireland, c.1540–1660', in *The Ideological Origins of the British Empire* (Cambridge: Cambridge University Press, 2000), pp. 24–60.
**7** Jace Weaver, *The Red Atlantic: American Indigenes and the Making of the Modern World, 1000–1927* (University of North Carolina Press, 2014), pp. 54–56.
**8** Peter C. Mancall, 'Native Americans and Europeans in English America, 1500–1700', in Nicholas Canny (ed.), *The Origins of Empire: British Overseas Enterprise to the Close of the Seventeenth Century* (Oxford History of the British Empire) (Oxford: Oxford University Press, 1998), pp. 328–32.
**9** Roxanne Dunbar-Ortiz, *An Indigenous Peoples' History of the United States* (Boston: Beacon Press, 2014), pp. xiii, 58–63.

## CHAPTER 1: 'NEW WORLDS': 1485–1505

**1** D. Wheeler, R. Garcia-Herrera, C. W. Wilkinson and C. Ward, 'Atmospheric Circulation and Storminess Derived from Royal Navy Logbooks: 1685 to 1750', *Climatic Change*, ci (2010), pp. 257–80; Y. Kushnir, G. Ottersen and M. Visbeck, 'An Overview of the North Atlantic Oscillation', in J. Hurrell et al. (eds), *North Atlantic Oscillation: Climatic Significance and Environmental Impact* (Washington, DC: American Geophysical Union, 2003), pp. 1–35.
**2** F. Fernández-Armesto, *Amerigo* (New York: Random House, 2007), pp. 74–83; *Pathfinders: a Global History of Exploration* (Oxford: Oxford University Press, 2007), pp. 141–45.
**3** F. Fernández-Armesto, 'The Origins of the European Atlantic', *Itinerario*, xxiv (2000), pp. 111–28.
**4** J. A. Williamson and R. Skelton, *The Cabot Voyages and Bristol Discovery Under Henry VII* (Cambridge: Cambridge University Press, 1962), pp. 188–89.
**5** F. Fernández-Armesto, 'Inglaterra y el atlántico en la baja edad media', in A. Béthencourt Massieu et al., *Canarias e Inglaterra a través de la historia* (Las Palmas: Ediciones del Cabildo Insular, 1995), pp. 65–92.
**6** Williamson and Skelton, *The Cabot Voyages*, pp. 19, 22–23.
**7** F. Fernández-Armesto, *Columbus* (Oxford: Oxford University Press, 1991), pp. 82–84.
**8** Fernández-Armesto, *Columbus*, pp. 95–99.
**9** Fernández-Armesto, *Before Columbus: Exploration and Colonization from the Mediterranean to the Atlantic*

(Philadelphia: University of Pennsylvania Press, 1987).
**10** Williamson and Skelton, *The Cabot Voyages*, pp. 203–12.
**11** Williamson and Skelton, *The Cabot Voyages*, pp. 52, 212–14; A. Ruddock, 'John Day of Bristol and the English Voyages across the Atlantic before 1497', *Geographical Journal*, 132 (1966), pp. 225–33.
**12** Cabot is beginning to gain the historical attention he deserves. 'The Cabot Project' at the University of Bristol has uncovered numerous documents about his life and thrown new light on his voyages. See http://www.bristol.ac.uk/history/research/cabot/
**13** Williamson and Skelton, *The Cabot Voyages*, pp. 84, 90–922, 202, 214–19; E. Jones, 'Henry VII and the Bristol Expeditions to North America: the Condon Documents', *Historical Research*, lxxxiii (2010), pp. 444–54.
**14** Williamson and Skelton, *The Cabot Voyages*, pp. 118, 225, 230–35.
**15** Williamson and Skelton, *The Cabot Voyages*, pp. 118, 225, 230–35.
**16** Williamson and Skelton, *The Cabot Voyages*, pp. 127–28, 219, 235–36, 249, 252.

## CHAPTER 2: ADVENTURERS: ENGLAND TURNS TO THE SEA, 1550–80

**1** Edward, Lord Herbert of Cherbury, *The Reign of Henry VIII* (London, 1649), p. 18, quoted in N. A. M. Rodger, *Safeguard of the Sea: a Naval History of Britain, 660–1649* (London: Allen Lane, 2004), p. 176.
**2** James Evans, *Merchant Adventurers: the Voyage of Discovery that Transformed Tudor England* (London: Weidenfeld and Nicolson, 2013); Stephen Alford, *London's Triumph: Merchant Adventurers and the Tudor City* (London: Allen Lane, 2017), pp. 80–91; Jerry Brotton, *This Orient Isle: Elizabethan England and the Islamic World* (London: Allen Lane, 2016), pp. 35–36, 45–47.
**3** P. E. H. Hair and Robin Law, 'The English in Western Africa to 1700', in Nicholas Canny (ed.), *The Origins of Empire: British Overseas Enterprise to the Close of the Seventeenth Century* (Oxford History of the British Empire) (Oxford: Oxford University Press, 1998), pp. 243, 247; P. E. H. Hair and J. D. Alsop, *English Seamen and Traders in Guinea, 1553–1565* (New York: Lewiston/Lampeter: E. Mellen Press, 1992); John C. Appleby, 'War, Politics, and Colonization, 1588–1625', in Canny, *The Origins of Empire*, p. 59.
**4** David Northrup, 'West Africans and the Atlantic', in Philip D. Morgan and Sean Hawkins, *Black Experience and the Empire* (Oxford: Oxford University Press, 2004), pp. 35–40.
**5** Appleby, 'War, Politics, and Colonization, 1588–1625', p. 59; Lucy Hughes-Hallett, *Heroes* (New York: Alfred A. Knopf, 2004), p. 179; Hair and Law, 'English in Western Africa', p. 246; Clement R. Markham (ed.), *The Hawkins Voyages*, vol. LVII (London: Hakluyt Society, 1878), p. 6.
**6** David Richardson, 'Through a Looking Glass: Olaudah Equiano and African Experiences of the British Atlantic Slave Trade', in Morgan and Hawkins, *Black Experience and the Empire*, p. 60; Hair and Law, 'English in Western Africa, pp. 246–47; N. Canny, 'The Origins of Empire: an Introduction', in Canny, *The Origins of Empire*, p. 28.
**7** Brotton, *This Orient Isle*, pp. 8, 40, 62.
**8** Brotton, *This Orient Isle*, pp. 13, 67, 110, 135–36.

**9** Rodger, *Safeguard of the Sea*, p. 79.

**10** Charles Carlton, *This Sea of Mars: War and the British Isles 1485–1746* (London and New Haven: Yale University Press, 2011), p. 44; David Scott, *Leviathan: the Rise of Britain as a World Power* (London: Harper Press, 2013), p. 77; Rodger, *Safeguard of the Sea*, p. 200.

**11** Rodger, *Safeguard of the Sea*, pp. 241–43; Hughes-Hallett, *Heroes*, pp. 180–90.

**12** For a more detailed biography of Diego, see Miranda Kauffman's book *Black Tudors: African lives in Renaissance England*, 2017.

**13** Hughes-Hallett, *Heroes*, pp. 192–94, 195–99, 200–11.

**14** Harry Kelsey, *Francis Drake: the Queen's Pirate* (New Haven and London: Yale University Press, 1998), pp. 137–71; Hughes-Hallett, *Heroes*, pp. 200–19.

**15** Kelsey, *Francis Drake*, pp. 207–39; Hughes-Hallett, *Heroes*, pp. 178, 206, 220–21, 225; Rodger, *Safeguard of the Sea*, pp. 244–45.

**16** Giovanni Botero, *The Travellers Breviat*, p. 17, quoted in Scott, *Leviathan*, p. 75.

**17** Rodger, *Safeguard of the Sea*, p. 77.

## CHAPTER 3: THE SPANISH ARMADA AND ENGLAND'S CONFLICT WITH SPAIN, 1585–1604

**1** For the origins of the conflict between England and Spain, see J. McDermott, *England and the Spanish Armada: the Necessary Quarrel* (New Haven and London: Yale University Press, 2005), chs. 1–3.

**2** McDermott, *England and the Spanish Armada*, p. 63.

**3** Quoted in S. Alford, *The Early Elizabethan Polity: William Cecil and the British Succession Crisis, 1558–1569* (Cambridge: Cambridge University Press, 1998), p. 184.

**4** Quoted in Rodger, 'Queen Elizabeth and the Myth of Sea-Power', p. 155.

**5** P. E. J. Hammer, *Elizabeth's Wars: War, Government and Society in Tudor England, 1544–1604* (Basingstoke: Palgrave Macmillan, 2003), p. 130.

**6** This paragraph is based on Rodger, 'Queen Elizabeth and the Myth of Sea-Power', and Rodger, *Safeguard of the Sea*, pp. 201–02, 239, 244, 305.

**7** McDermott, *England and the Spanish Armada*, p. 13.

**8** N. Hanson, *The Confident Hope of a Miracle: the True History of the Spanish Armada* (London: Doubleday, 2003), pp. 208–13.

**9** Quoted in G. Parker, *The Grand Strategy of Philip II* (New Haven and London: Yale University Press, 1998), p. 174.

**10** Quoted in Parker, *Grand Strategy*, p. 195.

**11** Quoted in Hanson, *Confident Hope*, p. 136.

**12** These figures are taken from Rodger, *Safeguard of the Sea*, pp. 263–64; Parker, *Grand Strategy*, p. 261.

**13** McDermott, *England and the Spanish Armada*, pp. 230–31, 255–57.

**14** Hanson, *Confident Hope*, pp. 299–300; McDermott, *England and the Spanish Armada*, pp. 231–33.

**15** These figures are taken from Hanson, *Confident Hope*, pp. 486–87.

**16** Rodger, *Safeguard of the Sea*, pp. 294–95.

## CHAPTER 4: BUILDING A NAVY

**1** C. S. L. Davies, 'Tudor: What's in a Name?', *History*, 97 (2012), pp. 24–42.

**2** J. D. Davies, *Kings of the Sea: Charles II, James II and the Royal Navy* (Barnsley: Seaforth, 2017).

**3** B. Capp, *Cromwell's Navy: the Fleet and the English*

*Revolution, 1648–60* (Oxford: Oxford University Press, 1989), p. 52.

**4** D. Loades, *The Tudor Navy: an Administrative, Political and Military History* (Aldershot: Scolar Press, 1992), pp. 36–37, 39, 72, 88–89, 91.

**5** C. S. Knighton and D. Loades (eds), *The Anthony Roll of Henry VIII's Navy* (Routledge, Navy Records Society, 2000).

**6** J. B. Hattendorf, R. J. B. Knight, A. W. H. Pearsall, N. A. M. Rodger and G. Till (eds), *British Naval Documents 1204–1960* (Aldershot: Scolar Press/Navy Records Society, 1993), pp. 63–64; D. Loades, *The Making of the Elizabethan Navy 1540–90: from the Solent to the Armada* (Woodbridge: Boydell and Brewer, 2009), p. 124.

**7** Ray Costello, *Black Salt: Seafarers of African Descent on British Ships* (Liverpool, 2012), pp. 3–8.

**8** Rodger, *Safeguard of the Sea*, p. 228.

**9** J. S. Wheeler, *The Making of a World Power: War and the Military Revolution in Seventeenth Century England* (Stroud: Sutton Publishing, 1999), p. 204.

**10** J. D. Davies, *Pepys's Navy: Ships, Men and Warfare, 1649–89* (Barnsley: Seaforth, 2008), pp. 25–28.

**11** Loades, *Making of the Elizabethan Navy*, pp. 39–55.

**12** For his naval career, see C. S. Knighton, *Pepys and the Navy* (Stroud: The History Press, 2003).

**13** Rodger, *Safeguard of the Sea*, pp. 223–34, 335–36.

**14** C. S. Knighton and D. Loades (eds), *Elizabethan Naval Administration* (Farnham: Ashgate/Navy Records Society, 2013), pp. 45–49.

**15** Davies, *Pepys's Navy*, p. 186.

**16** Davies, *Pepys's Navy*, pp. 189–90.

**17** Davies, *Pepys's Navy*, p. 35.

**18** F. L. Fox, *The Four Days' Battle of 1666: the Greatest Sea Fight of the Age of Sail* (Barnsley: Seaforth, 2009), pp. 287–88.

**19** G. Parker, 'The Dreadnought Revolution of Tudor England', *The Mariner's Mirror*, 82 (1996), p. 270.

**20** Rodger, *Safeguard of the Sea*, pp. 163, 205–06.

**21** Rodger, *Safeguard of the Sea*, pp. 208–12.

**22** Loades, *Making of the Elizabethan Navy*, p. 120.

**23** J. Stedall, 'Notes Made by Thomas Harriot (1560–1621) on Ships and Shipbuilding', *Mariner's Mirror*, 99 (2013), p. 326.

**24** B. Lavery (ed.), *Deane's Doctrine of Naval Architecture* (London: Conway, 1981).

**25** R. Endsor, *The Restoration Warship: the Design, Construction and Career of a Third Rate of Charles II's Navy* (London: Conway, 2009), pp. 31–35.

**26** M. Bellamy, 'David Balfour and Early Modern Danish Ship Design', *Mariner's Mirror*, 92 (2006), pp. 5–22.

**27** For all of these ships, see R. Winfield, *British Warships in the Age of Sail 1603–1714: Design, Construction, Careers and Fates* (Barnsley: Seaforth, 2014).

**28** A. Thrush, 'In Pursuit of the Frigate, 1603–40', *Historical Research*, 64 (1991), pp. 29–45.

**29** For a detailed study of the first of them, the *Lenox*, see Endsor, *Restoration Warship*.

**30** Davies, *Pepys's Navy*, pp. 53–54.

## CHAPTER 5: USING THE SEAS AND SKIES: NAVIGATION IN EARLY-MODERN ENGLAND

**1** Quoted in Susan Rose, *England's Medieval Navy, 1066–1509: Ships, Men and Warfare* (Barnsley: Pen and Sword, 2013), p. 107.

**2** William Bourne, *A Regiment for the Sea* (London, 1611): pp. vi-vii.

**3** Jim Egan, *The Works of John Dee: Modernizations of his Main Mathematical Masterpieces*, (Newport: Cosmopolite Press, 2010), p.190. Translated from John Dee, *The Mathematicall Praeface to the Elements of Geometrie of Euclid of Megara* (London: John Daye, 1570).

**4** Thomas Smith, 'Manuscript and Printed Sea Charts in Seventeenth Century London: the Case of the Thames School', in Norman Thrower (ed.), *The Compleat Plattmaker: Essays on Chart, Map and Globe Making in Seventeenth and Eighteenth Century England* (Berkeley: University of California Press, 1978), pp. 90–92.

**5** Quoted in Helen Wallis, 'Geographie is Better than Divinitie: Maps, Globes and Geography in the Days of Samuel Pepys', in Thrower, *Compleat Plattmaker*, p. 19.

**6** Jeanette Black, 'Mapping the English Colonies in North America: the Beginnings', in Thrower, *The Compleat Plattmaker*, p. 103.

**7** Coolie Verner, 'John Seller and the Chart Trade in Seventeenth Century England', in Thrower, *Compleat Plattmaker*, p. 139.

**8** Christine Petto, *Mapping and Charting in Early Modern England and France: Power, Patronage and Production* (Lanham: Lexington, 2015), p. 93.

**9** Quoted in N. Plumley, 'The Royal Mathematical School within Christ's Hospital: the Early Years – its Aims and Achievements', *Vistas in Astronomy*, vol. 20, pp. 51–59 (1976), p. 52.

## CHAPTER 6: ENCOUNTER AND EXPLOITATION: THE ENGLISH COLONIZATION OF NORTH AMERICA, 1585–1615

**1** Helge Ingstad and Anne Stine Ingstad, *The Viking Discovery of America* (Oslo: J. M. Stenersens, 1991).

**2** Brian Fagan, *Fish on Friday: Feasting, Fasting, and the Discovery of the New World* (New York: Basic Books, 2006).

**3** Richard Hakluyt, *Discourse Concerning Western Planting* (London, 1584), p. 11.

**4** Thomas Harriot, *A Briefe and True Report of the New Found Land of Virginia* (Frankfurt: De Bry, 1590), p. 45.

**5** Arthur Barlowe, *The First Voyage to Roanoke* (London, 1584), pp. 3–4.

**6** Barlowe, *First Voyage to Roanoke*, p. 9.

**7** Jace Weaver, *The Red Atlantic: American Indigenes and the Making of the Modern World, 1000–1927* (Chase Hill: University of North Carolina Press, 2014).

**8** Alden Vaughan, *Transatlantic Encounters: American Indians in Britain, 1500–1776* (Cambridge: Cambridge University Press, 2006).

**9** Roger M. Carpenter, *'Times are altered with us': American Indians from First Contact to the New Republic* (Chichester: Wiley Blackwell, 2015), p. 11.

**10** Carpenter, *Times are Altered With Us*, p. 82.

**11** Joan M. Marter, *The Grove Encyclopedia of American Art, Volume One* (Oxford and New York: Oxford University Press, 2011), pp. 357–58.

**12** Kim Sloan, *A New World: England's First View of America* (London: British Museum, 2006).

**13** Karen Ordahl Kupperman, *Roanoke: The Abandoned Colony* (Plymouth: Rowman & Littlefield, 2007).

**14** James Horn, *A Kingdom Strange: the Brief and Tragic History of the Lost Colony of Roanoke* (New York: Basic Books, 2010).

**15** Carpenter, *'Times are altered'*.

**16** John Smith, *Advertisements for the Unexperienced Planters of New England, or Anywhere* (London, 1631), pp. 21–22.

**17** Spencer Tucker, *The Encyclopedia of North American Indian Wars 1607–1890: a Political, Social, and Military History* (Santa Barbara: ABC-Clio, 2011).

**18** Seth Mallios, *The Deadly Politics of Giving: Exchange and Violence at Ajacan, Roanoke, and Jamestown* (Tuscaloosa: University of Alabama Press, 2006).

**19** Weaver, *Red Atlantic*, p. 146.

**20** Kelly Watson, *Insatiable Appetites: Imperial Encounters with Cannibals in the North Atlantic World* (New York and London: New York University, 2015).

**21** Helen Rountree, *Pocahontas's People: the Powhatan Indians of Virginia through Four Centuries* (Norman: University of North Carolina Press, 1990).

**22** Dunbar-Ortiz, *Indigenous Peoples' History*, p. 10. Dunbar-Ortiz's estimate is disputed, with many scholars estimating either higher or lower numbers. Most, however, seem to settle at somewhere between 12 and 18 million.

## CHAPTER 7: OF PROFIT AND LOSS: THE TRADING WORLD OF SEVENTEENTH-CENTURY ENGLAND

**1** William Oldys and Thomas Birch (eds), *The Works of Sir Walter Ralegh...* (8 vols) (Oxford: Oxford University Press, 1829), vol. 8, p. 325.

**2** Oldys and Birch, *Works of Sir Walter Ralegh*, vol. 8, p. 325.

**3** Clements R. Markham (ed.), *The Voyages of Sir James Lancaster...* (London: Hakluyt Society, 1877), p. 107.

**4** See H. V. Bowen, John McAleer and Robert J. Blyth, *Monsoon Traders: the Maritime World of the East India Company* (London: Scala, 2011), pp. 37–41; Cheryl Fury, 'The First English East India Company Voyage, 1601–1603: the Human Dimension', *International Journal of Maritime History*, vol. 24, no. 2 (2012), pp. 69–96.

**5** Robert Latham and William Matthews, *The Diary of Samuel Pepys* (11 vols) (London: Bell & Hyman, 1970–83), vol. 6, p. 300 (16 November 1665).

**6** Bowen, et al., *Monsoon Traders*, pp. 42–55.

**7** Niels Steensgaard, 'The Growth and Compensation of the Long-distance Trade of England and Dutch Republic before 1750', in James D. Tracy (ed.), *The Rise of Merchant Empires: Long-distance Trade in the Early Modern World, 1350–1750* (Cambridge: Cambridge University Press, 1990), pp. 142–43.

**8** W. E. Minchinton, *The Growth of English Overseas Trade in the 17th and 18th Centuries* (London: Methuen, 1969), pp. 32–34.

**9** B. R. Mitchell, *British Historical Statistics* (Cambridge: Cambridge University Press, 1988), pp. 492, 495.

## CHAPTER 8: THE BRITISH CIVIL WARS, 1638–53

**1** Ian Gentles, *The English Revolution and the Wars in the Three Kingdoms, 1638–1652* (Abingdon: Pearson Education Limited, 2014), p. 436.

**2** Charles I, *The Letters, Speeches and Proclamations of King Charles I*, ed. Charles Petrie (London: Cassell, 1968), p. 109.

**3** For an overview of the role of the navy in the outbreak of the civil wars, see Richard J. Blakemore and Elaine Murphy, *The British Civil Wars at Sea, 1638–1653* (Woodbridge: Boydell and Brewer, 2017), ch. 2; Edward Hyde, Earl of Clarendon, *The History of the Rebellion and Civil Wars in England Begun in the Year 1641*, ed. W. Dunn Macray (6 vols) (Oxford: Oxford University Press, 1888, reprinted 1992), ii, p. 224.

**4** Historical Manuscripts Commission, *Report on the Franciscan Manuscripts Preserved at the Convent, Merchants Quay, Dublin*, ed. G. D. Burtchaell and J. M. Rigg (London: Historical Manuscripts Commission, 1906), p. 208.

5 Historical Manuscripts Commission, *Thirteenth Report, Appendix, Part I: The Manuscripts of His Grace the Duke of Portland, Preserved at Welbeck Abbey*, ed. F. H. Blackburne Daniell et al. (London: Historical Manuscripts Commission, 9 vols, 1891–1923), i, p. 510.

6 *Moderate Intelligencer*, 233 (30 August–6 September 1649), pp. 2239–40.

7 TNA HCA 13/250, part i, examination of Antonio Vandermarche, 5 February 1649.

8 NMM AGC/34A/3; Henrietta Maria, *Letters of Queen Henrietta Maria: including her private correspondence with Charles the First*, ed. M. A. E. Green (London: Richard Bentley, 1857), p. 131.

9 *CSPV, 1643–47*, p. 34.

10 Historical Manuscripts Commission, *Report on the Pepys Manuscripts Preserved at Magdalene College, Cambridge*, ed. E. K. Purnell (London:Historical Manuscripts Commission, 1911), pp. 200–201, 204; J. R. Powell and E. J. Timings (eds), *Documents Relating to the English Civil War, 1642–1648* (London: Navy Records Society, 1963), pp. 91–92.

11 Blakemore and Murphy, *British Civil Wars at Sea*, ch. 4.

12 Anon, *Good and True Newes from Bedford* (London, 1643), np.

13; NMM, WYN 2/3, fos. 1–14; Blakemore and Murphy, *British Civil Wars at Sea*, ch. 3.

14 Bernard Capp, *Cromwell's Navy: the Fleet and the English Revolution, 1648–1660* (Oxford: Oxford University Press, 2001), pp. 15–41.

15 *A Perfect Diurnall*, 318 (27 August–3 September 1649), p. 2376.

16 NMM AND/27; NMM AND/45; NMM WYN 4/1; Blakemore and Murphy, *British Civil Wars at Sea*, ch. 7.

## CHAPTER 9: LIFE AT SEA

1 Martin Parker, *Saylors for my Money* (London, c.1630).

2 John Smith, *An Accidence or The Path-way to Experience. Necessary for All Young Sea-men* (London, 1626), pp. 37–38.

3 Edward Barlow, *Barlow's Journal of his Life at Sea in the King's Ships, East and West Indiamen & Other Merchantmen from 1659 to 1703*, ed. Basil Lubbock (London, 2 vols, 1934), vol. I, pp. 128, 166.

4 John Heminge and Henry Condell (eds), *Mr William Shakespeares Comedies, Histories, & Tragedies* (London, 1623), p. 1.

5 Richard Brathwaite, *Whimzies: or, a New Cast of Characters* (London, 1631), pp. 140–42.

6 William Ball, 'Might and Would Not', printed in Nelson P. Bard (ed.), 'The Earl of Warwick's Voyage in 1627' in N. A. M. Rodger (ed.), *The Naval Miscellany*, vol. V (London: Navy Records Society, 1984), p. 65.

7 The only published version of Barlow's journal remains as Basil Lubbock, *Barlow's Journal of His Life at Sea in King's Ships, East and West Indiamen & Other Merchantmen from 1659 to 1703*, 2 Vols (London: Hurst and Blackett, 1934). For a longer overview of Barlow's life, see J. D. Davies, 'Barlow, Edward (1642–c.1706)', *Oxford Dictionary of National Biography* (Oxford: Oxford University Press, 2004; online edn, Jan 2008 [http://www.oxforddnb.com/view/article/50179, accessed 15 June 2017]).

8 Lubbock, *Barlow's Journal*, I, pp. 23, 26, 29.

9 Edward Coxere, *Adventures by Sea of Edward Coxere*, ed. E. H. W. Meyerstein (Oxford, 1945), p. 4.

10 Smith, *An Accidence*, p. 7.

11 Smith, *An Accidence*, p. 40.

12 http://www.maryrose.org/discover-our-collection/story-of-the-ship/image-galleries/nggallery/image/87 (accessed 4 February 2017).

13 Smith, *An Accidence*, p. 7.

14 TNA HCA 13/62, deposition of Henry Cooper, 10 December 1649.

15 An example of such a suit survives: Museum of London, ID 53.101/1a.

16 Edward Barlow took over the command of the *Septer* in this way: 'it came to my lot to command the ship, being chief mate' (Lubbock, *Barlow's Journal*, II, p. 477).

17 TNA HCA 13/60, fos 110r-7v.

18 Luke Foxe, *North-West Fox; or, Fox from the North-West Passage* (1635), sig. A2r; Coxere, *Adventures by Sea*, pp. 108–09.

19 TNA PROB 11/197/441.

20 Lubbock, *Barlow's Journal*, II, 339.

21 Stadsarchief Rotterdam, Archives of the Scots Church, 962/01/305.

22 Coxere, *Adventures*, p. 51.

23 Lubbock, *Barlow's Journal*, II, p. 310.

24 TNA HCA 13/70, deposition of Magdalena Hendricx, 9 November 1654, fos 720r-4r.

25 Coxere, *Adventures by Sea*, pp. 108–9.

26 Anon, *The Seamans Wives Ranting Resolution* (London, 1680–82).

27 Stadsarchief Amsterdam, Archief van de Schout en Schepenen, 5061/299, fos 117r-v.

28 Lubbock, *Barlow's Journal*, vol.1, p. 226.

## CHAPTER 10: THE SEVENTEENTH-CENTURY ANGLO-DUTCH WARS

1 Jeremy Treglown (ed.), *The Letters of John Wilmot, Earl of Rochester* (Oxford: Blackwell, 1980), pp. 43–49.

2 State Papers 29/163 f.174.

3 Samuel Pepys, *The Diary of Samuel Pepys*, ed. Robert Latham and William Matthews, Vols i–ix (HarperCollins, 1995), 8 June 1665.

4 17 August 1665, Everett Green (ed.), *Calendar of State Papers 1664–5*, pp. 520–2

5 *The Diary of John Evelyn*, vol. 11, William Bray (ed.), (M. Walter Dunne, 1901), 18 June 1666.

6 See Elizabeth Staffell, 'The Horrible Tail-Man and the Anglo-Dutch Wars', *Journal of the Warburg and Courtauld Institutes*, vol. 63 (2000), p. 182.

7 Pepys's Diary, Wednesday 25 March 1668.

8 See Staffell, 'Horrible Tail-Man', p. 172.

## CHAPTER 11: A SEA OF SCOUNDRELS: PIRATES OF THE STUART ERA

1 Marcus Rediker, *Villains of All Nations: Atlantic Pirates in the Golden Age* (London: Verso, 2004).

2 Gabriel Kuhn, *Life Under the Jolly Roger: Reflections on Golden Age Piracy* (Oakland: PM Press, 2010).

3 John C. Appleby, *Under the Bloody Flag: Pirates of the Tudor Age* (Stroud: The History Press, 2009).

4 Peter Earle, *The Pirate Wars* (London: St Martin's Press, 2003).

5 C. M. Senior, *A Nation of Pirates: English Piracy in its Heyday* (Newton Abbot: David & Charles, 1976).

6 John C. Appleby, *Women and English Piracy, 1540–1720: Partners and Victims of Crime* (Woodbridge: Boydell & Brewer, 2013), pp. 79–81.

7 J. C. Appleby, 'Women and Piracy in Ireland: from Grainne

O'Malley to Anne Bonny', in M. MacCurtain and M. O'Dowd (eds), *Women in Early Modern Ireland* (Edinburgh: Edinburgh University Press, 1991).

**8** N. A. M. Rodger, 'The Law and Language of Private Naval Warfare', *Mariner's Mirror*, vol. 100, no. 1 (2014).

**9** Joe Moshenska, *A Stain in the Blood: the Remarkable Voyage of Sir Kenelm Digby* (London: William Heinemann, 2016).

**10** Roy Digby Thomas, *Digby: the Gunpowder Plotter's Legacy* (London: Janus, 2001), p. 106.

**11** Alan G. Jamieson, *Lords of the Sea: a History of the Barbary Corsairs* (London: Reaktion Books, 2012).

**12** Adrian Tinniswood, *Pirates of Barbary* (London: Vintage, 2011), p. 259.

**13** Des Ekin, *The Stolen Village: Baltimore and the Barbary Pirates* (Dublin: O'Brien Press, 2006); Robert C. Davis, *Christian Slaves, Muslim Masters: White Slavery in the Mediterranean, the Barbary Coast, and Italy, 1500–1800* (Basingstoke: Palgrave Macmillan, 2003).

**14** Daniel J. Vitkus, *Piracy, Slavery, and Redemption: Barbary Captivity Narratives from Early Modern England* (New York: Columbia University Press, 2001), p. 98.

**15** Vitkus, *Piracy, Slavery, and Redemption*, p. 185.

**16** Margarette Lincoln, *British Pirates and Society, 1680–1730* (Farnham: Ashgate, 2014).

**17** James H. Sweet, *Recreating Africa: Culture, Kinship, and Religion in the African-Portuguese World, 1441–1770* (Chapel Hill: University of North Carolina Press, 2003).

**18** Nabil Matar, *Britain and Barbary, 1589-1689* (Gainesville: University Press of Florida, 2005).

**19** Greg Bak, *Barbary Pirate: the Life and Crimes of John Ward, the Most Infamous Privateer of his Time* (Stroud: Sutton Publishing, 2006), p. 108.

**20** Bak, *Barbary Pirate*, p. 131.

**21** N. A. M. Rodger, *Command of the Ocean: a Naval History of Britain, 1649–1815* (London: Penguin, 2005), p. 88

**22** Kuhn, *Life Under the Jolly Roger*, p. 138.

**23** David Cordingly, *Life among the Pirates: the Romance and the Reality* (London: David Cordingly, 1995).

**24** Derek Howse and Norman J. W. Thrower (eds), *A Buccaneer's Atlas: Basil Ringrose's South Sea Waggoner: A Sea Atlas and Sailing Directions of the Pacific Coast of the Americas, 1682* (Berkeley: University of California Press, 1992), p. 22.

**25** Glyndwr Williams, *The Great South Sea: English Voyages and Encounters, 1570–1750* (New Haven: Yale University Press, 1997).

**26** Diana Preston and Michael Preston, *A Pirate of Exquisite Mind: the Life of William Dampier: Explorer, Naturalist and Buccaneer* (London: Berkley Books, 2005), p. 247.

**27** Kevin P. McDonald, *Pirates, Merchants, Settlers, and Slaves: Colonial America and the Indo-Atlantic World* (Oakland: Berkeley, 2015).

**28** Mark G. Hanna, *Pirate Nests and the Rise of the British Empire, 1570–1740* (Chapel Hill: University of North Carolina Press, 2015), p. 242.

## CHAPTER 12: ART AND THE MARITIME WORLD, 1550–1714

**1** Margarita Russell, *Visions of the Sea: Vroom and the Origins of Sea Painting* (Leiden: Leiden University Press, 1983), pp. 20–24.

**2** The two seascapes are later versions, probably painted in the late sixteenth century by a Dutch-trained artist working in England, that replicate, in a later style, the sixteenth-century subject matter underneath.

**3** Jenny Gaschke (ed.), *Turmoil and Tranquillity: the Sea through the Eyes of Dutch and Flemish Masters* (London: National Maritime Museum), p. 101.

**4** Catharine MacLeod (ed.), *The Lost Prince Henry, Prince of Wales (1594–1612)* (London: National Portrait Gallery, 2012), pp. 89–90.

**5** The portrait of Phineas Pett (NPG2035) is in the National Portrait Gallery collection, and that of Fisher Harding by Jonathan Richardson (BHC2743) is in the NMM collection.

**6** See *The Return of Prince Charles from Spain, 5 October 1623* (BHC0710) by Vroom in the NMM collection.

**7** Quoted in Stephen Orgel and Roy Strong, *Inigo Jones: Theatre of the Stuart Court* (London: Sotheby Parke Bernet, 1973), vol. 2, p. 574.

**8** Karen Hearn (ed.), *Van Dyck & Britain* (London: Tate Publishing, 2009), p. 116.

**9** Two of the portraits, representing Prince Rupert and Sir John Lawson, are in the Royal Collection; the rest were presented by George IV to Greenwich Hospital in 1824 and are now in the care of the National Maritime Museum.

**10** The portraits form part of the Greenwich Hospital Collection at the National Maritime Museum.

**11** Gaschke, *Turmoil and Tranquillity*, p. 140.

**12** See, for example, the pen and ink drawings PAJ2532 and PAJ2534 in the NMM Collection.

**13** The battle paintings remain in the Royal Collection and are on display at Hampton Court Palace.

**14** 'The Battle of the Texel', RCIN405306 Royal Collection Trust.

**15** For an exhaustive study on the context and iconography of the Painted Hall at Greenwich Hospital, see Richard Johns, 'James Thornhill and Decorative History Painting in England after 1688', PhD thesis, University of York, 2004, vol. I, pp. 156–201.

# Bibliography

**S. Alford,** *The Early Elizabethan Polity: William Cecil and the British Succession Crisis, 1558–1569* (Cambridge: Cambridge University Press, 1998) *London's Triumph: Merchant Adventurers and the Tudor City* (London: Allen Lane, 2017)

**John C. Appleby,** *Under the Bloody Flag: Pirates of the Tudor Age* (Stroud: The History Press, 2009)
*Women and English Piracy, 1540–1720: Partners and Victims of Crime* (Woodbridge: Boydell & Brewer, 2013)

**Greg Bak,** *Barbary Pirate: The Life and Crimes of John Ward, The Most Infamous Privateer of his Time* (Stroud: Sutton Publishing Limited, 2006)

**Edward Barlow,** *Barlow's Journal of his Life at Sea in the King's Ships, East and West Indiamen & Other Merchantmen from 1659 to 1703,* ed. Basil Lubbock (London, 2 vols, 1934)

**Arthur Barlowe,** *The First Voyage to Roanoke* (London, 1584)

**Richard J. Blakemore and Elaine Murphy,** *The British Civil Wars at Sea, 1638–1653* (Woodbridge: Boydell and Brewer, 2018)

**William Bourne,** *A Regiment for the Sea* (London, 1611)

**H.V. Bowen, John McAleer and Robert J. Blyth,** *Monsoon Traders: The Maritime World of the East India Company* (London: Scala, 2011)

**Richard Brathwaite,** *Whimzies: Or, a New Cast of Characters* (London, 1631)

**Jerry Brotton,** *This Orient Isle: Elizabethan England and the Islamic World* (London: Allen Lane, 2016)

**B. Capp,** *Cromwell's Navy: The Fleet and the English Revolution, 1648-60* (Oxford: Oxford University Press, 1989)

**Charles Carlton,** *This Sea of Mars: War and the British Isles 1485-1746* (London and New Haven: Yale University Press, 2011)

**Roger M. Carpenter,** *"Times are altered with us": American Indians from First Contact to the New Republic* (Chichester: Wiley Blackwell, 2015)

**David Cordingly,** *Life Among the Pirates: The Romance and The Reality* (London: David Cordingly, 1995)

**Edward Coxere,** *Adventures by Sea of Edward Coxere,* ed. E. H. W. Meyerstein (Oxford, 1945)

**J. D. Davies,** *Gentlemen and Tarpaulins: the Officers and Men of the Restoration Navy* (Oxford: Oxford University Press, 1991)
*Pepys's Navy: Ships, Men and Warfare, 1649–89* (Barnsley: Seaforth, 2008)
*Kings of the Sea: Charles II, James II and the Royal Navy* (Barnsley: Seaforth, 2017)

**Robert C. Davis,** *Christian Slaves, Muslim Masters: White Slavery in the Mediterranean, the Barbary Coast, and Italy, 1500-800* (Basingstoke: Palgrave Macmillan, 2003)

**Roxanne Dunbar-Ortiz,** *An Indigenous Peoples' History of the United States* (Boston: Beacon History, 2014)

**Richard Dunn,** *Ships, Clocks and Stars: the Quest for Longitude* (London: Collins, 2014)
*Navigational Instruments* (London: Bloomsbury Shire, 2016)

**Peter Earle,** *The Pirate Wars* (London: St Martin's Press, 2003)

**Jim Egan,** *The Works of John Dee: Modernizations of his Main Mathematical Masterpieces* (Newport: Cosmopolite Press, 2010)

**Des Ekin,** *The Stolen Village: Baltimore and the Barbary Pirates* (Dublin: O'Brien Press, 2006)

**R. Endsor,** *The Restoration Warship: The Design, Construction and Career of a Third Rate of Charles II's Navy* (London: Conway, 2009)

**James Evans,** *Merchant Adventurers: The voyage of discovery that transformed Tudor England* (London: Weidenfeld and Nicolson, 2013)

**Brian Fagan,** *Fish on Friday: Feasting, Fasting, and the Discovery of the New World* (New York: Basic Books, 2006)

**F. Fernández-Armesto,** *Columbus* (Oxford: Oxford University Press, 1991)
*Amerigo* (New York: Random House, 2007)
*Pathfinders: a Global History of Exploration* (Oxford: Oxford University Press, 2007)

**Frank L. Fox,** *The Four Days' Battle of 1666: the Greatest Sea Fight of the Age of Sail* (Barnsley: Seaforth, 2009)

**Luke Foxe,** *North-West Fox; Or, Fox from the North-West Passage* (1635)

**Jenny Gaschke (ed.),** *Turmoil and Tranquillity: The Sea through the Eyes of Dutch and Flemish Masters* (London: National Maritime Museum)

**Ian Gentles,** *The English Revolution and the Wars in the Three Kingdoms, 1638-1652* (Abingdon: Pearson Education Limited, 2014)

**P. E. H. Hair and J. D. Alsop,** *English Seamen and Traders in Guinea, 1553-1565* (Lewiston-Lampeter, 1992)

**P. E. H. Hair and Robin Law,** 'The English in Western Africa to 1700', in Nicholas Canny, ed. *The Origins of Empire: British Overseas Enterprise to the Close of the Seventeenth Century* (Oxford History of the British Empire) (Oxford: Oxford University Press, 1998)

**Richard Hakluyt,** *Discourse of Western Planting* (London, 1584)

**P. E. J. Hammer,** *Elizabeth's Wars: War, Government and Society in Tudor England, 1544-1604* (Basingstoke: Palgrave MacMillan 2003)

**Mark G. Hanna,** *Pirate Nests and the Rise of the British Empire, 1570-1740* (Chapel Hill, NC: University of North Carolina Press, 2015)

**N. Hanson,** *The Confident Hope of a Miracle: the True History of the Spanish Armada* (London: Doubleday, 2003)

**Thomas Harriot,** *A Briefe and True Report of the New Found Land of Virginia* (Frankfurt: De Bry, 1590)

**Karen Hearn (ed.),** *Van Dyck & Britain* (London: Tate Publishing, 2009)

**Henrietta Maria,** *Letters of Queen Henrietta Maria: including her private correspondence with Charles the First,* ed. M. A. E. Green (London: Richard Bentley, 1857)

**James Horn,** *A Kingdom Strange: The Brief and Tragic History of the Lost Colony of Roanoke* (New York: Basic Books, 2010)

**Derek Howse and Norman J. W. Thrower (eds),** *A Buccaneer's Atlas: Basil Ringrose's South Sea Waggoner: A Sea Atlas and Sailing Directions of the Pacific Coast of the Americas, 1682* (Berkeley, CA: University of California Press, 1992)

**Lucy Hughes-Hallett,** *Heroes* (New York: Alfred A. Knopf, 2004)

**Edward Hyde, Earl of Clarendon,** *The History of the Rebellion and Civil Wars in England Begun in the Year 1641,* ed. W. Dunn Macray (Oxford: Oxford University Press, 6 vols, 1888, reprinted 1992)

**Helge Ingstad and Anne Stine Ingstad,** *The Viking Discovery of America* (Oslo: J. M. Stenersens, 1991)

**Alan G. Jamieson,** *Lords of the Sea: A History of the Barbary Corsairs* (London: Reaktion Books, 2012)

**J.R. Jones,** *The Anglo-Dutch Wars of the Seventeenth Century* (London, New York: Longman, 1996)

**Miranda Kaufmann,** *Black Tudors: The Untold Story* (London: Oneworld Publications, 2017)

**Harry Kelsey,** *Francis Drake: The Queen's Pirate* (New Haven and London: Yale University Press, 1998)

**Peter Kirsh,** *Fireship: the Terror Weapon of the Age of Sail* (Barnsley: Seaforth Publishing, 2009)

**C. S. Knighton,** *Pepys and the Navy* (Stroud: The History Press, 2003)

**C. S. Knighton and D. Loades (eds),** *The Anthony Roll of Henry VIII's Navy* (Routledge, Navy Records Society, 2000)
*Elizabethan Naval Administration* (Routledge, Navy Records Society, 2013)

**Gabriel Kuhn,** *Life Under the Jolly Roger: Reflections on Golden Age Piracy* (Oakland, CA: PM Press, 2010)

**Karen Ordahl Kupperman,** *Roanoke: The Abandoned Colony* (Plymouth: Rowman & Littlefield, 2007)

**Robert Latham and William Matthews,** *The Diary of Samuel Pepys,* (11 vols., London: Bell & Hyman, 1970–83)

**B. Lavery (ed.),** *Deane's Doctrine of Naval Architecture* (London: Conway, 1981)

**Margarette Lincoln,** *British Pirates and Society, 1680–1730* (Farnham: Ashgate, 2014)

**D. Loades,** *The Tudor Navy: An Administrative, Political and Military History* (Aldershot: Scolar Press, 1992)
*The Making of the Elizabethan Navy 1540–90: from the Solent to the Armada* (Woodbridge: Boydell and Brewer, 2009)

**Catharine MacLeod (ed.),** *The Lost Prince Henry, Prince of Wales (1594–1612)* (London: National Portrait Gallery, 2012)

**Seth Mallios,** *The Deadly Politics of Giving: Exchange and Violence at Ajacan, Roanoke, and Jamestown* (Tuscaloosa: University of Alabama Press, 2006)

**Clement R. Markham, (ed.),** *The Hawkins Voyages,* Vol. LVII (London: Hakluyt Society, 1878)

**Nabil Matar,** *Britain and Barbary, 1589–1689* (Gainesville, FL: University Press of Florida, 2005)

**William Edward May,** *A History of Marine Navigation* (Henley-on-Thames: G. T. Foulis and Co., 1973)

**J. McDermott,** *England and the Spanish Armada: the Necessary Quarrel* (New Haven and London: Yale University Press, 2005)

**Kevin P. McDonald,** *Pirates, Merchants, Settlers, and Slaves: Colonial America and the Indo-Atlantic World* (Oakland, CA: Berkeley, 2015)

**W. E. Minchinton,** *The Growth of English Overseas Trade in the 17th and 18th Centuries* (London: Methuen, 1969)

**Philip D. Morgan & Sean Hawkins,** *Black Experience and the Empire* (Oxford: Oxford University Press, 2004)

**Joe Moshenska,** *A Stain in the Blood: The Remarkable Voyage of Sir Kenelm Digby* (London: William Heinemann, 2016)

**Matthew Neufeld,** 'The Framework of Casualty Care during the Anglo-Dutch Wars', *War in History* 19(4), 427–44

**David Northrup,** 'West Africans and the Atlantic' in Philip D. Morgan and Sean Hawkins, *Black Experience and the Empire* (Oxford: Oxford University Press, 2004)

**William Oldys and Thomas Birch (eds),** *The Works of Sir Walter Ralegh, Kt., Now First Collected: To Which Are Prefixed the Lives of the Author* (8 vols., Oxford: Oxford University Press, 1829)

**Stephen Orgel and Roy Strong,** *Inigo Jones: Theatre of the Stuart Court* (London: Sotheby Parke Bernet, 1973)

**G. Parker,** *The Grand Strategy of Philip II* (New Haven and London: Yale University Press, 1998)

**Martin Parker,** *Saylors for my Money* (London, c.1630)

**Christine Petto,** *Mapping and Charting in Early Modern England and France: Power, Patronage and Production* (Lanham: Lexington, 2015)

**Charles Petrie (ed.),** *The Letters, Speeches and Proclamations of King Charles I* (London: Cassell, 1968)

**Steven Pincus,** 'Popery, Trade and Universal Monarchy: the Ideological Context of the Outbreak of the Second Anglo-Dutch War', *English Historical Review,* 107(422) (January 1992), pp. 1–29

**Diana Preston and Michael Preston,** *A Pirate of Exquisite Mind: The Life of William Dampier: Explorer, Naturalist and Buccaneer* (London, 2005)

**Marcus Rediker,** *Villains of All Nations: Atlantic Pirates in the Golden Age* (London: Verso, 2004)

**N. A. M. Rodger,** *Safeguard of the Sea: A Naval History of Britain, 660–1649* (London: Allen Lane, 2004)
*The Command of the Ocean: A Naval History of Britain, 1649–1815* (London: Penguin, 2005)

**Susan Rose** *England's Medieval Navy, 1066–1509: Ships, Men and Warfare* (Barnsley: Pen and Sword, 2013)

**Helen Rountree,** *Pocahontas's People: The Powhatan Indians of Virginia through Four Centuries* (Norman: University of North Carolina Press, 1990)

**Margarita Russell,** *Visions of the Sea: Vroom and the Origins of Sea Painting* (Leiden University Press, 1983)

**David Scott,** *Leviathan: the Rise of Britain as a World Power* (London: Harper Press, 2013)

**C. M. Senior,** *A Nation of Pirates: English Piracy in its Heyday* (Newton Abbot: David & Charles, 1976)

**Kim Sloan,** *A New World: England's First View of America* (London: British Museum, 2006)

**John Smith,** *An Accidence or The Path-way to Experience. Necessary for All Young Sea-men* (London, 1626)

**Elizabeth Staffell,** 'The Horrible Tail-Man and the Anglo-Dutch Wars', *Journal of the Warburg and Courtauld Institutes,* 63 (2000)

**James H. Sweet,** *Recreating Africa: Culture, Kinship, and Religion in the African-Portuguese World, 1441–1770* (Chapel Hill, NC: University of North Carolina Press, 2003)

**E. G. R. Taylor,** *The Mathematical Practitioners of Tudor and Stuart England* (Cambridge: Cambridge University Press, 1968)

**Roy Digby Thomas,** *Digby: The Gunpowder Plotter's Legacy* (London: Janus Publishing Company, 2001)

**Norman Thrower (ed.),** *The Compleat Plattmaker: Essays on Chart, Map and Globe Making in England in the Seventeenth and Eighteenth Centuries* (Berkeley: University of California Press, 1978)

**Adrian Tinniswood,** *Pirates of Barbary* (London: Vintage, 2011)

**James D. Tracy (ed.),** *The Rise of Merchant Empires: Long-distance Trade in the Early Modern World, 1350–1750* (Cambridge: Cambridge University Press, 1990)

**Jeremy Treglown (ed.),** *The Letters of John Wilmot, Earl of Rochester* (Blackwell, 1980)

**Spencer Tucker,** *The Encyclopedia of North American Indian Wars 1607–1890: A Political, Social, and Military History* (California: ABC-Clio, 2011)

**Sarah Tyacke,** 'Chart Making in England and its Context', in D. Woodward (ed.), *Cartography in the European Renaissance*

(Chicago: University of Chicago Press, 2007)

**Alden Vaughan,** *Transatlantic Encounters: American Indians in Britain, 1500-1776* (Cambridge: Cambridge University Press, 2006)

**Daniel J. Vitkus,** *Piracy, Slavery, and Redemption: Barbary Captivity Narratives from Early Modern England* (New York: Columbia University Press, 2001)

**David W. Waters,** *The Art of Navigation in England in Elizabethan and Early Stuart Times* (London: National Maritime Museum, 1978)

**Kelly Watson,** *Insatiable Appetites: Imperial Encounters with Cannibals in the North Atlantic World* (New York and London: New York University, 2015)

**Jace Weaver,** *The Red Atlantic: American Indigenes and the Making of the Modern World, 1000-1927,* (Chase Hill: University of North Carolina Press, 2014)

**J. S. Wheeler,** *The Making of a World Power: War and the Military Revolution in Seventeenth Century England* (Stroud: Sutton Publishing, 1999)

**Glyndwr Williams,** *The Great South Sea: English Voyages and Encounters, 1570-1750* (New Haven, CT: Yale University Press, 1997)

**J. A. Williamson and R. Skelton,** *The Cabot Voyages and Bristol Discovery Under Henry VII* (Cambridge: C.U.P., 1962)

**R. Winfield,** *British Warships in the Age of Sail 1603-1714: Design, Construction, Careers and Fates* (Barnsley: Seaforth, 2014)

# Index